# CONTENTS

**Targeting Homework**
**Year 4 New Edition**

Copyright © 2024 Blake Education
ISBN: 978 1 92572 646 6

Published by Pascal Press
PO Box 250
Glebe NSW 2037
www.pascalpress.com.au
contact@pascalpress.com.au

Author: Frances Mackay
Publisher: Lynn Dickinson
Editors: Marie Theodore & Ruth Schultz
Cover and Text Designer: Leanne Nobilio
Typesetter: Ruth Schultz
Proofreader: Tim Learner
Images & Illustrations: Dreamstime (unless otherwise indicated)
Printed by Wai Man Book Binding (China) Ltd

**Acknowledgements**
Thank you to the publishers, authors and illustrators
who generously granted permission for their work
to be reproduced in this book.

# Introduction

**Targeting Homework** aims to build and reinforce English and Maths skills. This book supports the ACARA Australian Curriculum for Year 4 and helps children to revise and consolidate what has been taught in the classroom. ACARA codes are shown on each unit and a chart explaining their content descriptions is on pages v and vi. The inside back cover (Maths) and front cover (English) show the topics in each unit.

## The structure of this book

This book has 32 carefully graded double-page units on English and Maths. The English units are divided into three sections:

★ Grammar and Punctuation

★ Spelling and Phonic Knowledge

★ Reading and Comprehension — includes a wide variety of literary and cross-curriculum texts.

This also includes a Reading Review segment for children to record and rate their home reading books.

The Maths units are divided between:

★ Number and Algebra

★ Measurement and Space

★ Statistics and Probability

★ Problem Solving.

**My Book Review**

Title _____

Author _____

Rating ☆☆☆☆☆

Comment _____

_____

## Assessment

Term Reviews follow Units 1–8, 9–16, 17–24 and 25–32 to test work covered during the term, and allow parents and carers to monitor their child's progress. Children are encouraged to mark each unit as it is completed and to colour in the traffic lights at the end of each segment. These results are then transferred to the Marking Grid. Parents and carers can see at a glance if their child is excelling or struggling!

● **Green** = Excellent — 2 or fewer questions incorrect

● **Orange** = Passing — 50% or more questions answered correctly

● **Red** = Struggling — fewer than 50% correct and needs help

SCORE /18 ( 0-6 ) ( 8-14 ) ( 16-18 )  Score 2 points for each correct answer!

## How to Use This Book

The activities in this book are specifically designed to be used at home with minimal resources and support. Helpful explanations of key concepts and skills are provided throughout the book to help understand the tasks. Useful examples of how to do the activities are provided.

Regular practice of key concepts and skills will support the work your child does in school and will enable you to monitor their progress throughout the year. It is recommended that children complete 8 units per school term (one a week) and then the Term Review. Every unit has a Traffic Light scoreboard at the end of each section.

Score 2 points for each correct answer!

You or your child should mark each completed unit and then colour the traffic light that corresponds to the number of correct questions. This process will enable you to see at a glance how your child is progressing and to identify weak spots. The results should be recorded at the end of each term on the Marking Grid on page 1. The Term Review results are important for tracking progress and identifying any improvements in performance. If you find that certain questions are repeatedly

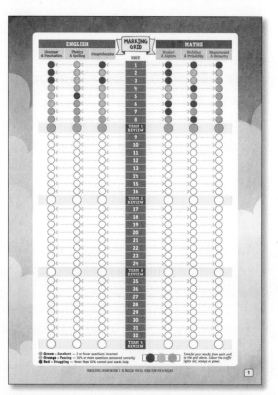

NOTE: The Maths Problem Solving questions do not appear on the Marking Grid as they often have multiple or subjective answers that cannot be easily scored.

causing difficulties and errors, then there is a good reason to discuss this with your child's teacher and arrange for extra instruction in that problem area.

### Home Reading Journal

Each English unit provides space for your child to log, review and rate a book they have read during the week. These details can then be transferred to the handy Reading Journal Summary on page 146, which can be photocopied and shared with their teacher or kept as a record.

### Answers

The answer section on pages 147–162 can be removed, stapled together and kept somewhere safe. Use it to check answers when your child has completed each unit. Encourage your child to colour in the Traffic Light boxes when the answers have been calculated.

TARGETING HOMEWORK 4 © PASCAL PRESS ISBN 9781925726466

## Australian Curriculum Correlations: Year 4 English

| CODE | CODE DESCRIPTION | Grammar & Punctuation UNITS | Phonic Knowledge & Spelling UNITS | Reading Comprehension UNITS |
|---|---|---|---|---|
| **LANGUAGE** | | | | |
| AC9E4LA01 | Explore language used to develop relationships in formal and informal situations | 30 | | 28 |
| AC9E4LA02 | Identify the subjective language of opinion and feeling, and the objective language of factual reporting | 17 | | 17 |
| AC9E4LA03 | Identify how texts across the curriculum have different language features and are typically organised into characteristic stages depending on purposes | 29 | | 3, 9, 13, 17, 23, 27, 28 |
| AC9E4LA04 | Identify how text connectives including temporal and conditional words, and topic word associations are used to sequence and connect ideas | 9, 10, 11, 18, 22, 26, 32 | | 22, 32 |
| AC9E4LA06 | Understand that complex sentences contain one independent clause and at least one dependent clause typically joined by a subordinating conjunction to create relationships, such as time and causality | 21 | | |
| AC9E4LA07 | Investigate how quoted (direct) and reported (indirect) speech are used | 15, 16, 27 | | |
| AC9E4LA08 | Understand how adverb groups/phrases and prepositional phrases work in different ways to provide circumstantial details about an activity | 19, 20, 31 | | |
| AC9E4LA09 | Understand past, present and future tenses and their impact on meaning in a sentence | 8, 28 | 8 | |
| AC9E4LA11 | Expand vocabulary by exploring a range of synonyms and antonyms, and using words encountered in a range of sources | 12 | 8, 10, 29 | 8 |
| AC9E4LA12 | Understand that punctuation signals dialogue through quotation marks and that dialogue follows conventions for the use of capital letters, commas and boundary punctuation | 15, 16, 27 | | |
| **LITERATURE** | | | | |
| AC9E4LE02 | Describe the effects of text structures and language features in literary texts when responding to and sharing opinions | | | 29, 31 |
| AC9E4LE03 | Discuss how authors and illustrators make stories engaging by the way they develop character, setting and plot tensions | | | 2 |
| AC9E4LE04 | Examine the use of literary devices and deliberate word play in literary texts, including poetry, to shape meaning | | 11 | 5 |
| **LITERACY** | | | | |
| AC9E4LY04 | Read different types of texts, integrating phonic, semantic and grammatical knowledge to read accurately and fluently, re-reading and self-correcting when needed | 11 | | |
| AC9E4LY05 | Use comprehension strategies such as visualising, predicting, connecting, summarising, monitoring and questioning to build literal and inferred meaning, to expand topic knowledge and ideas, and evaluate texts | | | ALL UNITS |
| AC9E4LY06 | Plan, create, edit and publish written and multimodal imaginative, informative and persuasive texts, using visual features, relevant linked ideas, complex sentences, appropriate tense, synonyms and antonyms, correct spelling of multisyllabic words and simple punctuation | 1, 2, 3, 4, 5, 6, 7, 13, 14, 23, 24, 25, 29 | | |
| AC9E4LY09 | Understand how to use and apply phonological and morphological knowledge to read and write multisyllabic words with more complex letter combinations, including a variety of vowel sounds and known prefixes and suffixes | | 3, 4, 5, 7, 8, 9, 11-14, 16, 17, 18, 20, 22, 23, 24, 26, 27, 29, 30, 31, 32 | |
| AC9E4LY10 | Understand how to use knowledge of letter patterns, including double letters, spelling generalisations, morphological word families, common prefixes and suffixes, and word origins, to spell more complex words | | ALL UNITS | |
| AC9E4LY11 | Read and write high frequency words including homophones and know how to use context to identify correct spelling | | 2, 3, 5, 6, 7, 9, 11, 20, 23, 27 | |
| **CROSS CURRICULAR COMPREHENSION TEXTS** | | | | |
| **SCIENCE** | | | | |
| AC9S4H02 | Consider how people use scientific explanations to meet a need or solve a problem | | | 1, 19, 30 |
| AC9S4U03 | Identify how forces can be exerted by one object on another and investigate the effect of frictional, gravitational and magnetic forces on the motion of objects | | | 18 |
| AC9S4U04 | Examine the properties of natural and made materials including fibres, metals, glass and plastics and consider how these properties influence their use | | | 10 |
| **HISTORY** | | | | |
| AC9HS4K01 | The diversity of First Nations Australians, their social organisation and their continuous connection to Country/Place | | | 26 |
| AC9HS4K02 | The causes of the establishment of the first British colony in Australia in 1788 | | | 4 |
| AC9HS4K03 | The experiences of individuals and groups, including military and civilian officials, and convicts involved in the establishment of the first British colony | | | 11, 17 |
| AC9HS4K04 | The effects of contact with other people on First Nations Australians and their Countries/Places following the arrival of the First Fleet and how this was viewed by First Nations Australians as an invasion | | | 24 |
| **GEOGRAPHY** | | | | |
| AC9HS4K05 | The importance of environments, including natural vegetation and water sources, to people and animals in Australia and on another continent | | | 20 |
| AC9HS4K06 | Sustainable use and management of renewable and non-renewable resources, including the custodial responsibility First Nations Australians have for Country/Place | | | 9, 23, 27 |
| **CIVICS & CITIZENSHIP** | | | | |
| AC9HS4K07 | The differences between "rules" and "laws", why laws are important and how they affect the lives of people | | | 12 |
| AC9HS4K08 | The roles of local government and how members of the community use and contribute to local services | | | 7 |

Australian CURRICULUM

## Australian Curriculum Correlations: Year 4 Maths

| ACARA CODE | CONTENT DESCRIPTION | Number & Algebra<br>UNITS | Statistics & Probability<br>UNITS | Measurement & Space<br>UNITS | Problem Solving<br>UNITS |
|---|---|---|---|---|---|
| **NUMBER** | | | | | |
| AC9M4N01 | Recognise and extend the application of place value to tenths and hundredths and use the conventions of decimal notation to name and represent decimals | 1, 2, 16, 30 | | | 32 |
| AC9M4N02 | Explain and use the properties of odd and even numbers | 3, 17, 23 | | | 30, 32 |
| AC9M4N03 | Find equivalent representations of fractions using related denominators and make connections between fractions and decimal notation | 6, 11, 13, 16, 20, 21 | | | 21 |
| AC9M4N04 | Count by fractions including mixed numerals; locate and represent these fractions as numbers on number lines | 13, 31 | | | 13 |
| AC9M4N05 | Solve problems involving multiplying or dividing natural numbers by multiples and powers of 10 without a calculator, using the multiplicative relationship between the place value of digits | 12, 24 | | 19 | |
| AC9M4N06 | Develop efficient strategies and use appropriate digital tools for solving problems involving addition and subtraction, and multiplication and division where there is no remainder | 2, 8, 12 | | | 3, 5, 6, 17 |
| AC9M4N07 | Choose and use estimation and rounding to check and explain the reasonableness of calculations including the results of financial transactions | 7, 22 | | | |
| AC9M4N08 | Use mathematical modelling to solve practical problems involving additive and multiplicative situations including financial contexts; formulate the problems using number sentences and choose efficient calculation strategies, using digital tools where appropriate; interpret and communicate solutions in terms of the situation | 9, 11, 27, 29 | | | 8, 19, 28 |
| AC9M4N09 | Follow and create algorithms involving a sequence of steps and decisions that use addition or multiplication to generate sets of numbers; identify and describe any emerging patterns | 5, 14, 18, 32 | | | 20 |
| **ALGEBRA** | | | | | |
| AC9M4A01 | Find unknown values in numerical equations involving addition and subtraction, using the properties of numbers and operations | 10, 15, 25 | | | 2, 9, 14, 16, 25 |
| AC9M4A02 | Recall and demonstrate proficiency with multiplication facts up to 10 x 10 and related division facts; extend and apply facts to develop efficient mental strategies for computation with larger numbers without a calculator | 4, 10, 19, 23, 28 | | | 4, 23 |
| **MEASUREMENT** | | | | | |
| AC9M4M01 | Interpret unmarked and partial units when measuring and comparing attributes of length, mass, capacity, duration and temperature, using scaled and digital instruments and appropriate units | | | 1, 3, 5, 6, 11, 13, 14, 19, 22, 29, 32 | 22 |
| AC9M4M02 | Recognise ways of measuring and approximating the perimeter and area of shapes and enclosed spaces, using appropriate formal and informal units | | | 7, 12, 15 | 1, 15, 26 |
| AC9M4M03 | Solve problems involving the duration of time including situations involving "am" and "pm" and conversions between units of time | | | 2, 10, 18, 25, 26 | 10, 18, 27 |
| AC9M4M04 | Estimate and compare angles using angle names including acute, obtuse, straight angle, reflex and revolution, and recognise their relationship to a right angle | | | 20, 28 | |
| **SPACE** | | | | | |
| AC9M4SP01 | Represent and approximate composite shapes and objects in the environment, using combinations of familiar shapes and objects | | | 4, 7, 24, 27 | 7, 12 |
| AC9M4SP02 | Create and interpret grid reference systems using grid references and directions to locate and describe positions and pathways | | | 8, 16, 17 | 29 |
| AC9M4SP03 | Recognise line and rotational symmetry of shapes and create symmetrical patterns and pictures, using dynamic geometric software where appropriate | | | 21, 24, 31 | 24 |
| **STATISTICS** | | | | | |
| AC9M4ST01 | Acquire data for categorical and discrete numerical variables to address a question of interest or purpose using digital tools; represent data using many-to-one pictographs, column graphs and other displays or visualisations; interpret and discuss the information that has been created | | 1, 11, 15, 25, 30 | | |
| AC9M4ST02 | Analyse the effectiveness of different displays or visualisations in illustrating and comparing data distributions, then discuss the shape of distributions and the variation in the data | | 3, 9, 17, 19, 22, 23, 29 | | |
| AC9M4ST03 | Conduct statistical investigations, collecting data through survey responses and other methods; record and display data using digital tools; interpret the data and communicate the results | | | | |
| **PROBABILITY** | | | | | |
| AC9M4P01 | Describe possible everyday events and the possible outcomes of chance experiments and order outcomes or events based on their likelihood of occurring; identify independent or dependent events | | 5, 7, 13, 21, 27, 31 | | |
| AC9M4P02 | Conduct repeated chance experiments to observe relationships between outcomes; identify and describe the variation in results | | | | 31 |

Australian CURRICULUM

TARGETING HOMEWORK 4 © PASCAL PRESS ISBN 9781925726466

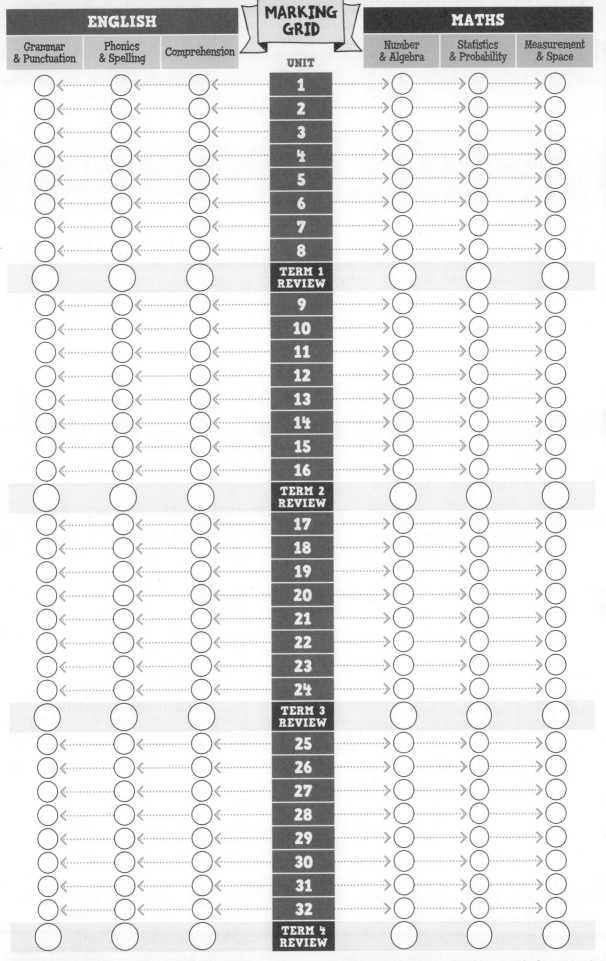

# MARKING GRID

## ENGLISH

| Grammar & Punctuation | Phonics & Spelling | Comprehension |

## MATHS

| Number & Algebra | Statistics & Probability | Measurement & Space |

### UNIT

1
2
3
4
5
6
7
8
**TERM 1 REVIEW**
9
10
11
12
13
14
15
16
**TERM 2 REVIEW**
17
18
19
20
21
22
23
24
**TERM 3 REVIEW**
25
26
27
28
29
30
31
32
**TERM 4 REVIEW**

● **Green** = Excellent — 2 or fewer questions incorrect
● **Orange** = Passing — 50% or more questions answered correctly
● **Red** = Struggling — fewer than 50% correct and needs help

*Transfer your results from each unit to the grid above. Colour the traffic lights red, orange or green.*

# Grammar & Punctuation

AC9E4LY06

TERM 1 ENGLISH

## Simple sentences – subjects and verbs

A **sentence** is a group of words that states a complete thought. It makes sense on its own. A **simple sentence** has a **subject** and a **verb**.

*Example:* The dogs chased the ball.
        subject    verb

A **statement** is a sentence that tells us about everyday things, facts and ideas. Statements begin with a capital letter and end with a **full stop (.)**.

**Underline the subjects and circle the verbs in these statements.**

① Our supermarket sells organic fruit and vegetables.

② The battered old car crawled up the hill.

③ Yesterday, Penny cycled all the way into town.

## Objects

Many sentences also contain an **object**. An object is someone or something that receives the action of the subject.

        subject    verb        object
*Example:* My aunty baked a huge birthday cake for my birthday.

**Underline the objects in these statements.**

④ Jamie painted the kitchen ceiling and walls.

⑤ A huge ship sailed into the harbour last night.

## Questions

A **question** is a sentence that asks for information. It begins with a capital letter and ends with a **question mark (?)**. Questions can begin with **who, what, which, how, when, where** or **why**.

**Add a question word to complete these questions.**

⑥ _____ do you make a cake?

⑦ _____ sat on my hat?

**The verbs do, does, did, has and have are also useful for asking questions. Complete these questions using one of these verbs.**

⑧ _____ you enjoy the movie last night?

⑨ _____ Riley finished his homework yet?

*Score 2 points for each correct answer!*  **SCORE** **/18**  0-6  8-14  16-18

# Phonic Knowledge & Spelling

AC9E4LY10

## Short vowel sounds – a, e, i, o, u

**Say each word. They all contain a short vowel sound — the sound is short and snappy!**

| drag | grab | crack | splash |
|------|------|-------|--------|
| smell | step | mend | stretch |
| skip | thick | pinch | blink |
| drop | rock | frost | strong |
| crust | plump | junk | bunch |

**Choose words from the word bank to complete these sentences.**

① I often cut the _____ off my sandwich.

② "Do you want thin or _____ toast for your breakfast?" asked Dad.

③ I had to reach over and _____ their towels before they got wet.

**Circle two words with short vowels in each line.**

④ **short a**   stamp   lace   crack

⑤ **short e**   been   shell   spend

⑥ **short i**   mice   bring   mist

⑦ **short o**   trot   joke   stop

⑧ **short u**   mute   shrug   truck

## The doubling rule

When a word ends in a short vowel followed by a **single consonant**, double the last consonant before adding **–ed** or **–ing**.

**Remember!** Consonants are all the letters that are not vowels.

*Examples:*  drag, dragged, dragging
           strap, strapped, strapping

If a word has more than one consonant after the short vowel, you do not double the last consonant.

*Examples:*  crack, cracked, cracking
           stretch, stretched, stretching

**Add –ed and –ing to these words. Decide if you need to double the last consonant.**

|  | –ed | –ing |
|---|---|---|
| ⑨ test | _____ | _____ |
| ⑩ stop | _____ | _____ |

**Add step to make compound words.**

⑪ _____brother   ⑫ _____ladder

*Score 2 points for each correct answer!*  **SCORE** **/24**  0-10  12-18  20-24

## Mosquito life cycle

**Informative text** – Explanation
**Author** – Lisa Nicol

Mosquitoes undergo complete **metamorphosis** during their life cycle.

**Egg** Mosquitoes mate while flying. After mating, the female looks for a meal of blood to nourish the fertilised egg. She lays them in **stagnant** water, such as swamps or puddles, or on damp soil. Depending on the **species**, mosquitoes lay eggs separately or attached in rafts of hundreds of eggs.

**Larva** The eggs hatch within 48 hours. Mosquito larvae, often called wrigglers, emerge. They usually hang from the surface of the water, breathing through a tube. They feed on algae, bacteria and other **microorganisms**. They shed their skin (moult) as they grow. After 5–7 days, on the fourth moult, the larva changes into a pupa.

**Pupa** Pupae float on the surface of the water. They do not eat but breathe through horn-like tubes called 'trumpets'. In 1–4 days, the pupa becomes an adult.

**Adult** The pupal case splits open and an adult mosquito emerges. It rests on the surface of the water while its body and wings dry and harden. After a few days the adult mosquito can mate. Depending on the temperature and species, a mosquito may live 4–40 days.

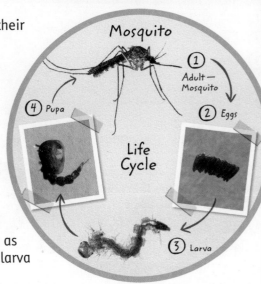

Source: *Life Cycles*, Go Facts, Blake Education.

---

Write or circle the correct answers.

1. 'The female mosquito nourishes the eggs with blood.' What does **nourish** mean?

   a provide with food

   b cover up

   c hide

2. An example of **stagnant** water is:

   a a flowing river.

   b a swamp.

   c the sea.

3. Mosquito larvae **emerge** from the eggs. This means they:

   a swim away.    b come out.    c hide.

4. Name two things that mosquito larvae eat.

   _____

   _____

5. How many moults do the larvae go through before they change into a pupa?

   a 1    b 4    c We are not told.

6. What is a **microorganism**?

   a a very small plant or animal

   b a feeding tube

7. What are the breathing tubes of pupae called?

   a wrigglers    b trumpets    c moults

8. What does **metamorphosis** mean?

   a an underwater life cycle

   b a complete change in form from one stage of the life cycle to another

   c a species of mosquito

### My Book Review

Title _____

Author _____

Rating ☆ ☆ ☆ ☆ ☆

Comment _____

_____

*Score 2 points for each correct answer!*  SCORE /16  0-6  8-12  14-16

# Number & Algebra

AC9M4N01

## Exploring numbers

Write the missing numbers.

① 58, 59, 60, 61, ___, ___, ___, ___

② 499, _____, _____, _____, _____, 504

③ 1233, 1234, 1235, _____, _____, _____, _____

④ 5000, 4999, 4998, 4997, _____, _____, _____, _____

⑤ 9867, 9866, 9865, 9864, _____, _____, _____, _____

How do you write these numbers?
Circle the correct answer.

⑥ fifty-nine
   a 95          b 59          c 509

⑦ one thousand, eight hundred
   a 1080        b 1008        c 1800

⑧ twenty-four thousand, nine hundred and six
   a 24 906      b 24 960      c 24 690

⑨ seventy-eight thousand, five hundred and ninety-nine
   a 78 995      b 78 599      c 78 950

Write the numbers in order from smallest to largest.

⑩ 47   63   98   25   72

_____

⑪ 780   708   718   781   788

_____

⑫ 5490   5940   5090   5040   5904

_____

⑬ 24 600   24 700   24 650   24 690   24 605

_____

Write these numbers in words.

⑭ 89 _____

⑮ 152 _____

_____

⑯ 708 _____

_____

⑰ 1500 _____

_____

⑱ 5608 _____

_____

⑲ 12 504 _____

_____

Score 2 points for each correct answer!   **SCORE** **/38**   (0-16) (18-32) (34-38)

# Statistics & Probability

AC9M4ST01

## Picture graphs

A **picture graph** uses pictures to represent data gathered.

In this picture graph, the larger book represents 10 books sold. The smaller book represents 3 books sold.

**Number of books sold at Greenfield Primary School book fair**

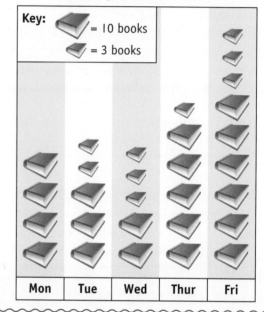

Key:
= 10 books
= 3 books

| Mon | Tue | Wed | Thur | Fri |

Use the graph to answer the questions.

① On which day was the largest number of books sold? _____

② On which day was the smallest number of books sold? _____

③ How many books were sold on Wednesday? _____

④ How many more books were sold on Friday than on Wednesday? _____

⑤ On which day were 53 books sold? _____

⑥ On which days were fewer than forty books sold? _____

⑦ How many fewer books were sold on Wednesday than on Tuesday? _____

⑧ The sales target on Thursday was 60 books. How many books did they miss their target by? _____

⑨ How many books were sold altogether? _____

⑩ Each book was sold for $2. How much money did they raise? _____

Score 2 points for each correct answer!   **SCORE** **/20**   (0-8) (10-14) (16-20)

## Measurement & Space

AC9M4M01

### Length

> We measure length in millimetres (mm), centimetres (cm) and metres (m).
>
> 10 mm = 1 cm          100 cm = 1 m
>
> A school ruler is usually 30 cm long.
>
> To estimate is to make a good guess.

**Which is the best estimate for the length of each thing? Circle the correct answer.**

1. ironing board
   a 115 mm          b 115 cm          c 115 m

2. small car
   a 4 mm          b 4 cm          c 4 m

3. birthday card
   a 18 mm          b 18 cm          c 18 m

**Estimate the length of each line to the nearest cm.**
**Then measure to see if you are correct.**

_____

4. My estimate _____          5. Measurement _____

_____

6. My estimate _____          7. Measurement _____

_____

8. My estimate _____          9. Measurement _____

**Follow the instructions to draw a robot.**

10. Colour the rectangle red.

11. At the base of the rectangle, draw two triangles in each corner. Make each side of the triangles 2 cm long. Colour both triangles green.

12. On the top of the rectangle, draw a square. Draw each side of the square 2 cm long. Colour the square red.

13. Draw two eyes, a nose and a mouth inside the square. Use black.

14. Draw an ear on two sides of the square. Draw the ears as triangles with sides of 1 cm. Colour them green.

15. Draw a semi-circle on top of the red square. You can decide its size. Colour this blue.

16. To draw the arms, measure down 2 cm from the top of the red rectangle and draw an arm on each side. The arms should be 2 cm wide by 1 cm high. Colour these blue.

17. Finish your robot by drawing dials, buttons and levers on its body in black.

*Score 2 points for each correct answer!*  SCORE  | /34 | (0-14) (16-28) (30-34)

## Problem Solving

AC9M3M02

### Robot order

Zuri has five robots and she lined them up in a row in order from tallest to shortest.

- Red Robot is 42 cm and that's the tallest one.
- Green Robot is in the middle.
- Purple Robot is 4 cm shorter than Yellow Robot, which isn't the shortest.
- Pink Robot is 6 cm shorter than Red Robot.
- Yellow Robot is 12 cm shorter than Pink Robot.
- Green Robot is 12 centimetres taller than Purple Robot.

Colour the robots to show the order.
Write how tall each one is.

**TERM 1 ENGLISH**

## Grammar & Punctuation

AC9E4LY06

### Simple sentences – commands

Some sentences are **commands**. A command tells someone to do something. The subject of a command is always 'you'. Some commands have objects and some don't. Commands begin with a capital letter and end with a **full stop (.)** or an **exclamation mark (!)**.

Commands begin with a doing word or **verb**.

*Examples:* **Pack** your suitcase.
**Label** your diagram.
**Eat** your lunch.

**Most instructions are written as commands. Number these instructions in the correct order from 1–5. Circle the verbs.**

**How to make pancakes**

① ___ Remove the pancake from the pan and eat!

② ___ Beat the ingredients together in a bowl.

③ ___ Brush some butter onto a hot pan.

④ ___ Gather your ingredients.

⑤ ___ Pour some batter into the pan and cook until lightly golden.

### Exclamations

An **exclamation** is a sentence that shows surprise, fear, happiness or excitement. Exclamations begin with a capital letter and end with an **exclamation mark (!)**. Sometimes, commands are exclamations.

*Examples:* I hate you!
Wow! You came first!
Clean your bedroom — NOW!
Ouch — that hurt!

**Are these sentences statements (S), questions (Q), exclamations (E) or commands (C)? Write S, Q, E or C next to each sentence.**

⑥ I played rugby at the park. ___

⑦ Draw a graph of your results. ___

⑧ Hooray! We're going on holiday tomorrow! ___

⑨ Do you know how to get to the cinema? ___

*Score 2 points for each correct answer!* **SCORE** **/18** (0-6) (8-14) (16-18)

## Phonic Knowledge & Spelling

AC9E4LY10, AC9E4LY11

### Long vowel sounds – a, e, i, o, u

**Say each word from the word bank. What sound does the vowel make? The vowel and the e at the end of the word work together to make a long vowel sound.**

| brake | scrape | safe | whale | trade |
|-------|--------|------|-------|-------|
| fire | tide | spice | whine | shine |
| chose | globe | stroke | erode | explode |
| amuse | accuse | refuse | confuse | excuse |

**Choose words from the word bank to complete these sentences.**

① "_____ me, can you push the door open? Thanks."

② Please put your money in the bank where it will be _____.

**Circle two words with long vowels in each line.**

③ **long a**    plant    chase    trade

④ **long i**    wise    slide    film

⑤ **long o**    stop    nose    vote

⑥ **long u**    shut    prune    flute

### Adding –ed, –ing and –y to words that end in 'e'

When a word ends in **e**, you usually drop the **e** before adding **–ing** or **–y**. When you add **–ed**, you just add **–d** because the word already has an **e**.

*Examples:* tast**e**, taste**d**, tast**ing**, tast**y**

**Add –ed and –ing to these words.**

| | –ed | –ing |
|---|-----|------|
| ⑦ whine | _____ | _____ |
| ⑧ explode | _____ | _____ |

**Add –y to these words.**

⑨ spice _____

⑩ haze _____

⑪ stone _____

⑫ slime _____

*Score 2 points for each correct answer!* **SCORE** **/24** (0-10) (12-18) (20-24)

TARGETING HOMEWORK 4 © PASCAL PRESS ISBN 9781925726466

# Disaster Christmas

**Imaginative text** – Narrative
**Author** – Lisa Thompson, **Illustrator** – Greg Turra

*It's Christmas Eve, 1974, and Cyclone Tracy is heading towards Darwin. Mandy and her brother Davey are asleep in their bedroom. Mandy's mum, dad and Uncle Lou are also in the house.*

Mandy looked out her bedroom window and watched what she thought were great sheets of silver tissue fly across the yard and down the street. Only it wasn't silver tissue. They were sheets of roof tin that had peeled off homes like ripe banana skins. A tree fell and smacked the side of the house so hard the house shook.

Mandy screamed. Davey startled awake. Branches from the tree scraped across the window glass. The bedroom door swung open. Uncle Lou shone a torch into the room.

"Cyclone Tracy's here. She's a monster alright and it doesn't sound like she's mucking about. Mandy, get away from the window and onto the floor with Davey."

Dad rushed in shining another torch.

"Power's gone," said Dad.

With a loud bang, one of the windows in the kitchen smashed. Mum screamed as wind and rain rushed in. Cyclone Tracy was in the house.

"Get to the bathroom!" yelled Uncle Lou.

Source: *Disaster Christmas*, Sparklers, Blake Education.

Write or circle the correct answers.

① **The purpose of this text is to make the reader:**

a smile.

b feel anxious for the characters.

c cry.

② **What is a cyclone?**

a a storm with destructive winds and heavy rainfall

b a heatwave

③ **What hit the house and made it shake?**

a sheets of tin roofing

b the wind

c a tree

④ **Why did Uncle Lou tell Mandy to get away from the window?**

_____

⑤ **Which one of these is the odd word out?**

a yelled          c whispered

b screamed     d roared

⑥ **What does the author mean by the sentence, 'Cyclone Tracy was in the house'?**

a Everyone in the house was talking about the cyclone.

b The wind and rain had come inside the house.

⑦ **Uncle Lou told everyone to 'get to the bathroom'. Why do you think he did this?**

a The bathroom was small and the walls were less likely to collapse.

b He wanted everyone to have a wash.

*Score 2 points for each correct answer!*  SCORE  **/14**  (0-4) (6-10) (12-14)

## My Book Review

Title _____

Author _____

Rating ☆☆☆☆☆

Comment _____

_____

# Number & Algebra

AC9M4N01, AC9M4N06

## Place value

The position of digits in numbers tells us what they represent. We call this **place value**.

24 785

- The **2** is two lots of ten thousand which equals 20 000.
- The **4** is four lots of one thousand which equals 4000.
- The **7** is seven lots of one hundred which equals 700.
- The **8** is eight lots of ten which equals 80.
- The **5** is five lots of one which equals 5.

**Hint:** the value of **0** is always 0, no matter what position it is in. For example, 702 has 0 lots of ten. This is another way of saying $0 \times 10$, which equals **0**.

**Complete the place value table.**

| | Ten thousands | Thousands | Hundreds | Tens | Ones |
|---|---|---|---|---|---|
| ① 25 | | | | | |
| ② 89 | | | | | |
| ③ 984 | | | | | |
| ④ 5906 | | | | | |
| ⑤ 12 891 | | | | | |
| ⑥ 24 785 | | | | | |

**Write the value of the digit in red.**

⑦ 69 _____  ⑬ 1682 _____

⑧ 124 _____  ⑭ 7002 _____

⑨ 508 _____  ⑮ 5905 _____

⑩ 582 _____  ⑯ 12 865 _____

⑪ 750 _____  ⑰ 72 698 _____

⑫ 999 _____  ⑱ 89 006 _____

## Using place value to add

You can use place value to add big numbers.
*Example:*  243 + 156

Split the numbers into hundreds, tens and ones. Then add them.

243 = 200 + 40 + 3   156 = 100 + 50 + 6

Add the hundreds together, add the tens together and add the ones together:

200 + 100 = **300**   40 + 50 = **90**   3 + 6 = **9**

300 + 90 + 9 = **399**

You can write this using brackets:

**243 + 156**

= (200 + 100) + (40 + 50) + (3 + 6)

= 300 + 90 + 9

= **399**

**Split the numbers into their place value to add them. Show your working out.**

⑲ 312 + 186

_____

_____

⑳ 541 + 357

_____

_____

㉑ 730 + 269

_____

_____

## Using place value to subtract

You can use the same split method to subtract numbers.
*Example:*  **569 – 248**

500 – 200 = **300**   60 – 40 = **20**   9 – 8 = 1

300 + 20 + 1 = **321**

When you subtract one number from another number, the answer is called the **difference**.

You can check your answer by adding the difference (321) to the number subtracted (248). It should equal 569.

**Split the numbers into their place value to subtract them. Show your working out.**

㉒ 785 – 463

_____

_____

㉓ 498 – 164

_____

_____

_____

㉔ 668 – 102

_____

_____

_____

Score 2 points for each correct answer!

**SCORE**  **/48**  (0–22)  (24–42)  (44–48)

## Statistics & Probability

*There are no statistics & probability activities in this unit.*

## Measurement & Space

AC9M4M03

### Analogue and digital time

When we tell the time using an **analogue clock**, we use these terms:

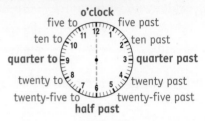

When we tell the time using a **digital clock**, we say the hour first and then the minutes past the hour.

6 o'clock = 6:00
$\frac{1}{4}$ past 5 = 5:15
$\frac{1}{2}$ past 12 = 12:30
$\frac{1}{4}$ to 9 = 8:45
25 past 2 = 2:25
20 to 6 = 5:40
5 to 10 = 9:55

**Write these analogue times as digital times.**

1. 3 o'clock = _____

2. $\frac{1}{4}$ past 7 = _____

3. 25 past 8 = _____

4. $\frac{1}{4}$ to 10 = _____

5. 10 to 5 = _____

6. 5 past 3 = _____

7. $\frac{1}{2}$ past 1 = _____

8. 20 to 8 = _____

**Write these digital times as analogue times.**

9. 8:30 = _____

10. 7:15 = _____

11. 9:00 = _____

12. 6:45 = _____

13. 2:25 = _____

14. 8:50 = _____

15. 2:20 = _____

16. 4:40 = _____

**Draw the time on these clocks.**

17. 8:15

21. 8:29

18. 7:35

22. 6:43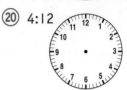

19. 2:50

23. 3:56

20. 4:12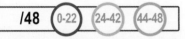

24. 1:26

*Score 2 points for each correct answer!* SCORE **/48** (0-22) (24-42) (44-48)

## Problem Solving

AC9M4A01

### Addition squares

This is an addition square.

| + | 3 | 9 |
|---|---|---|
| 8 | 11 | 17 |
| 5 | 8 | 14 |

These addition squares have some answers. Work out the questions.

1.
| + | | |
|---|---|---|
| | 10 | 12 |
| | 11 | |

2.
| + | | |
|---|---|---|
| | 15 | 17 |
| | | 11 |

3. Now try this multiplication square.

| × | | |
|---|---|---|
| | 15 | 12 |
| | 20 | |

# Grammar & Punctuation

AC9E4LY06

## Common nouns

> **Common nouns** are words used to name people, animals, places and things.
>
> *Examples:* butterfly, mountain, dentist, elephant, daughter

**Sort the nouns in the word box to complete the table.**

| scientist | park |
|---|---|
| fridge | teacher |
| calculator | school |
| family | bicycle |
| tadpole | joey |
| zoo | shark |
| ferry | hotel |
| spider | grandad |

| ① People | ② Animals |
|---|---|
|  |  |
|  |  |
|  |  |
|  |  |

| ③ Places | ④ Things |
|---|---|
|  |  |
|  |  |
|  |  |
|  |  |

## Concrete and abstract nouns

> Common nouns are either **concrete** or **abstract**. **Concrete nouns** name the things we can see, taste, hear and touch.
>
> *Examples:* chair, music, snake, gardener
>
> **Abstract nouns** name ideas and feelings.
>
> *Examples:* happiness, fear, success, anger

**Are the nouns in bold abstract (A) or concrete (C)? Write A or C.**

⑤ I kept my **promise** to help Mum clean the house. ___

⑥ The hideous **monster** lay in wait for its victim. ___

⑦ I saved enough **money** to go on holiday. ___

# Phonic Knowledge & Spelling

AC9E4LY09, AC9E4LY10, AC9E4LY11

## Letter teams that make the long 'a' sound

**Say each word from the word bank. The letter teams a–e, ai, ay and ei work together to make one sound — the long 'a' sound.**

| plane | mane | tale | wade |
|---|---|---|---|
| raise | explain | contain | obtain |
| display | relay | delay | decay |
| weigh | sleigh | rein | eight |

**Choose words from the word bank to complete these sentences.**

① Dad does not like to _____ himself on the scales!

② I had to _____ why I had not done my homework.

③ _____ is the next even number after six.

**Make new words by choosing from these beginnings. One has been done for you.**

| sh | dr | br | st | sn | fl | tr | gr | sl | pl |

| ④ –ay | ⑤ –ai | ⑥ a–e |
|---|---|---|
| s<u>w</u>ay | <u>br</u> ain | q<u>u</u> ake |
| _ _ ay | _ _ ain | _ _ ake |
| _ _ ay | _ _ ain | _ _ ake |
| _ _ ay | _ _ ain | _ _ ake |

## Homophones

> Homophones are words that sound the same but have a different spelling and meaning.

**Circle the correct homophone in each sentence.**

⑦ We used (plane  plain) flour to bake the cakes.

⑧ We lost our (weigh  way) coming back home.

⑨ The queen's (reign  rein) has been long.

⑩ The cat had a short (tale  tail)

⑪ The town's (mane  main ) road is wide.

## Book review
## – *The Key to Rondo by Emily Rodda*

**Persuasive text** – Book review
**Author** – Merryn Whitfield

Omnibus Books, 2007

*Have you ever broken the rules? Leo never thought he would. He was always the sensible one in the family — he never took any risks. That was why Aunt Bethany left him the old wooden music box when she died.*

But Leo's calm and ordered life changes forever when his young cousin Mimi comes to visit. She turns his world upside down with her wilful and unpredictable ways.

When Leo's parents leave the two children alone in the house, Mimi snatches the music box from Leo and, ignoring the age-old rule of only turning the key three times, Mimi adds an extra turn. What happens next is beyond the children's wildest dreams. The music box is not what it seems. It is in fact its own little world, a real world, where amazing and magical things happen, but not all of them good. The land of Rondo is ruled by the evil Blue Queen who wants the key and nothing will stand in her way.

As Leo and Mimi travel through Rondo, they learn of its many secrets, and we learn more about our two main characters and their hidden fears and wishes. It seems as though there is much more to Mimi than meets the eye, and her abrupt personality hides a lonely young girl.

*The Key to Rondo* is unlike Emily Rodda's previous Deltora Quest series, and some of her fans may be disappointed with this book and its lack of atmosphere. But children of all ages are sure to enjoy the many fairytale and nursery rhyme characters that pop up regularly throughout the story. And many older readers will take pleasure in following Leo and Mimi's quest through Rondo and their battle with the evil Blue Queen. It's a pleasant read, but not one you can't put down. I'll give it 6 out of 10.

RATING

**6** out of **10**

Source: *Writing Centres: Persuasive Texts*, Middle Primary, Blake Education.

**Write or circle the correct answers.**

1. **Why does the reviewer begin her review of the book with a question?**

   a She likes starting reviews with a question.

   b She wants to gain the attention of the reader.

   c I don't know.

2. **Who arrives at Leo's house and turns his life upside down?**

   a Aunt Bethany

   b the Blue Queen

   c cousin Mimi

3. **Which is the odd word?**

   a wilful          b stubborn          c willing

4. **How many times does Mimi turn the music box key?**

   a 1          b 2          c 3          d 4

5. **What does abrupt mean in this text?**

   a rude and curt          b sudden          c quick

6. **Which line in the text tells you that readers of *The Key to Rondo* may not like this book as much as the Deltora Quest series?**

   _____

   _____

Score 2 points for each correct answer! | SCORE | **/12** | 0-4 | 6-8 | 10-12

**My Book Review**

Title _____

Author _____

Rating ☆☆☆☆☆

Comment _____

_____

TERM 1 MATHS

# Number & Algebra

AC9M4N02

## Odd and even numbers

An **even number** can be shared or divided into two equal parts.
Even numbers end in **0, 2, 4, 6** or **8**.

An **odd number** cannot be shared or divided into two equal parts.
Odd numbers end in **1, 3, 5, 7** or **9**.

**Write these numbers.**

① Odd numbers between 20 and 36

_____

② Even numbers between 561 and 585

_____

_____

③ Odd numbers between 4530 and 4540

_____

④ Even numbers between 13 381 and 13 391

_____

**Will the answer be odd or even?**

⑤ odd + odd = _____

⑥ even + even = _____

⑦ odd + even = _____

⑧ odd – odd = _____

⑨ even – even = _____

⑩ odd – even = _____

⑪ even – odd = _____

⑫ even × even = _____

⑬ odd × odd = _____

⑭ even × odd = _____

**Use the numbers in the box to answer these questions.**

| 5687 | 4500 | 12 679 | 24 562 | 3843 |
| 456 | 24 | 805 | 5901 | 766 |

**What is:**

⑮ the largest odd number? _____

⑯ the largest even number? _____

⑰ the smallest odd number? _____

⑱ the smallest even number? _____

⑲ the even number closest to 800? _____

⑳ the odd number closest to 5900? _____

㉑ the even number that's double 2250?

_____

㉒ the even number that's half of 48? _____

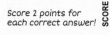
# Statistics & Probability

AC9M4ST02

## Recording data in a picture graph

Sam did a survey of the children in his school to find out the month of their birthday.

He recorded his results in this table.

| Birthday month | No. of children |
|---|---|
| January | 31 |
| February | 20 |
| March | 42 |
| April | 50 |
| May | 24 |
| June | 34 |
| July | 30 |
| August | 40 |
| September | 33 |
| October | 15 |
| November | 31 |
| December | 12 |

① **Use Sam's results to complete the picture graph. Look carefully at the key.**

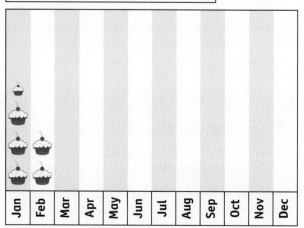

**Key:** 🧁 = 10 children  🧁 = 1 child

**Write or circle the correct answers.**

② What would be the best title for the graph?
  **a** Birthdays of the Children in Sam's Class
  **b** Birthday Months of the Children in Sam's School
  **c** Most Popular Birthdays in Sam's School

③ Which month had the most birthdays?

_____

④ Which month had the fewest birthdays?

_____

⑤ Would it be helpful for this graph to have a symbol for 100 children? _____

⑥ Which two months had the same number of birthdays? _____

⑦ What question do you think Sam asked the children in his school?

  a What is your favourite month in the year?

  b In what month is your birthday?

  c How old are you?

  d What did you do for your birthday?

Score 2 points for each correct answer!

SCORE **/14** 0-4 6-10 12-14

## Measurement & Space

AC9M4M01

### Mass

Mass is measured in grams and kilograms.

A paperclip weighs approximately 1 gram.

A 1 litre bottle of water weighs approximately 1 kilogram.

1 kg = 1000 g

1 kilogram = 1000 grams

$\frac{1}{2}$ kg = 500 g

half of a kilogram = 500 grams

$\frac{1}{4}$ kg = 250 g

quarter of a kilogram = 250 grams

**Number these items from the smallest mass (1) to the largest mass (9).**

①  tennis ball: 58 g

②  cricket ball: 163 g

③  cricket bat: 1 kg

④  tennis racquet: 280 g

⑤  badminton racquet: 90 g

⑥  softball bat: 94 g

⑦  dart board: 5 kg

⑧  basketball: 624 g

⑨  table tennis bat: 85 g

**Use the items to answer the questions.**

⑩ Which item has the greatest mass?

_____

⑪ Which item has the smallest mass?

_____

⑫ Which items are heavier than $\frac{1}{2}$ kilogram?

_____

_____

⑬ Which items weigh less than $\frac{1}{2}$ kilogram?

_____

_____

_____

⑭ What is the total mass of a tennis racquet and a tennis ball? _____

⑮ What is the total mass of a cricket bat and a cricket ball? _____

⑯ What is the total mass of three badminton racquets? _____

⑰ Which item weighs more than $\frac{1}{4}$ kg but less than $\frac{1}{2}$ kilogram?

_____

Score 2 points for each correct answer!

SCORE **/34** 0-14 16-28 30-34

## Problem Solving

AC9M4N06

### Find the largest

**What is the largest number you can make using these three digits?**

3  5  4

- You can only use each digit once.
- You can add or multiply.
- Use a calculator to help you.

*Possible answers:*

3 + 5 + 4 = 12     35 + 4 = 39     54 + 3 = 57

3 × 54 = 162     53 × 4 = 212     5 × 43 = 215

**What is the largest number you can make using these three digits?**

5  8  4

**Write down all the possible combinations.**

_____

_____

_____

# Grammar & Punctuation

AC9E4LY06

## Proper nouns

> **Proper nouns** are the special names given to people, places and things. They begin with a capital letter.
>
> *Examples:* Sydney, Mississippi, Mrs Jones, August, Easter, Jack

**Is the word in bold a common noun (C) or a proper noun (P)? Write C or P.**

① My teacher is called **Mrs Sirett**. ___

② My sister's **teacher** is called Mr Black. ___

③ **Children** must be supervised at the pool.
___

④ **London** is the capital city of England. ___

**Give all the proper nouns a capital letter.**

⑤ michael plays basketball for the franklin dodgers.

⑥ My dog, max, likes to play with my friend's dog, spot.

⑦ We like to eat lunch at ted's café in border street.

**Match each proper noun in the box to a common noun. The first one has been done for you.**

| Africa | Cockatoo | Mercedes | Paul |
|---|---|---|---|
| Amazon | Everest | Paris | Star Wars |

| Common noun | Proper noun |
|---|---|
| month | May |
| ⑧ car | _____ |
| ⑨ mountain | _____ |
| ⑩ movie | _____ |
| ⑪ city | _____ |
| ⑫ continent | _____ |
| ⑬ boy's name | _____ |
| ⑭ river | _____ |
| ⑮ parrot | _____ |

---

# Phonic Knowledge & Spelling

AC9E4LY09, AC9E4LY10

## Letter teams that make the long 'e' sound

**Say each word in the word bank. The letter teams ee and ea work together to make one sound — the long 'e' sound.**

**When the letter r is added to these letter teams, it makes an ear sound.**

| agree | sneeze | squeeze | coffee |
|---|---|---|---|
| cease | season | reason | creature |
| near | gear | clear | beard |
| cheer | deer | peer | steer |

**Choose words from the word bank to complete these sentences.**

① Early one morning, we saw a _____ crossing the road.

② When I am sad, I like to have people to _____ me up.

③ My dad likes to have a cup of _____ every morning.

**Make words by adding the word ending to each line.**

| −eep | −ear |
|---|---|
| bl e e p | r e a r |
| ④ sw _ _ _ | ⑥ sp _ _ _ |
| ⑤ cr _ _ _ | ⑦ g _ _ _ |

## Plurals

> **Remember!** To make a word **plural** (more than one), you usually just add **s**. For words that end in **ch, sh, s, ss, x, z** or **zz** you add **−es** to make them plural.
>
> *Examples:*
> coffee – coffee**s**       chur**ch** – church**es**
> di**sh** – dish**es**       gas – gas**es**
> class – class**es**       box – box**es**
> waltz – waltz**es**       buzz – buzz**es**
>
> **NOTE** – Some words do not follow the rules, such as **ox – oxen** and **quiz – quizzes**. Some words do not change for the plural.
>
> *Examples:* aircraft, spacecraft

**Write these words in the plural.**

⑧ peach _____      ⑩ leash _____

⑨ guess _____      ⑪ lynx _____

AC9E4LY05, AC9HS4K02

## Dirk Hartog

**Informative text**
Author – Carolyn Tate

Europeans had long believed there was a great land mass in the Southern **Hemisphere**. They called it, in Latin, *Terra Australias Incognita* – Unknown South Land. Dirk Hartog proved that it existed.

Hartog (1580–1621) was a Dutch sailor and explorer. He set sail in 1616 with a fleet of ships to trade in Batavia (today's Jakarta, Indonesia). Hartog's ship, *Eendracht*, became separated from the fleet in a storm. When the ship rounded the Cape of Good Hope (the southern tip of Africa), it mistakenly sailed too far east.

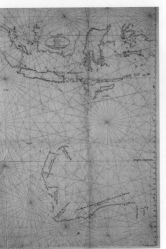

On 25 October 1616, the *Eendracht* dropped anchor off what is now known as Dirk Hartog Island. Less than one kilometre away was the west coast of Australia – Hartog realised he had discovered a new land. He scratched a short record of his visit on a **pewter** dinner plate. He then nailed the plate to a post and left it on a cliff top.

Hartog then sailed north, **charting** the coastline as he went. He named the new land *'t Landt van de Eendracht* (The Land of the Eendracht). Later Dutch explorers changed this to *Hollandia Nova* (New Holland). The British named it *Australia*, just over 200 years after Hartog's journey.

Source: *Explorers*, Go Facts, Blake Education.

---

Write or circle the correct answers.

① **Dirk Hartog was born in Holland in 1580. How old was he when he set sail for Batavia?**

a 25     b 36     c We are not told.

② **Which word in the text means 'half of the earth'?**

_____

③ **What is Latin?**

a the language of Ancient Rome

b a name

c a type of Dutch boat

④ **Why was Australia called *Terra Australis Incognita* in the 1500s?**

a People liked the sound of the name.

b The name is close to the word 'Australia'.

c Australia was unknown then and the words mean 'Unknown South Land'.

⑤ **What is the southern tip of Africa called?**

_____

⑥ **What is pewter?**

a a type of decoration

b a type of metal

c an expensive plate

⑦ **Why did Hartog scratch a record of his visit on a plate and leave it on a cliff top?**

a He wanted to prove that he had been there.

b He wanted to say how good the ship's meals were.

c He wanted to warn any enemies to stay away.

⑧ **Charting means:**

a photographing.

b drawing.

c mapping.

Score 2 points for each correct answer!   SCORE  /16  0-6  8-12  14-16

### My Book Review

Title _____

Author _____

Rating ☆☆☆☆☆

Comment _____

_____

# Number & Algebra

AC9M4A02

## Multiplication and division facts

If you know the multiplication facts, you also know the division facts.

5 × 4 = 20    20 ÷ 4 = 5

4 × 5 = 20    20 ÷ 5 = 4

**Complete these multiplications and divisions.**

① 4 × 3 = _____
② 3 × _____ = 12
③ 12 ÷ 4 = _____
④ 12 ÷ _____ = 3
⑤ 3 × 5 = _____
⑥ _____ × 3 = 15
⑦ 15 ÷ 5 = _____
⑧ 15 ÷ _____ = 3
⑨ 6 × 2 = _____
⑩ _____ × 6 = 12

⑪ 12 ÷ _____ = 6
⑫ 12 ÷ 2 = _____
⑬ 7 × 4 = _____
⑭ 4 × _____ = 28
⑮ 28 ÷ 4 = _____
⑯ 28 ÷ _____ = 4
⑰ 9 × 3 = _____
⑱ 3 × 9 = _____
⑲ 27 ÷ _____ = 3
⑳ 27 ÷ 9 = _____

㉑ **This is a multiplication grid for the 2, 3, 4 and 5 times tables. Complete the grid.**

| × | 2 | 3 | 4 | 5 |
|---|---|---|---|---|
| 1 | 2 | 3 | 4 | 5 |
| 2 | 4 | 6 | | 10 |
| 3 | 6 | 9 | | 15 |
| 4 | 8 | | 16 | 20 |
| 5 | 10 | | 20 | |
| 6 | 12 | 18 | | |
| 7 | 14 | 21 | | 35 |
| 8 | 16 | | | |
| 9 | | | | 45 |
| 10 | | 30 | 40 | |

**Use the grid to answer the questions.**

㉒ What do you notice about the numbers in the ×2 column? What is the pattern?

_____

_____

㉓ What do you notice about the numbers in the ×4 column? What is the pattern?

_____

_____

㉔ What do you notice about the numbers in the ×5 column? What is the pattern?

_____

_____

**Write the missing numbers.**

㉕ 12, 14, 16, 18, _____, _____, _____, _____

㉖ 30, 33, 36, 39, _____, _____, _____, _____

㉗ 40, 44, 48, 52, _____, _____, _____, _____

㉘ 55, 60, 65, 70, _____, _____, _____, _____

㉙ 124, 126, 128, 130, _____, _____, _____,

_____

㉚ 152, 156, 160, 164, _____, _____, _____,

_____

Score 2 points for each correct answer!

SCORE  /60  ( 0-28 )  ( 30-54 )  ( 56-60 )

## Statistics & Probability

*There are no statistics & probability activities in this unit.*

## Measurement & Space

AC9M4SP01

### 2D shapes

2D shapes can be **regular** or **irregular**.

The **sides** of a **regular shape** are equal – they are all the same length.

The **angles** of a **regular shape** are equal – they are all the same size.

The **sides** of an **irregular shape** are different lengths.

The **angles** of an **irregular shape** are different sizes.

A **quadrilateral** is a shape with **four sides**. Squares and rectangles are quadrilaterals.

A square is a regular quadrilateral – all the sides and angles are equal.

A rectangle is an irregular quadrilateral.

TARGETING HOMEWORK 4 © PASCAL PRESS ISBN 9781925726466

TERM 1 MATHS

**Name these shapes. Use the word bank to help you. Circle if the shapes are regular or irregular.**

triangle: 3 sides
quadrilateral: 4 sides
pentagon: 5 sides
hexagon: 6 sides
heptagon: 7 sides
octagon: 8 sides
nonagon: 9 sides
decagon: 10 sides

① _____
② **a** regular    **b** irregular

③ _____
④ **a** regular    **b** irregular

⑤ _____
⑥ **a** regular    **b** irregular

⑦ _____
⑧ **a** regular    **b** irregular

⑨ _____
⑩ **a** regular    **b** irregular

⑪ _____
⑫ **a** regular    **b** irregular

⑬ _____
⑭ **a** regular    **b** irregular

⑮ _____
⑯ **a** regular    **b** irregular

⑰ _____
⑱ **a** regular    **b** irregular

⑲ _____
⑳ **a** regular    **b** irregular

*Score 2 points for each correct answer!*

SCORE /40   0-18   20-34   36-40

## Multiplication grids

**Multiply each number in the grid by 3. Write the answers in the second grid. How quickly can you complete it?**

| 4 | 3 | 5 | 2 | 9 |
|---|---|---|---|---|
| 10 | 2 | 8 | 4 | 7 |
| 1 | 6 | 10 | 5 | 1 |
| 9 | 4 | 2 | 8 | 10 |
| 2 | 3 | 7 | 4 | 9 |
| 5 | 8 | 10 | 2 | 6 |

**×3**

| 12 | | | | 27 |
|---|---|---|---|---|
| | | | | |
| | | | | |
| | | 6 | | |
| | | | | |
| 15 | | | | 18 |

Now try it ×5!

**×5**

| 20 | | | | 45 |
|---|---|---|---|---|
| | | | | |
| | | | | |
| | | 10 | | |
| | | | | |
| 25 | | | | 30 |

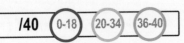

# Grammar & Punctuation

AC9E4LY06

## Noun groups

> A **noun group** is a group of words built around a **noun**. The noun is the main word and the words in the noun group tell us more about the noun.
>
> *Examples:*  a tall, handsome **prince**
> noun group        **noun**
>
> an **octopus** with eight dangly **legs**
> noun group  **noun**        noun group  **noun**
>
> A **noun group** may contain two or more nouns connected by **and**, which is known as a joining word.
>
> *Example:* The old house had **broken windows, a damaged door and a leaky roof.**

**Circle the nouns and underline the noun groups in these sentences. (*Hint:* There may be more than one in each sentence.)**

1. A large, heavy parcel was delivered to our neighbour.
2. The rain poured into the old, haunted house.
3. The model wore a long, flowing dress at the photoshoot.
4. An elephant with huge feet stomped into the circus ring.

**Underline the noun groups in these sentences. (*Hint:* There may be more than one in each sentence.)**

5. The clown wore huge brown shoes, a funny hat and a red nose.
6. Mike and his best friend are staying with us on Saturday and Sunday.
7. The supermarket had apples, bananas and melons on special offer.
8. My brother is a tall boy with red hair and a freckled face.

*Score 2 points for each correct answer!*  **SCORE** **/16**  (0-6) (8-12) (14-16)

# Phonic Knowledge & Spelling

AC9E4LY09, AC9E4LY10, AC9E4LY11

## Letter teams o–e, oa and ow

**Say each word in the word bank. The letter teams o–e, oa and ow work together to make the long 'o' sound.**

| nose | close | rode | whole |
|------|-------|------|-------|
| loaf | load | coax | coast |
| borrow | shadow | elbow | meadow |

**Choose words from the word bank to complete these sentences.**

1. Can you find a _____ bottle in amongst the broken ones?
2. If you are poor, you sometimes need to _____ money.
3. My _____ was not broken, it was only bruised.

**Make compound words that end in load. The first one has been done for you.**

bus load

4. down_____
5. ship_____
6. over_____
7. work_____
8. truck_____

**Circle the correct homophone to complete these sentences.**

9. The man (rode   road) his horse to the stable.
10. My nan can eat a (whole   hole) cake at once!
11. I stubbed my big (tow   toe) on a rock.

*Score 2 points for each correct answer!*  **SCORE** **/22**  (0-8) (10-16) (18-22)

**Imaginative text** – Humorous poems and word play
**Author** – Anonymous

## Raising Frogs for Profit

Raising frogs for profit
Is a very sorry joke.
How can you make money
When so many of them croak?

## A Sea-Serpent Saw a Big Tanker

A sea-serpent saw a big tanker,
Bit a hole in her side and sank her.
It swallowed the crew
In a minute or two,
And then picked its teeth with the anchor.

## Betty Botter

Betty Botter bought some butter,
But, she said, this butter's bitter;
If I put it in my batter,
It will make my batter bitter,
But a bit of better butter
Will make my batter better.
So she bought a bit of butter
Better than her bitter butter
And she put it in her batter,
And it made her batter better,
So 'twas better Betty Botter
Bought a bit of better butter.

## Well, Hardly Ever

Never throw a brick at a drownin' man
Outside a grocery store —
Always throw him a bar of soap —
And he'll wash himself ashore.

---

Write or circle the correct answers.

① A pun is a joke that makes a play on words that can have several different meanings. In the poem *Raising Frogs for Profit*, the word **croak** has two different meanings. What are they?

a to hop away and to hide

b the sound a frog makes and to die

c to sing and to hop

② What's funny about the last line in the poem *Well, Hardly Ever*?

_____

All the poems use words that rhyme.
Which words in the texts rhyme with these?

③ joke _____

④ crew _____

⑤ *Betty Botter* is a tongue twister. What does this mean?

a It twists your tongue when you say it.

b The words can be difficult to pronounce if you say them quickly.

c I'm not sure.

⑥ What is another word for **bitter**?

a sour          b tasty          c sweet

⑦ What does **profit** mean?

a to have fun

b to begin a hobby

c to make money

⑧ What was Betty Botter trying to do?

_____

Score 2 points for each correct answer!  SCORE  **/16**  (0-6)  (8-12)  (14-16)

## My Book Review

Title _____

Author _____

Rating ☆☆☆☆☆

Comment _____

_____

## Number & Algebra

AC9M4N09

### Number patterns

Use the rule to fill in the blanks in these number patterns.

**(rule)    pattern**

① (+5)  120, 125, _____, _____, 140, 145, _____

② (+3)  255, _____, _____, 264, _____

③ (–5)  1350, 1345, 1340, _____, _____, _____

④ (+4)  1824, 1828, _____, _____, _____, 1844

⑤ (–4)  3000, _____, _____, _____, 2984

Complete these number patterns. Write the rule.

⑥ 890, 892, 894, _____, _____, _____

rule = _____

⑦ 6000, 5997, 5994, _____, _____, _____

rule = _____

⑧ 12 105, 12 100, 12 095, _____, _____, _____

rule = _____

⑨ 56, 66, 76, 86, _____, _____, _____

rule = _____

⑩ 568, 564, 560, _____, _____, _____

rule = _____

⑪–⑭ **Join the boxes that have the same answers.**

(2 × 10) + 1

double 8

8 lots of 2

7 × 3

half of 24

half of 72

24 ÷ 2

9 times 4

## Statistics & Probability

AC9M4P01

### How likely is it?

We can use a **likely scale** to predict how likely something is to happen.

impossible   very unlikely    likely    very likely    certain

*Examples:*

You will go to school in a hot air balloon: very unlikely or impossible

You will eat lunch tomorrow: very likely or certain

You will fly to Mars today: impossible

You will have a drink today: certain

**Write the labels from the likely scale to show the chance of each thing happening.**

① You will ride an elephant to school tomorrow. _____

② You will do some writing at school this week.

_____

③ You will talk to someone today.

_____

④ You will eat some fruit this week.

_____

⑤ An alien spaceship will land in the school grounds. _____

⑥ Your parents will receive some mail today.

_____

⑦ You will go to the beach this summer.

_____

⑧ You will get younger every day.

_____

**Number these events from 1 to 5 with 1 being impossible and 5 being certain.**

⑨ This year you will grow older.

___

⑩ This year your family will win the lottery.

___

⑪ This year you will become Prime Minister.

___

⑫ This year you will meet someone new.

___

⑬ This year you will go on a family outing.

TARGETING HOMEWORK 4 © PASCAL PRESS ISBN 9781925726466

## Measurement & Space

AC9M4M01

## Capacity

Capacity is the amount a container can hold.
When we measure capacity, we use millilitres and litres.

1000 millilitres = 1 litre
500 millilitres = $\frac{1}{2}$ litre
250 millilitres = $\frac{1}{4}$ litre
This jug contains 250 mL or $\frac{1}{4}$ litre of water.

How much water is in each jug?
Write the answer in mL.

① _____

③ _____

② _____

④ _____

Colour each measuring jug to match the quantity.

⑤ 100 mL

⑦ 250 mL

⑥ 325 mL

⑧ 50 mL

Write true or false.

⑨ $\frac{1}{2}$ litre = 250 mL _____
⑩ 1 litre = 1000 mL _____
⑪ 250 mL + 250 mL = $\frac{1}{2}$ litre _____
⑫ 3 litres + 200 mL = 3200 mL _____

Score 2 points for each correct answer!

SCORE 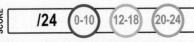 /24  (0-10) (12-18) (20-24)

## Problem Solving

AC9M4N06

### Down to zero

Look at this puzzle.

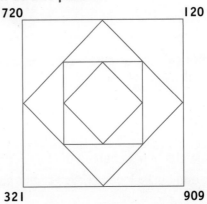

Find the difference between the numbers in the corners to get the middle numbers. For example in the top row, 720 – 120 = 600.
Repeat until you reach zero.
Your square should look like this:

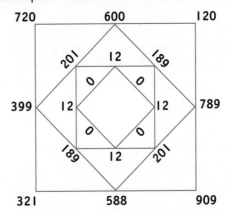

**Your challenge:** Is it possible to find four corner numbers that cannot be reduced to zero?

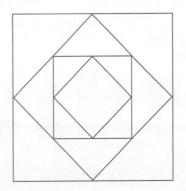

# Grammar & Punctuation

AC9E4LY06

## Verbs

Every sentence has a **verb**. Verbs are words that tell us what is happening in a sentence. They tell us what the **subject** of the sentence is doing, thinking, saying and feeling.

*Example:* The man **dived** into the swimming pool.

The man is the **subject**.

What was the man doing?
He **dived**.
The **verb** is 'dived'.

**Underline the subject of each sentence. Then circle the verb.**

① The footballers practised their skills every Thursday.

② I studied the painting on the wall.

③ Two huge elephants charged at the tourists.

④ Georgie and Jack played cricket at the park.

**Choose a suitable verb from the box to complete this paragraph.**

| | | |
|---|---|---|
| hope | said | placed |
| broke | put | scooped |
| finished | opened | enjoy |
| turned | | |

Jamal's mother _____ ⑤
mixing the ingredients for his birthday cake,
_____ ⑥ the oven on and put
the cake in. She then _____ ⑦
a large bar of chocolate, _____ ⑧
it into pieces and _____ ⑨
it in a bowl. She then _____ ⑩
out some ice cream into ten small bowls and
_____ ⑪ them on the table.

"Right, I'm finished," she _____ ⑫.
"I _____ ⑬ Jamal and his friends
_____ ⑭ his birthday treats."

---

# Phonic Knowledge & Spelling

AC9E4LY10, AC9E4LY11

## Letter teams that make the long 'i' sound

Say each word in the word bank. The letter teams **i–e**, **ie** and **igh** work together to make one sound — **the long 'i' sound**. Many words that end in the **letter y** also make the long 'i' sound. In one syllable words, the letter i usually makes a long 'i' sound.

| | | | |
|---|---|---|---|
| bite | hike | shine | life |
| cry | dry | fly | fry |
| pie | tie | lie | die |
| kind | wind | blind | wild |
| fight | right | slight | might |

**Choose words from the word bank to complete these sentences.**

① "Who broke the baby's _____ up toy?" asked Mum.

② I do not know why I turned left instead of _____.

③ Dad couldn't remember when he bought his polka dot _____.

## Adding endings to words that end in y

**Remember!** When a word ends in **y**, we keep the **y** when we add **–ing**.

*Examples:* fry, fry**ing** cry, cry**ing**

But, we change the **y** to **i** before adding **–es** or **–ed**.

*Examples:* fry – fr**ies**, fr**ied**
cry – cr**ies**, cr**ied**

**Note:** fly – fly**ing**, fl**ies**, **flew**

**Add –ing, –es and –ed to these words.**

| | –ing | –es | –ed |
|---|---|---|---|
| ④ dry | _____ | _____ | _____ |
| ⑤ spy | _____ | _____ | _____ |
| ⑥ pry | _____ | _____ | _____ |
| ⑦ try | _____ | _____ | _____ |

---

## Getting Rid of Wrinkles

**Imaginative text** – Humorous
**Author** – Teena Raffa-Mulligan
**Illustrator** – Craig Smith

*Tessa's Great Grandma Em wanted to get rid of the wrinkles on her face before her old friend, Amelia, came to visit. Tessa decided to help her.*

Tessa bounced down off the fence. "Don't worry, I'll help."

They hurried indoors. Great Gran let Tessa draw a big circle on the calendar around the date when Amelia was due to arrive.

They ate the rest of the super-special chocolate cake and a whole tub of ice-cream to help them think.

"I've got an idea," said Tessa. "If you stand on your head, you might unwrinkle, like when Mum hangs creased clothes on a hanger."

Great Gran nodded. "That might work. But it's been such a long time since I did anything like that, you'd better catch my legs."

Tessa missed.

"Timber!" cried Great Grandpop when Great Gran toppled sideways.

Now she had a headache as well as wrinkles, and had to lie on the sofa for a while before they tried something else.

That gave Tessa time to think. "Steam," she said at last. "That gets the crinkles out really well when Mum's doing the ironing."

It didn't work on Great Gran's face. She leaned over a bowl of steaming water with a towel covering her head for an hour. Afterwards, she felt so hot that she almost fainted and had to lie down again.

She felt worse when Great Grandpop marched about the house singing, 'Emma, the Red-faced Grandma' to the tune of 'Rudolf the Red-nosed Reindeer'.

Source: *Getting Rid of Wrinkles*, Gigglers, Blake Education.

---

**Write or circle the correct answers.**

① **What is the meaning of bounced in this text?**

a rebounded

b recovered

c jumped

② **Why did Great Gran want to get rid of her wrinkles before her friend arrived?**

a She wanted to fill in the time while she waited.

b She wanted to look her best for her friend.

c She wanted to impress her great granddaughter.

③ **What other two words in the text mean the same as wrinkle?**

_____

④ **How did Great Gran feel when Great Grandpop marched about singing 'Emma, the Red-faced Grandma'?**

a proud      b unhappy      c embarrassed

*Score 2 points for each correct answer!* SCORE /8  0-2  4-6  8

### My Book Review

Title _____

Author _____

Rating

Comment _____

_____

**TERM 1 MATHS**

# Number & Algebra

AC9M4N03

## Fractions

When we share an object into **equal parts**, each part is called a **fraction**.

This shape has been divided up into 6 equal parts.

Each part is $\frac{1}{6}$ of the whole shape. **4 out of 6 parts** are shaded, so we say $\frac{4}{6}$ of the shape is shaded.

**Write the fraction of the shape that is shaded.**

① ____

④ ____

② ____

⑤ ____

③ ____

⑥ ____

**Colour the shapes to show the fractions.**

⑦ $\frac{2}{6}$

⑪ $\frac{4}{10}$

⑧ $\frac{2}{5}$

⑫ $\frac{1}{3}$

⑨ $\frac{2}{8}$

⑬ $\frac{4}{8}$

⑩ $\frac{2}{3}$

⑭ $\frac{5}{6}$

**Complete this fraction wall by writing the missing fractions.**

| 1 | | | |
| $\frac{1}{2}$ | | $\frac{1}{2}$ | |

⑮ $\frac{1}{3}$

⑯ $\frac{1}{4}$

⑰

⑱

⑲

⑳

SCORE Score 2 points for each correct answer! **/40**  (0-18) (20-34) (36-40)

# Statistics & Probability

*There are no statistics & probability activities in this unit.*

# Measurement & Space

AC9M4M01

## Measuring temperature

**Temperature** is a measure of **how cold or hot** things are. We use a thermometer to measure temperature in **degrees Celsius (°C)**.

The larger the number in degrees Celsius, the hotter it is. So 30 °C is hotter than 10 °C.

**Write these temperatures in order from coldest to hottest.**

① 12 °C   40 °C   35 °C   8 °C

_____

② 18 °C   12 °C   20 °C   17 °C

_____

③ 0 °C   32 °C   100 °C   25 °C

_____

**Write these temperatures in numerals and use the symbol for degrees Celsius.**

④ twenty-eight degrees Celsius   _____

⑤ fifteen degrees Celsius   _____

⑥ one hundred and ten degrees Celsius   _____

⑦ two hundred degrees Celsius   _____

⑧ ninety-two degrees Celsius   _____

⑨ one hundred and five degrees Celsius   _____

TARGETING HOMEWORK 4 © PASCAL PRESS  ISBN 9781925726466

**Write these temperatures in words.**

⑩ 27 °C _____

⑪ 109 °C _____
_____

⑫ 181 °C _____
_____

*Example:*
This thermometer shows a temperature of 30 °C.

**Write the temperatures shown on each thermometer.**

⑬ _____

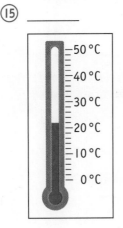

⑭ _____

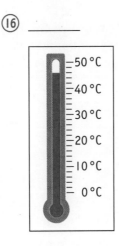

⑮ _____

⑯ _____

## Tree diagrams

**Read this problem. A tree diagram has been used to solve it.**

Jan always wears either pink socks or white socks. She wears her socks with black, white or pink trainers.

How many different choices of footwear does she have?

**pink socks**

| pink socks & black trainers | pink socks & white trainers | pink socks & pink trainers |
|---|---|---|

**white socks**

| white socks & black trainers | white socks & white trainers | white socks & pink trainers |
|---|---|---|

Jan has **6** choices of footwear that she can wear.

**Use a tree diagram to solve this problem.**

Ben likes two types of pizza: tomato base and cheese base.

He likes three types of toppings: ham, pineapple and anchovies.

He always has only one topping on his pizza.

How many different choices does Ben have for his pizzas?

*Score 2 points for each correct answer!*

SCORE **/32** ⟨0-14⟩ ⟨16-26⟩ ⟨28-32⟩

# Grammar & Punctuation

AC9E4LY06

TERM 1 ENGLISH

## Commands

Some sentences are **commands**. They request or demand that the listener or reader do something. Commands begin with a **doing verb** and end with a full stop. The subject of a command is always **you**.

*Examples:* **Choose** your favourite book.
**Map** your journey to school.

Sometimes an **exclamation mark (!)** can give extra emphasis to a **command**. Exclamations are sentences where people suddenly cry out in surprise, fear or anger.

*Examples:* **Get** out of my way!
**Remove** the saucepan — it's boiling over!

**Choose a verb to begin each sentence.**

| Run | Watch | Wash |
| --- | --- | --- |

1 _____ out for that truck!

2 _____ your hands after using the toilet.

3 _____ for your life!

## Commas

**Commas (,)** are used to:

* separate items in a list.
  *Example:* This recipe requires eggs, milk, butter and flour.

* show the reader where to make a small break between words.
  *Example:* Melt the butter, add the beaten eggs and stir in the flour.

**Add commas in this recipe.**
**(*Hint:* There are 8 commas in total. Not all the steps have commas!)**

4 – 11  **Rock cakes**

* Collect the ingredients: flour sugar butter dried fruit egg and milk.

* Mix the flour sugar and melted butter in a bowl.

* Beat the egg and milk together.

* Add the milk mixture to the flour mixture stir until smooth and then add the dried fruit.

* Scoop up some of the mixture shape it into a ball and place it on a baking tray.

* Bake in a moderate oven until brown.

*Score 2 points for each correct answer!*  SCORE  **/22**  (0-8) (10-16) (18-22)

# Phonic Knowledge & Spelling

AC9E4LY09, AC9E4LY10, AC9E4LY11

## Letter teams oo and ew

Say each word in the word bank. The letter team **oo** can make a **short sound**, such as in **book** or a **long sound**, such as in **noon**. The letter team **ew** makes a **long oo** sound.

| wood | good | hook | shook | foot |
| --- | --- | --- | --- | --- |
| noon | soon | roof | proof | tooth |
| chew | crew | screw | knew | jewel |

**Choose words from the word bank to complete these sentences.**

1 "I can't find any _____ to light the fire," said Dad.

2 I don't think that is a real _____ in that necklace.

3 "Isn't that a _____ idea," said Mum.

**Circle the words that have the same long oo sound as noon.**

4 food   took   mood   broom   crook

**Complete the rhyming words.**

5 few      6 book      7 boot
  d _ _      t _ _ _      r _ _ _
  st _ _     l _ _ _      sh _ _ _

**Add tooth to the beginning of these words to make compound words.**

8 _____ paste

9 _____ ache

10 _____ brush

11 _____ pick

**Make new words by adding the endings. Write the new words.**

12 wood + en = _____

13 roof + ing = _____

14 good + ness = _____

15 chew + ed = _____

16 soon + er = _____

*Score 2 points for each correct answer!*  SCORE  **/32**  (0-14) (16-26) (28-32)

TARGETING HOMEWORK 4 © PASCAL PRESS ISBN 9781925726466

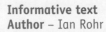
TERM 1 ENGLISH

# The Australian Government

**Informative text**
**Author – Ian Rohr**

Australia is a parliamentary constitutional monarchy — it has a parliament, a **constitution** and the British monarch is the head of state.

Australia has a federal system of government. This means States make their own local decisions and join together to give major powers to a central, Federal Government.

### Federal Government

The Australian Constitution contains the rules for governing Australia. It lists the specific areas that the Federal Government can control. The Federal Government passes laws that affect the whole country.

### State and Territory Governments

State and Territory governments have the power to make laws in areas not covered by the constitution. Their powers are not set out in the Australian constitution, and Federal law overrules State law if they conflict on an issue.

### Local Government

Local governments run **municipalities** through local councils. Councillors are elected and hold regular meetings to make decisions on local issues and funding. State governments give control over certain functions to local councils. However, they can dismiss a council and call for a new election if a council acts irresponsibly or breaks the law.

Source: *Government*, Go Facts, Blake Education.

---

**Write or circle the correct answers.**

① **What is a monarch?**

  a a Prime Minister

  b the head of state such as a king or queen

  c a member of parliament

② **What does the Australian constitution contain?**

  a decisions

  b parliament

  c the rules for governing Australia

③ **What is a municipality?**

  a a town or district that has local government

  b a meeting

  c a type of government

④ **What is the meaning of overrule?**

  a to rule over   b to reject   c to agree

⑤ **What is the meaning of dismiss?**

  a govern   b elect   c order to leave

⑥ **What happens if the State government dismisses a local council?**

_____

_____

Score 2 points for each correct answer!

SCORE **/12**  ( 0-4 ) ( 6-8 ) ( 10-12 )

### My Book Review

Title _____

Author _____

Rating ☆☆☆☆☆

Comment _____

_____

# Number & Algebra

AC9M4N07

## Rounding money

In Australia, the smallest amount of money you can spend is five cents. This means you need to know how to **round** a number up or down.

When rounding money, always look at the **cent place value**.

If the cent place value is:

- **1** or **2** then you **round down** to the nearest dollar
- **3** or **4** then you **round up** to 5 cents
- **6** or **7** then you **round down** to 5 cents
- **8** or **9** then you **round up** to 10 cents

*Examples*:

$1.01 and $1.02: round down to $1.00

$1.03 and $1.04: round up to $1.05

$1.06 and $1.07: round down to $1.05

$1.08 and $1.09: round up to $1.10

**Round these amounts to the nearest 5 cents. Circle the correct answer.**

1. $3.61    a $3.65    b $3.60
2. $12.52   a $12.50   b $12.55
3. $22.74   a $22.70   b $22.75
4. $61.83   a $61.80   b $61.85
5. $80.26   a $80.30   b $80.25
6. $104.49  a $104.50  b $104.45
7. $238.77  a $238.80  b $238.75

**Work out the change from $20.00 for each amount. The first one has been done for you.**

| | Price | Nearest 5 cents | Change from $20.00 |
|---|---|---|---|
| | $1.62 | $1.60 | $18.40 |
| 8 | $5.31 | | |
| 9 | $8.59 | | |
| 10 | $10.75 | | |
| 11 | $16.49 | | |
| 12 | $11.27 | | |
| 13 | $17.18 | | |
| 14 | $14.36 | | |
| 15 | $10.33 | | |
| 16 | $8.84 | | |

**Solve these money problems. Calculate the change to the nearest 5 cents.**

17. Ben bought 3 pens for $1.99 each. He paid $10.00. How much change did he receive?

_____

18. A dozen eggs cost $6.29. How much change from $20.00 if you buy two dozen eggs?

_____

19. Apples cost 57 cents each. How much change from $10.00 if you buy 4 apples?

_____

20. Jade bought a book for $5.99, a pen for $4.58 and a writing pad for $1.97. How much change did Jade get from $20.00?

_____

*Score 2 points for each correct answer!*   SCORE  **/40**  ( 0-18 )  ( 20-34 )  ( 36-40 )

# Statistics & Probability

AC9M4P01

## Probability of events

Sometimes, an event cannot happen if another event happens. In other words, some events **cannot happen at the same time.**

*Examples*:

- If it is raining, it cannot be dry.
- If a girl is born, it cannot be a boy.
- If you only have a blue and a red pencil, you cannot draw a yellow flower.

**Write the letter of the event that cannot happen at the same time. The first one is done for you.**

The bath will overflow. __b__

1. I will buy some red shoes from my favourite shoe shop. ___
2. I will draw a red car. ___
3. I will get 10 out of 10 in my maths test this week. ___
4. Dad will buy a new blue car. ___

   **a** No new cars come in blue.

   **b** The plug was not put in the bath.

   **d** I only have yellow and green pencils.

   **e** My favourite shoe shop doesn't sell red shoes.

   **f** My teacher cancelled the maths test this week.

TERM 1 MATHS

**Circle the correct answer.**

⑤ There are 5 coloured marbles in a bag: 3 red ones, 1 green one and 1 blue one. Abby takes a blue marble out of the bag. What cannot happen next?

a Ben takes out a blue marble.

b Ben takes out a red marble.

c Ben takes out a green marble.

⑥ I own three pairs of shoes: one black pair, one white pair and one red pair. I pack two pairs of my shoes to go away on holiday. What cannot happen?

a I pack one white and one black pair of shoes.

b I pack one pink and one black pair of shoes.

c I pack one red and one black pair of shoes.

*Score 2 points for each correct answer!* **SCORE** **/12** ⟨0-4⟩ ⟨6-8⟩ ⟨10-12⟩

## Measurement & Space

AC9M4M02, AC9M4SP01

## Area

Area is the amount of space inside a shape. Shape A has 8 squares inside it. Shape B has 14 squares. Shape B has a larger area than shape A.

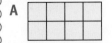 A  B

**Use the areas of these shapes to answer the questions. Write the correct answer.**

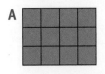 A  B 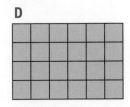 D

C

① Which shape has the largest area? _____

② Which shape has the smallest area? _____

③ Which shapes have an area less than 10 squares? _____

④ Which shapes have an area larger than 10 squares? _____

⑤ Which shape has an area that is half of 24 squares? _____

⑥ Which shape is more than double the area of shape B? _____

⑦–⑨ **Draw three different straight-sided shapes, each with an area of 12 squares.**

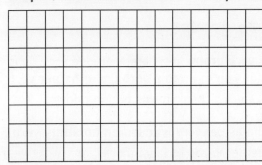

Sometimes, a shape covers half squares.
*Example:*

 There are six full squares and four half squares shaded. Two halves make one, so this shape has a total area of **8** squares.

**What is the area of these shapes? Remember that two half squares make one whole square.**

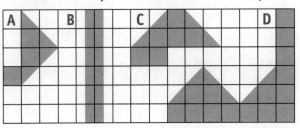

⑩ A = _____ squares

⑪ B = _____ squares

⑫ C = _____ squares

⑬ D = _____ squares

*Score 2 points for each correct answer!* **SCORE** **/26** ⟨0-10⟩ ⟨12-20⟩ ⟨22-26⟩

## Problem Solving

AC9M4SP01

## Join the dots

**Can you join all 9 dots with four straight lines without taking your pencil off the paper? You cannot go over any line twice.**

**What kind of shape did you end up with?**

_____

_____

# Grammar & Punctuation

AC9E4LA09

## Verb groups

A **verb group** has more than one verb. It is made up of a **main verb** and a **helper verb**.

*Example:* The rain **was** <u>pouring</u> down.
**helper verb**  main verb

The helper verb is called an **auxiliary verb**.

**Helper verbs** include: am, is, are, was, were, be, being, been, do, does, did, has, have, had, will and shall.

**Underline the verb group in these sentences.**

① Jasmine is going to university this year.

② The boys were playing football in the park.

③ Michelle has cut her hair shorter.

④ My brother will travel to Europe next month.

## Auxiliary verbs

Some **auxiliary (helper) verbs** tell us about time — whether things are happening in the **present**, the **past** or the **future**.

*Examples:*  Suzie **is** <u>eating</u> her lunch. **present**
Suzie **was** <u>eating</u> her lunch. **past**
Suzie **will** <u>eat</u> her lunch. **future**

**Underline the verb group in these sentences. Then write if they are happening in the present, past or future.**

⑤ Our class will sing at a concert tomorrow.

_____

⑥ Jamie was building a cubby house.

_____

⑦ I am reading an exciting book.

_____

⑧ I shall ride my bike to Nan's on Monday.

_____

# Phonic Knowledge & Spelling

AC9E4LA11, AC9E4LY09, AC9E4LY10

## Letter teams ou and ow

Say each word in the word bank. In these words, the letter teams **ou** and **ow** work together to make the same **sound 'ou'** as in **mouse** and **'ow'** as in **cow**.

| | | | |
|---|---|---|---|
| proud | cloud | hour | flour |
| found | sound | mountain | fountain |
| bow | browse | down | town |
| growl | howl | eyebrow | anyhow |

**Choose words from the word bank to complete these sentences.**

① I managed to get _____ all over me when I made the cake.

② Can you find someone to climb the _____ with me?

③ I kept falling _____ when I tried to ice skate.

④ When I leant on the dog's kennel, the dog started to _____.

**Add down to the beginning of these words to make compound words.**

⑤ _____load

⑥ _____fall

⑦ _____grade

⑧ _____pipe

## Word origins

The word **fountain** comes from an early English word, 'fontayne' which means 'a spring of water that collects in a pool'. It also derives from an old French word, 'fontaine' which means 'natural spring'.

**We use some French words in our language. Match the French word to its meaning.**

| café | ballet | croissant | rendezvous |
|---|---|---|---|

⑨ to meet someone at a specific time and place: _____

⑩ a type of dance: _____

⑪ a small restaurant: _____

⑫ a type of pastry: _____

*Score 2 points for each correct answer!* **SCORE** /16 ( 0-6 ) ( 8-12 ) ( 14-16 )

*Score 2 points for each correct answer!* **SCORE** /24

TARGETING HOMEWORK 4 © PASCAL PRESS  ISBN 9781925726466

**TERM 1 ENGLISH**

## Australian English

**Informative text**
**Author** – Frances Mackay

The first European settlers in Australia came from Britain, so Australian English originated from there, but it has been influenced by many other languages.

One of the most important influences on Australian English has been Aboriginal languages. When the First Fleet arrived in 1788, there were over 200 Aboriginal languages spoken and during the first 100 years of European settlement, about 400 Aboriginal words were adopted by Australian English. Most of these words are the names of places, plants and animals. These words include: Canberra, Ballarat, kangaroo, boomerang, budgerigar, wallaby, wombat, corroboree, dingo, koala, galah, kookaburra, billabong and woomera.

Many of the convicts who were transported from England, Ireland, Scotland and Wales had a language all of their own, called 'flash language', and some of these words were incorporated into Australian English and are still used today — such as **plant** (to hide stolen goods) and **swag** (a thief's stolen goods). The word 'swag' came to mean the belongings of a traveller, wrapped up in a bed roll.

Gold was discovered in 1851 and this brought a huge influx of immigrants hoping to find a fortune. The Gold Rush attracted people from all over the world — China, France, Italy, Poland, Hungary and America. Some of the words used by the gold miners are still in use today and include **digger**, **fossick**, **roll-up** and **mullock**.

As the nation continued to grow and develop, so too did its language. Today, Australian English, like other languages all over the world, continues to evolve and change. Some words will decline in their usage and new words will be added as the language continues to be influenced by world events and the latest trends.

---

Write or circle the correct answers.

① **Another word for originated is:**

 a finished.  b started.  c continued.

② **Which is the odd word?**

 a impacted  b influenced  c unaffected

③ **Name two places in Australia where the name has been borrowed from the Aboriginal language.**

_____

_____

④ **True or false? Over 400 Aboriginal words have been incorporated into Australian English.**

_____

⑤ **What is a convict?**

 a a prisoner

 b an early settler

 c a traveller

⑥ **Another word for fossick is:**

 a travel.  b search.  c speak.

⑦ **A modern-day word that would be unfamiliar to Australians in the 1800s is:**

 a wagon.  b walkabout.  c email.

⑧ **Where did the word swag originate from?**

_____

*Score 2 points for each correct answer!*

**SCORE** /16  0-6  8-12  14-16

**My Book Review**

Title _____

Author _____

Rating ☆☆☆☆☆

Comment _____

_____

# Number & Algebra

AC9M4N06

## Using multiplication for problem solving

*Example:*
How many books does Jake have if he has four times as many as Riley who has eight books?

How to work it out as a number sentence:

4 × 8 = 32 books

Jake has 4 times the number Riley has.

Riley has 8 books.

**Write a number sentence for each multiplication problem to help you solve it.**

① How many strawberries does Su have if she has five times as many as Ria who has ten strawberries?

_____

② Ben ate two hamburgers every day for each day in June. How many did he eat altogether?

_____

③ Megan started with eight figurines. She went to the market and bought some more. She now has triple the number of figurines she originally had. How many does she have?

_____

④ One hundred elephants walked past the safari tourists. How many elephant feet went past?

_____

⑤ Five giants ate four baked potatoes and five boiled potatoes each. How many potatoes were eaten altogether?

_____

⑥ There were 21 people at a party. One third of them ate five sausage rolls each. How many sausage rolls were eaten?

_____

# Problem solving using division

*Example:*
Tim needs 24 cans of cola for his party. The cola comes in packs of six. How many packs does he need?

How to work it out as a number sentence:

24 ÷ 6 = 4 packs

total number of cans needed

number of cans in a pack

**Write a number sentence for each division problem to help you solve it.**

⑦ The volunteer at the charity shop is sorting the shoes. There are 48 shoes. How many pairs of shoes are there?

_____

⑧ There are twenty-five chairs in the hall. When they are put away, they are stacked in fives. How many stacks of chairs will there be?

_____

⑨ Tessa sorted her eighteen hairclips evenly into three containers. How many hairclips in each container?

_____

⑩ Forty people from the care home are going to a concert. They are travelling in taxis. Each taxi can take five passengers. How many taxis do they need?

_____

Score 2 points for each correct answer! | SCORE | /20 | 0-8 | 10-14 | 16-20

# Statistics & Probability

*There are no statistics & probability activities in this unit.*

## Measurement & Space

AC9M4SP02

## Map reading

**Symbols** are used on maps because there is not enough space to draw pictures of everything. Symbols are shown in the **key** (or legend).

This map shows where Emma lives.

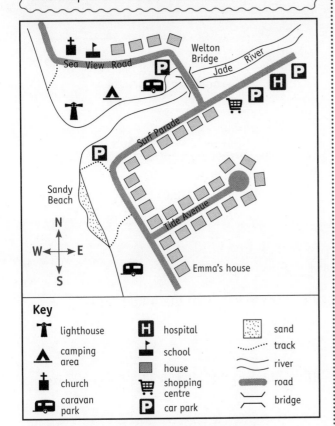

**Key**

| | | | | | |
|---|---|---|---|---|---|
| lighthouse | | hospital | | sand | |
| camping area | | school | | track | |
| church | | house | | river | |
| caravan park | | shopping centre | | road | |
| | | car park | | bridge | |

**Use the key to answer these questions. Write or circle the correct answers.**

① What is opposite Emma's house?

_____

② How many houses are in Tide Avenue? _____

③ In which street is the hospital?

_____

④ In which street is the school?

_____

⑤ What is the name of the road that crosses the river?

_____

⑥ Where is the camping ground?

　a near the lighthouse

　b near Sandy Beach

　c on Surf Parade

⑦ How many parking areas are there in the town? _____

⑧ What is the name of the bridge?

_____

⑨ Emma's mum drives her to school. What roads do they travel on to get there?

_____

_____

Maps use a **compass symbol** to show direction.

N = north, **E** = east, **S** = south and **W** = west

**Use the compass symbol on the map to answer these questions. Write or circle the correct answers.**

⑩ What is north of the lighthouse?

　a shopping centre

　b hospital

　c church

⑪ Is the camping area north or south of the river? _____

⑫ Is Emma's house north or south of the bridge? _____

⑬ In which direction is Sandy Beach from the lighthouse? _____

*Score 2 points for each correct answer!* | **SCORE** | **/26** (0-10) (12-20) (22-26)

## Problem Solving

AC9M4N08

## Multiplying larger numbers

**You can use the grid method to multiply larger numbers.**

*Example:* 31 × 26

Split the numbers. Then use the grid.

31 × 26

30  1    20  6

| × | **20** | **6** |
|---|---|---|
| **30** | 600 | 180 |
| **1** | 20 | 6 |

600 + 180 = 780

20 + 6 = 26

**Total = 806**

**Use the grid method to work out 45 × 23.**

| × | **40** | **5** |
|---|---|---|
| **20** | | |
| **3** | | |

## Grammar & Punctuation

**Underline the subject and then circle the verb in this statement.**

① Yesterday, our class visited the museum.

**Underline the object in this statement.**

② Beth painted the bedroom ceiling and walls.

**Add a question word to complete these questions.**

③ _____ do you make a scarf?

④ _____ is your favourite food?

**Write if these sentences are statements (S), questions (Q), exclamations (E) or commands (C).**

⑤ We went to the cinema last week. ____

⑥ Chop the vegetables into small pieces. ____

⑦ Why didn't you call in on Saturday? ____

⑧ This is fantastic! ____

**Write if the nouns in bold are abstract (A) or concrete (C).**

⑨ I kept my **promise** to help Dad wash the car. ____

⑩ The angry **giant** chased after Jack. ____

**Write capital letters for all the proper nouns in this sentence.**

⑪ harry potter was written by j. k. rowling.

**Underline the noun group in this sentence.**

⑫ The man wore shiny black shoes, a top hat and a bow tie.

**Add the missing commas in this sentence.**

⑬ Chop the tomatoes lettuce spring onions and celery into small pieces.

**Underline the verb group in this sentence. Write if it is happening in the past, present or future.**

⑭ The boys were playing cricket in the park. _____

**Match the common nouns in the box to the proper nouns.**

| city | car | country |
|------|-----|---------|

⑮ New Zealand _____

⑯ Ford _____

⑰ Las Vegas _____

*Score 2 points for each correct answer!*  **SCORE** /34  (0-14)  (16-28)  (30-34)

## Phonic Knowledge & Spelling

**Circle two words with short vowels in each line.**

① **short** a   stack   pace   lamp   made

② **short** e   been   shell   spend   mean

**Add –ed and –ing to these words. Decide if you need to double the last consonant.**

  –ed            –ing

③ check _____ _____

④ drag _____ _____

**Add –ed and –ing to this word.**

  –ed            –ing

⑤ vote _____ _____

**Circle the correct homophone to complete these sentences.**

⑥ We caught the (plane   plain) at 10 o'clock.

⑦ We rode on a (slay   sleigh) in the snow.

**Add –y to this word.**

⑧ spice _____

**Write these words in the plural form.**

⑨ atlas _____

⑩ speech _____

**Add –ing, –es and –ed to this word.**

  –ing        –es        –ed

⑪ dry _____ _____ _____

**Write two different meanings for this homonym.**

⑫ tie _____

_____

**Complete the rhyming words.**

⑬ few   d _ _   st _ _   ch _ _

**Match the words in the box to make compound words.**

| pick | cake | shelf |
|------|------|-------|

⑭ tooth_____

⑮ book_____

⑯ pan_____

*Score 2 points for each correct answer!*  **SCORE** /32  (0-14)  (16-26)  (28-32)

TARGETING HOMEWORK 4 © PASCAL PRESS  ISBN 9781925726466

**Informative text**
**Author** – Claire Craig

# When One Thing Leads to Another

Sometimes an idea that doesn't work can lead to an idea that does. Levi Strauss didn't set out to become the most famous maker of jeans in history, but that's what happened.

Strauss went to San Francisco in 1853 when the California gold rush was in full swing. He hoped to sell canvas to the **prospectors** so they could use this thick, sturdy material to make tents and wagon covers. But he made a mistake. Nobody wanted to buy his canvas.

What the prospectors really needed was trousers. People worked hard in the goldfields and their trousers wore out quickly. So Levi Strauss made trousers out of the brown canvas he couldn't sell. They quickly sold out. Then Strauss switched to a heavy blue fabric. Today, Levi's blue jeans are worn in every country in the world.

Source: *Whose Crazy Idea was That?*, Brainwaves, Blake Education.

*Pants that don't wear aren't worth a hoot in the diggings!*

**Write or circle the correct answers.**

① **What is a prospector?**

_____

② **Where is San Francisco?**

_____

③ **Why did Levi Strauss go to the goldfields?**

a to prospect for gold
b to sell canvas cloth
c to make jeans

④ **Which word in the text means well-known?**

_____

⑤ **What is a wagon?**

a a storage box
b a cart, often drawn by horses
c equipment used for gold mining

⑥ **Levis Strauss 'made the best of a bad thing'. What does this saying mean?**

_____

Score 2 points for each correct answer!

SCORE /12   0-4   6-8   10-12

**My Book Review**

Title _____

Author _____

Rating ☆☆☆☆☆

Comment _____

_____

# Number & Algebra

**How do you write these numbers? Circle the correct answer.**

① seventy-nine

    a 97        b 79        c 709

② one thousand, six hundred

    a 1060    b 1006    c 1600

③ forty-four thousand, eight hundred and six

    a 44 806    b 44 860    c 44 680

**Write the value of the digit in red.**

④ 29 _____

⑤ 765 _____

⑥ 5602 _____

⑦ 58 520 _____

⑧ Split the numbers into their place value to add them. Show your working out.

$$512 + 175$$

_____

_____

_____

⑨ Use the split method to subtract these numbers. Show your working out.

$$694 - 232$$

_____

_____

_____

⑩ Write all the odd numbers between 5410 and 5420.

_____

**Complete these multiplications and divisions.**

⑪ $4 \times 3 =$ _____

⑫ $3 \times$ _____ $= 12$

⑬ $12 \div 4 =$ _____

⑭ $12 \div$ _____ $= 3$

⑮ $5 \times 6 =$ _____

⑯ _____ $\times 5 = 30$

⑰ $30 \div 5 =$ _____

⑱ $30 \div$ _____ $= 5$

**Use the rule to fill in the blanks in these number patterns.**

    **(rule) pattern**

⑲ (+5)  130, 135, _____, _____, 150, 155, _____

⑳ (+3)  655, _____, _____, 664, _____

㉑ (−5)  2345, 2340, _____, _____, _____

**What fraction of these shapes is coloured?**

㉒ _____

㉓ _____

**Solve these money problems. Calculate the change to the nearest 5 cents.**

㉔ Jaz bought 3 books for $1.49 each. She paid the shopkeeper $10.00. How much change did she receive?

_____

㉕ A dozen eggs cost $5.23. How much change from $20.00 if you buy two dozen?

_____

**Write a number sentence for each division problem to help you solve it.**

㉖ Thirty people are coming to May's party. She is going to divide them into five equal groups to play a game. How many people will be in each group?

_____

㉗ Our class of thirty-two students are going to the zoo tomorrow. Only four students at a time can go into the gorilla enclosure. How many groups will it take for the whole class to see the gorillas?

_____

Score 2 points for each correct answer!

SCORE /54  0-24  26-48  50-54

# Statistics & Probability

**How likely are these statements? Write impossible, very unlikely, likely, very likely or certain.**

① There will be kangaroos in Australia tomorrow.

_____

② I will travel to Mars tomorrow.

_____

③ You will go to bed at exactly the same time as your friend.

_____

④ A chef will wear a hat.

_____

⑤ The day after Thursday will be Friday.

_____

⑥ There are 6 coloured marbles in a bag: 3 red ones, 2 green ones and 1 blue one. Abby takes two green marbles out of the bag. What **cannot** happen next?

    a Tanya takes out a red marble

    b Tanya takes out a blue marble

    c Tanya takes out a green marble

TARGETING HOMEWORK 4 © PASCAL PRESS ISBN 9781925726466

Jade surveyed the children in her class to find out what month they had their birthday.

She recorded her results in this table.

| Birthday Month | No. of children |
|---|---|
| January | 1 |
| February | 4 |
| March | 5 |
| April | 3 |
| May | 2 |
| June | 4 |
| July | 3 |
| August | 4 |
| September | 3 |
| October | 3 |
| November | 2 |
| December | 1 |

⑦ Use the information in Jade's table to complete the picture graph.

Key: 🧁 = 2 children  🧁 = 1 child

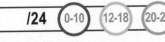

| Jan | Feb | Mar | Apr | May | Jun | Jul | Aug | Sep | Oct | Nov | Dec |

**Write or circle the correct answers.**

⑧ In which month were most children born?

_____

⑨ Which two months had the fewest birthdays?

_____

⑩ How many children took part in the survey?

_____

⑪ Would it be helpful for this graph to have a symbol for 10 children? _____

⑫ What question do you think Jade asked?

 **a** Which is your favourite month?

 **b** In which month were you born?

 **c** How old are you?

*Score 2 points for each correct answer!* SCORE **/24** (0-10) (12-18) (20-24)

## Measurement & Space

**Write these analogue times as digital times.**

① 8 o'clock = _____

② $\frac{1}{4}$ past 5 = _____

③ 25 past 6 = _____

④ $\frac{1}{4}$ to 8 = _____

⑤ 10 to 4 = _____

⑥ 5 past 12 = _____

Estimate the length of the line to the nearest cm. Then measure to see if you are correct.

_____

⑦ My estimate _____

⑧ Measurement _____

**Answer the questions about these items.**

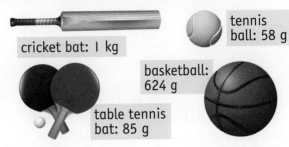

cricket bat: 1 kg

tennis ball: 58 g

basketball: 624 g

table tennis bat: 85 g

⑨ Write the items in order from lightest to heaviest.

_____

_____

⑩ What is the total mass of a tennis ball, a basketball and a table tennis bat?

_____

⑪ Which shape is an irregular quadrilateral?

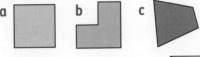

 a   b   c

How much water is in the jug? Write the answer in mL.

⑫ _____

**Write the temperature shown on each thermometer.**

⑬ _____

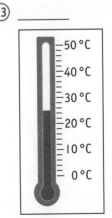

⑭ _____

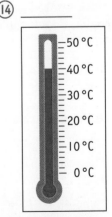

⑮ What is the area of this shape?

_____ squares

**Draw the time on each clock.**

⑯ 4:15

⑰ 5:35

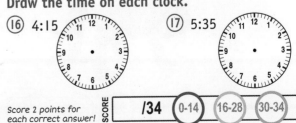

*Score 2 points for each correct answer!* SCORE **/34** (0-14) (16-28) (30-34)

# Grammar & Punctuation

AC9E4LA04

## Personal pronouns

Pronouns take the place of nouns. **Personal pronouns** replace the names of people, places, animals and things. We use pronouns in sentences so we don't have to repeat the same noun over again.

*Example:*

My dog has a favourite toy. My dog likes to cuddle the toy, bury the toy and sleep with the toy.

My dog has a favourite toy. **He** likes to cuddle **it**, bury **it** and sleep with **it**.

The pronoun **he** replaces **my dog**.

The pronoun **it** replaces the noun **toy**.

Pronouns must **agree** with the nouns they replace in number and gender. Gender refers to male, female or neutral (it).

**Singular:** I, he, she, it, him, her, me, you

**Plural:** we, us, you, they, them

**Replace the nouns in bold with a pronoun. Rewrite the sentences.**

① Matty threw the ball so hard **the ball** went flying over the fence.

_____

_____

_____

② Jack wanted to go fishing so **Jack** asked his mum if **Jack** could go.

_____

_____

_____

**Circle the correct pronoun in each sentence.**

③ (She   Her) went to the cinema with us.

④ Please take (I   me) to the park with you.

⑤ Mum took (us   we) to see Gran.

⑥ "Why aren't (she   you) up yet?" asked Mum.

Score 2 points for each correct answer!   SCORE   /12   ( 0-4 )   ( 6-8 )   ( 10-12 )

# Phonic Knowledge & Spelling

AC9E4LY09, AC9E4LY10, AC9E4LY11

## Letter teams au, aw, oar and ore

**Say each word in the word bank. The letter teams au, aw, oar and ore work together to make one sound — or.**

| | | | |
|---|---|---|---|
| pause | cause | caught | applaud |
| draw | drawer | prawn | awful |
| roar | soar | coarse | board |
| shore | score | bore | ignore |

**Choose words from the word bank to complete these sentences.**

① Dad had to mend the _____ in my desk because it was broken.

② Jackson _____ the ball before it hit the ground.

③ Mum sat beside me as we watched the surfer ride into the _____ .

**Circle the correct homophone in each sentence.**

④ My dog hurt his front (paws   pause).

⑤ The lion's (roar   raw) was very loud.

⑥ "I'm (board   bored)," said Sam.

⑦ I cannot (drawer   draw) very well.

**Add the correct ending. Choose from –s, –ed, –ing or –er.**

⑧ The audience applaud_____ the musicians.

⑨ These prawn_____ are not fresh.

⑩ Jason was ignore _____ me so I bore____ my finger into his back!

⑪ The material was much coarse_____ than I expected.

**Complete the rhyming words.**

⑫ saw   l _ _      p _ _      j _ _      cl _ _

⑬ core   m _ _ _      s _ _ _      sh _ _ _      st _ _ _

Score 2 points for each correct answer!   SCORE   /26   ( 0-10 )   ( 12-20 )   ( 22-26 )

TARGETING HOMEWORK 4 © PASCAL PRESS ISBN 9781925726466

**Persuasive text** – Letter
**Author** – Merryn Whitfield

## Letter to the Editor of *Water Watchers Daily*

Dear Editor

Gurgle, gurgle, gurgle. That's the sad sound of water, the life-blood of our planet, disappearing down the drain. The lack of awareness in our community of the ongoing need to care for our valuable water resources is deeply concerning. When is our community of guzzlers going to recognise that they hold the key to our children's future?

It saddens me to think that we seem to have forgotten the two child-easy rules of good water management.

Firstly, reduce the amount of water that we consume on a daily basis. Lowering water consumption can be easily achieved by using dual-flush toilets, having shorter showers and not doing the washing until you have a full load.

Secondly, the use of 'grey' water is an underdeveloped resource in our community. People have long rejected the idea of using dirty bath water or water from their washing machines for other purposes. Why not use it to water your garden or wash the car? It's not rocket science but it is a clever way of saving our precious resources.

I urge all members of our community to follow these simple steps so that our children's water supply will be secured in the years to come, because I certainly don't want to explain to my grandchildren why we didn't act when we had the chance.

Yours faithfully,

*Doris Dripp*

Mrs D. Dripp

Source: *Writing Centres: Persuasive Texts*, Middle Primary, Blake Education.

Write or circle the correct answers.

① **Who is the intended audience for the letter?**

a the editor

b the readers of *Water Watchers Daily*

c Mrs Dripp

② **The letter was written to:**

a complain.

b inform.

c persuade.

③ **What does the word consume mean in this text?**

a to eat food or take a drink

b to use something up

④ **What does the phrase 'our community of guzzlers' mean?**

a people who drink a lot of water

b people who use a lot of water

⑤ **List three ideas Mrs Dripp suggests to save water.**

_____

_____

_____

⑥ **Which is the odd word?**

a consume          c deplete

b use               d save

⑦ **What did Mrs Dripp hope she would achieve by writing this letter?**

_____

_____

Score 2 points for each correct answer!

SCORE /14   0-4   6-10   12-14

TERM 2 ENGLISH

# Number & Algebra

AC9M4N08

## Using the split method to add large numbers

You can use the **split method** when you need to **add a new ten**.

*Example:* **457 + 329**

= (400 + 50 + 7) + (300 + 20 + 9)

=           700 + 70 + 16

Split 16 into a new 10 + 6.

= 700 + (70 + 10) + 6

= 700 + 80 + 6

= **786**

**Use the split method to add. Show your working out.**

① 548 + 237

_____

_____

_____

_____

② 652 + 229

_____

_____

_____

_____

Sometimes you need to add **a new hundred** as well as **a new ten**.

*Example:* **345 + 287**

= (300 + 40 + 5) + (200 + 80 + 7)

= 500 + 120 + 12

= 500 + 100 + 20 + 10 + 2

= (500 + 100) + (20 +10) + 2

= 600 + 30 + 2

= **632**

**Use the split method to add. Show your working out.**

③ 428 + 285

_____

_____

_____

_____

_____

④ 587 + 146

_____

_____

_____

_____

_____

Score 2 points for each correct answer!  **SCORE** **/8**  ( 0-2 )  ( 4-6 )  ( 8 )

# Statistics & Probability

AC9M4S102

## Survey questions

When you carry out a **survey**, it is important to ask questions that will get the information you need.

Milly wanted to find out about the TV habits of the students in her class. She wanted to know if they watched TV every day, how many hours a week they watched TV and how often they watched TV with their families.

**Which questions should Milly include in her survey to collect the data she needs? Circle the correct answers.**

① What is your favourite TV program?
   **a** include      **b** don't include

② Do you watch TV every day?
   • yes  • no
   **a** include      **b** don't include

③ Do you have a TV in your bedroom?
   **a** include      **b** don't include

④ How many hours of TV do you usually watch each day?
   0  1  2  3  4  5  6  7  8
   **a** include      **b** don't include

⑤ Which TV channel do you watch most?
   **a** include      **b** don't include

⑥ How often do you watch TV with your family?
   • never    • sometimes    • always
   **a** include      **b** don't include

⑦ Do you do your homework watching TV?
   **a** include      **b** don't include

⑧ Do you record TV programs and watch them later?
   **a** include      **b** don't include

TARGETING HOMEWORK 4 © PASCAL PRESS ISBN 9781925726466

Once Milly had chosen her questions, she had to decide how to carry out the survey. Circle the correct answers.

⑨ What is the best way for Milly to collect the data?

    **a** Ask all the students in her school.

    **b** Ask all the students in her class.

    **c** Ask the parents of the students in her class.

    **d** Ask the teacher.

⑩ What equipment could Milly use to collect the data?

    **a** a questionnaire sheet, a clipboard and a pencil

    **b** a TV guide

    **c** not sure

⑪ What is the best way for Milly to present the results of her survey?

    **a** a drawing

    **b** video

    **c** tally charts and graphs

*Score 2 points for each correct answer!* **SCORE** /22 ( 0-8 ) ( 10-16 ) ( 18-22 )

## Measurement & Space

AC9M4N08

## Length

> 10 millimetres = 1 centimetre
> 100 centimetres = 1 metre
> 1000 metres = 1 kilometre

Convert these measurements.

① 40 mm = _____ cm

② 2 metres = _____ cm

③ 3000 m = _____ km

④ 5 cm = _____ mm

⑤ 170 mm = _____ cm

⑥ $\frac{1}{2}$ km = _____ m

⑦ $\frac{1}{4}$ m = _____ cm

⑧ 6000 m = _____ km

**Read this problem.**

Three pencils are laid in a line, one after the other. The first one is 55 mm in length, the second is 14 cm and the third is 160 mm. What is the total length of the three pencils, in millimetres?

---

> This is an adding problem. To work out the answer in millimetres, all three measurements must be in mm. 14 cm = 140 mm, so pencil 2 is 140 mm long.
>
> Total = 55 mm + 140 mm + 160 mm
>       = **355 mm**

Write a number sentence to help you solve these length word problems.

⑨ Tad had a one metre length of string. He cut off 30 cm to tie up a package. How much string did he have left?

⑩ The bakery is 1 km from Su's house. Su sets off to buy some bread. She walks 600 metres and calls at her friend's house on the way. How much further is it to the bakery?

⑪ Each side of a regular quadrilateral is 25 mm long. What is the total length of all the sides of the shape?

⑫ Jason is 142 cm tall. Riley is 135 cm tall. How much shorter than Jason is Riley?

⑬ The length of the swimming pool is 50 m. Marie swims 250 metres every morning. How many laps of the pool does she swim?

⑭ Alice had a length of wood 42 cm long. She cut it into 6 equal lengths. How long was each piece?

*Score 2 points for each correct answer!* **SCORE** /28 ( 0-12 ) ( 14-22 ) ( 24-28 )

## Problem Solving

AC9M4A01

### Make a match

Match the boxes that have the same answers.

| the sum of 12 and 13 | | 50 + 50 + 20 |

| $\frac{1}{2}$ of 200 | 10 × 10 | 160 − 40 |

| 5 × 4 | 100 − 52 | 100 ÷ 5 |

| double 24 | | quarter of 100 |

# Grammar & Punctuation

AC9E4LA04

## Pronoun determiners

TERM 2 ENGLISH

Some **pronouns** are **determiners**. They come before a noun and are used to show which thing is being referred to. The determiner must **agree** with the nouns they refer to in number and gender.

*Example:* Sara put on **her** jacket.

Pronoun determiners are: my, your, her, his, its, our and their.

**Add a pronoun determiner to each sentence. Make sure it agrees with the noun or noun group in bold.**

① **Mike** took out _____ reading glasses to read _____ book.

② **Lynne and Jayne** went to visit _____ grandmother.

③ "Please take off _____ shoes, **Eli**," said Mum.

④ **I** prefer to wash _____ hair in the shower.

⑤ A **rabbit** can dig a long burrow with _____ claws.

**Underline the noun or noun group that the pronoun in bold is referring to.**

*Example:* I visited <u>London</u> last year.
**It** was a busy city.
'It' is referring to the place, 'London'.

⑥ Yesterday, I went to see my doctor. **He** is really nice.

⑦ Jack has a younger sister, Georgia. **She** goes to ballet every week.

⑧ My brother and I took a bus to see **our** friend in hospital.

⑨ "Can I get some milk for **you**, Luke?" asked Tom.

⑩ Mustafa and Greg hung **their** coats in Ali's wardrobe.

# Phonic Knowledge & Spelling

AC9E4LA11, AC9E4LY10

## Tricky letter 'a' words

Say each word in the word bank. The letter **a** can make a **short 'a'** sound as the word **bat**. It can make a **long 'a'** sound as in the word **cake**, but in this list of words, it makes two different sounds.

The letter **a** in the first two rows of words makes an **'ah'** sound. The letter **a** in the last two rows of words makes an **'o'** sound, as in **'hop'**.

| last | half | calf | class |
|------|------|------|-------|
| task | mask | calm | palm |
| wash | squash | halt | scald |
| wand | wasp | waltz | wallet |

**Choose words from the word bank to complete these sentences.**

① Mum told me to _____ my hair before going out.

② I go to a gym _____ every Thursday.

## Plurals

**Remember!** To make the plural of words, you usually just add –s, but to words that end in s, ss, sh, ch, x, z and zz, you add –es.
*Examples:*  gas – gas**es**     box – box**es**
buzz – buzz**es**

**Write the plurals of these words.**

③ glass _____

④ waltz _____

## Word origins

Some of the words we use in English today come from the German language.
*Examples:* fest, pretzel, hound, rucksack, waltz

**Match the words in the box to their meanings.**

| waltz | fest | pretzel |
|-------|------|---------|

⑤ a biscuit in the shape of a knot: _____

⑥ a festival: _____

⑦ a type of dance: _____

Score 2 points for each correct answer!  SCORE  **/20**  (0-8) (10-14) (16-20)

Score 2 points for each correct answer!  SCORE  **/14**  (0-4) (6-10) (12-14)

## The Fashion Show

**Imaginative text** – A play
**Author** – Frances Mackay

**Characters**

**Penny Plastic   Wendy Wool   Will Wood
Georgina Glass   Rob Rubber   Steve Steel
Announcer**

**Will:** Will you two hurry up? We're going to be late!

**Steve:** *(giggling)* OK Will, don't get your knots in a twist! We're almost ready.

**Penny:** *(doing a twirl)* Look at me, everybody! Look at my beautiful colours. You're so dull, Will, in your boring browns. I'm so much more versatile. Everyone will be amazed at how many designs and shapes I can be.

**Will:** What do you mean, boring browns? People love my warm, natural tones, which is more than I can say for you, Penny, you're not natural at all. I can be cut into lots of different shapes. I'm very hard-wearing.

**Penny:** So am I!

**Will:** Yes — but I'm renewable — you're not!

**Wendy:** Come on you two — stop fighting. After all, I'm the best material here by a long way. I can be used for all sorts of things such as clothes, furniture and carpets. I can be dyed all kinds of colours and I'm renewable too — so there! *(pokes out her tongue)*

**Georgina:** True — but not one of you has my beauty. I'm the most beautiful of all. I can be made into gorgeous vases and works of art. I'm stunning!

**Rob:** Yes — but we can all see right through you, Georgina. If I stand behind you, everyone will be able to see ME — not you! Besides, you break into millions of dangerous shards. Eek! I shudder to think! Whereas I'm nice and warm and I smell heavenly *(points nose in the air)*.

**Steve:** You smell like a farmyard, more like! I'm the only one who's beautiful round here. I'm the strongest too. I make all the important stuff like cars and skyscrapers and ...

**Announcer:** *(cuts in, in a loud voice)* And now, ladies and gentlemen, I present to you the world's most stunning materials. *(audience claps)*

Source: *Science Comprehension & Writing Centres*, Middle Primary, Blake Education.

TERM 2 ENGLISH

---

**Write or circle the correct answers.**

**Find words in the text that have these meanings.**

① made by nature, not humans:

n_____

② can be created again:

r_____

③ does not wear out easily:

h_____

④ Which is the odd word?

a exciting          c dull

b boring           d unexciting

⑤ Which two characters tell us they are made from renewable materials?

_____

_____

⑥ List the four properties of wood that Will tells us about.

_____

_____

⑦ Which character is made from the most fragile material?

a Will          b Georgina          c Wendy

**My Book Review**

Title _____

Author _____

Rating ☆ ☆ ☆ ☆ ☆

Comment _____

_____

*Score 2 points for each correct answer!*   **SCORE**   /14   0-4   6-10   12-14

# UNIT 10

## Number & Algebra

AC9M4A01, AC9M4A02

### Multiplication and division facts

> If you know the **multiplication facts**, you also know the **division facts**.
>
> 5 × 6 = 30    30 ÷ 6 = 5
> 6 × 5 = 30    30 ÷ 5 = 6

**Complete these multiplications and divisions.**

1. 4 × 6 = _____
2. 6 × _____ = 24
3. 24 ÷ 4 = _____
4. 24 ÷ _____ = 6
5. 3 × 7 = _____
6. _____ × 3 = 21
7. 21 ÷ 3 = _____
8. 21 ÷ _____ = 7
9. 6 × 9 = _____
10. _____ × 6 = 54
11. 54 ÷ _____ = 6
12. 54 ÷ 9 = _____
13. 7 × 8 = _____
14. 8 × _____ = 56
15. 56 ÷ 8 = _____
16. 56 ÷ _____ = 7
17. 5 × 6 = _____
18. 6 × 5 = _____
19. 30 ÷ _____ = 5
20. 30 ÷ 6 = _____

21. **This is a multiplication grid for the 6, 7, 8 and 9 times tables. Complete the grid.**

| ×  | 6  | 7  | 8  | 9  |
|----|----|----|----|----|
| 1  | 6  | 7  | 8  | 9  |
| 2  | 12 | 14 |    | 18 |
| 3  | 18 | 21 |    | 27 |
| 4  | 24 |    | 32 | 36 |
| 5  | 30 |    | 40 |    |
| 6  | 36 | 42 |    |    |
| 7  | 42 | 49 |    | 63 |
| 8  | 48 |    |    |    |
| 9  | 54 |    |    | 81 |
| 10 | 60 | 70 | 80 |    |

22. What do you notice about the numbers in the ×6 column? What is the pattern?

_____

_____

23. What do you notice about the numbers in the ×8 column? What is the pattern?

_____

_____

24. What do you notice about the numbers in the ×9 column? What is the pattern?

_____

_____

**Write the next numbers in the sequences.**

25. 12, 18, 24, 30, ____, ____, ____, ____
26. 40, 48, 56, 64, ____, ____, ____, ____
27. 90, 81, 72, 63, ____, ____, ____, ____
28. 161, 168, 175, 182, _____, _____, _____, _____
29. 210, 204, 198, 192, _____, _____, _____, _____
30. 400, 392, 384, 376, _____, _____, _____, _____

Score 2 points for each correct answer! **SCORE** | **/60** | 0-26 | 28-52 | 54-60

## Statistics & Probability

*There are no statistics & probability activities in this unit.*

## Measurement & Space

AC9M4M03

### Converting time

> 60 seconds = 1 minute
> 60 minutes = 1 hour
> To convert minutes into seconds, **multiply by 60.**
> *Example:*
> 4 minutes = ____ seconds
> To solve this, multiply 4 minutes by 60 seconds.
> The easy way is to multiply: 4 × 6 = 24
> Then add a zero: 240.

**Convert these times.**

① 2 minutes = _____ seconds

② 3 minutes = _____ seconds

③ 5 minutes = _____ seconds

④ 10 minutes = _____ seconds

⑤ 8 minutes = _____ seconds

⑥ 7 minutes = _____ seconds

**To convert hours into minutes, multiply by 60.**
**Convert these times.**

⑦ 1 hour = _____ minutes

⑧ 2 hours = _____ minutes

⑨ 4 hours = _____ minutes

⑩ 5 hours = _____ minutes

⑪ 10 hours = _____ minutes

⑫ 9 hours = _____ minutes

To convert seconds into minutes,
**divide** by 60.
180 seconds = ___ minutes
To solve this, divide 180 by 60.
The easy way is to ignore the zero on the end
of each number and calculate:
$18 \div 6 = 3$ minutes

**Convert these times.**

⑬ 120 seconds = ____ minutes

⑭ 240 seconds = ____ minutes

⑮ 360 seconds = ____ minutes

⑯ 180 seconds = ____ minutes

⑰ 420 seconds = ____ minutes

⑱ 540 seconds = ____ minutes

**To convert minutes into hours, divide by 60.**
**Convert these times.**

⑲ 60 minutes = ____ hour

⑳ 180 minutes = ____ hours

㉑ 240 minutes = ____ hours

㉒ 360 minutes = ____ hours

㉓ 300 minutes = ____ hours

㉔ 600 minutes = ____ hours

## Time problems

Work out the answers to these problems.
Show your working out.

**The Maddock family went for a long walk last Saturday. They started out at 8 o'clock and they finished the walk at 1 o'clock.**

① How many hours did the walk take?

_____

② How many minutes did the walk take?

_____

**In 2016, Aleix Vendrell held the world record for holding your breath. He held his breath for 24 minutes!**

③ For how many seconds did Aleix hold his breath?

_____

_____

④ Mandy's dental appointment was at 5 pm. She arrived at the dentist at 4:40 pm. Was she late or early?

_____

By how many minutes?

_____

⑤ Reece thought his dental appointment was 25 minutes later than the actual appointment which was at 12:30 pm. What time did Reece think his appointment was?

_____

⑥ Ellissa was 45 minutes late for her hairdressing appointment. Her appointment was at 11:15 am. What time did Ellissa arrive at the hairdresser?

_____

**TERM 2 MATHS**

# Grammar & Punctuation

AC9E4LA04, AC9E4LY04

## Possessive pronouns

> **Possessive pronouns** show ownership.
>
> *Example:* That book is **mine**, not **hers**.
>
> Singular possessive pronouns: mine, yours, hers, his
>
> Plural possessive pronouns: ours, yours, theirs
>
> **WATCH OUT!** Don't confuse possessive pronouns with contractions! Possessive pronouns <u>never</u> need an apostrophe.

**Circle the possessive pronouns. Then underline what they own.**

① I think these garden magazines are yours.

② That tall house over there is ours.

③ The boys claimed that the skateboard was theirs.

④ Those coats are theirs and so are the shoes.

**Add a possessive pronoun to each sentence.**

⑤ I bought that book, so it's _____.

⑥ I've left _____ at home, can I borrow _____?

⑦ That bicycle is _____, so she should take it home.

> We can use **possessive pronouns** to avoid unnecessary repetition of words.
>
> *Example:*
>
> That book is not your book, it's his book.
>
> We can rewrite this as:
>
> That book is not **yours**, it's **his**.

**Rewrite these sentences to avoid unnecessary repetition.**

⑧ Are those plates your plates or our plates?

_____

_____

⑨ Is this coat your coat?

_____

# Phonic Knowledge & Spelling

AC9E4LY09, AC9E4LY10, AC9E4LY11, AC9E4LE04

## Letter teams or, ear and ar

Say each word in the word bank. All the words in this list have tricky letter teams! The words with **or** and **ear** make an 'er' sound. The words with **ar** make an 'or' sound.

| worm | word | world | work |
| early | earth | earn | learn |
| war | warm | warn | wharf |

**Choose words from the word bank to complete these sentences.**

① "I haven't _____ from Mia since yesterday," said Tina.

② The builder had to _____ quickly to finish the fence on time.

③ Once I got inside, I started to feel _____ again.

④ Can a sheep _____ how to dance in a tutu?

**Add work to the beginning of these words to make compound words.**

⑤ _____ book

⑥ _____ shop

⑦ _____ load

⑧ _____ force

## Alliteration

> An **alliteration** is a sentence or group of words where each word begins with the same letter or sound.
>
> *Example:* Sammy snake slithered soundlessly along the smooth sandstone.

**Make up alliterations using words from the word bank that begin with w. Write sentences or phrases.**

*Example:* warty world

⑨ _____

_____

⑩ _____

_____

⑪ _____

_____

# Ships of the First Fleet

**Informative text** – Report
**Author** – Frances Mackay and Neil Johnson

A fleet of 11 ships left Portsmouth, England, on 13 May 1787. They were sailing for Botany Bay in New South Wales in order to establish a new colony there. In command on the flagship the HMS *Sirius* was Captain Arthur Phillip, a British Royal Naval Officer. He was later appointed Governor of New South Wales.

The First Fleet carried more than 750 convicts and around 700 officers, crew, mariners and their families. The ships arrived in Botany Bay on 18 January 1788. On 26 January, they moved to Port Jackson, as Botany Bay had poor soil and no fresh water.

| Type of ship | Ship name | Year built | Captain / Skipper | Passengers |
|---|---|---|---|---|
| Naval ship | HMS *Sirius* (Flagship) | 1781, rebuilt 1786 | Captain Arthur Phillip (commander of the First Fleet), Captain John Hunter | 198 officers, crew, mariners & families |
| | HMS *Supply* (Smallest ship) | 1759 | Captain Henry Lidgbird Ball | 55 officers, crew & mariners; 2 convicts |
| Transport ship | *Alexander* (Largest ship) | 1783 | Master Duncan Sinclair | 30 crew, 41 mariners, 191 male convicts |
| | *Charlotte* | 1781 | Master Thomas Gilbert | 30 crew, 42 mariners, 88 male convicts, 24 female convicts |
| | *Friendship* | 1784 | Master Francis Walton | 25 crew, 40 mariners, 73 male convicts, 21 female convicts |
| | *Lady Penrhyn* | 1786 | Master William Cropton Sever | 32 crew, 18 mariners, 2 male convicts, 102 female convicts, 12 children |
| | *Prince of Wales* | 1786 | Master John Mason | 25 crew, 29 mariners, 3 male convicts, 64 female convicts, 3 convicts' children |
| | *Scarborough* | 1782 | Master John Marshall | 30 crew, 50 mariners, 202 male convicts |
| Store ship | *Borrowdale* | 1785 | Master Readthorn Hobson Reed | 22 crew |
| | *Fishburn* | 1780 | Master Robert Brown | 22 crew |
| | *Golden Grove* | 1780 | Master William Sharpe | 22 crew, 4 civilians |

Source: *Australian History Centres*, Middle Primary, Blake Education.

**TERM 2 ENGLISH**

**Write or circle the correct answers.**

① **How many months was the journey from England to Botany Bay for the First Fleet?**

_____

② **What is another word for colony?**

a prison    b settlement    c country

③ **Who was the first Governor of New South Wales?**

_____

**Match the words in the box to their meanings.**

| officer   marine   convict   crew |

④ a prisoner: _____

⑤ people who work on a ship:

_____

⑥ a soldier trained to work on land and sea:

_____

⑦ senior person in the navy:

_____

⑧ **Which ship carried the most convicts?**

a *Scarborough*    b *Charlotte*    c *Alexander*

⑨ **Which ship was the oldest in the fleet?**

a *Golden Grove*    b *Sirius*    c *Supply*

⑩ **Who was the Captain of the *Scarborough*?**

_____

*Score 2 points for each correct answer!* **SCORE** /20   0-8   10-14   16-20

## My Book Review

Title _____

Author _____

Rating ☆☆☆☆☆

Comment _____

_____

# Number & Algebra

AC9M4N03

## Equivalent fractions

Equivalent fractions are fractions with the same value.

These shapes are all coloured to show one half.

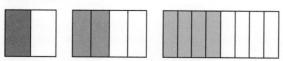

The number of parts shaded is equal to the number of parts not shaded. The total number of parts has been divided by two.

$\frac{1}{2}$ is equal to $\frac{2}{4}$.     $\frac{1}{2}$ is also equal to $\frac{4}{8}$.

**Write the equivalent fractions. Use the diagrams to help you.**

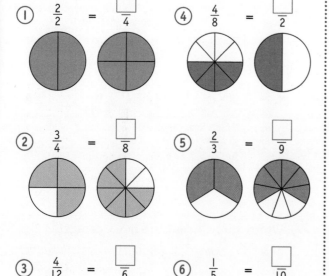

① $\frac{2}{2}$ = $\frac{\square}{4}$     ④ $\frac{4}{8}$ = $\frac{\square}{2}$

② $\frac{3}{4}$ = $\frac{\square}{8}$     ⑤ $\frac{2}{3}$ = $\frac{\square}{9}$

③ $\frac{4}{12}$ = $\frac{\square}{6}$     ⑥ $\frac{1}{5}$ = $\frac{\square}{10}$

**This is a fraction wall.** You can use it to work out equivalent fractions.

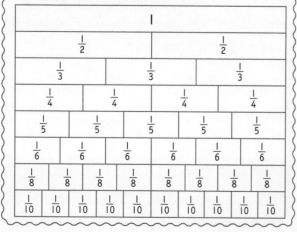

**Use the wall to write the equivalent fractions.**

⑦ $\frac{1}{2}$ = $\frac{\square}{8}$     ⑪ $\frac{2}{3}$ = $\frac{\square}{6}$     ⑮ $\frac{2}{5}$ = $\frac{\square}{10}$

⑧ $\frac{1}{2}$ = $\frac{\square}{6}$     ⑫ $\frac{3}{3}$ = $\frac{\square}{6}$     ⑯ $\frac{1}{5}$ = $\frac{\square}{10}$

⑨ $\frac{1}{2}$ = $\frac{\square}{10}$     ⑬ $\frac{1}{4}$ = $\frac{\square}{8}$     ⑰ $\frac{3}{5}$ = $\frac{\square}{10}$

⑩ $\frac{1}{3}$ = $\frac{\square}{6}$     ⑭ $\frac{2}{4}$ = $\frac{\square}{8}$     ⑱ $\frac{4}{4}$ = $\frac{\square}{8}$

Score 2 points for each correct answer! | SCORE /36 | 0-16 | 18-30 | 32-36

# Statistics & Probability

AC9M4ST01

## Column or bar graphs

A **column graph** can show two types of data.

This graph shows the favourite music of the students in Class 4B. The graph uses a key to show that the red columns represent girls and the blue columns represent boys.

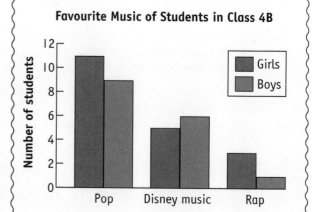

**Favourite Music of Students in Class 4B**

**Use the music graph to answer the questions. Write or circle the correct answers.**

① Which type of music do the students prefer?
_____

② Which type of music do the students like the least?
_____

③ How many students took part in the survey?
**a** We are not told.
**b** 35
**c** 19

④ How many boys preferred pop music? _____

⑤ How many girls preferred Disney music?
_____

TARGETING HOMEWORK 4 © PASCAL PRESS ISBN 9781925726466

⑥ How many more girls than boys preferred rap music? _____

⑦ How many boys took part in the survey? _____

⑧ How many girls took part in the survey? _____

## Measurement & Space

AC9M4M01

## Measuring mass

This is a **balance scale**. It is used to measure small masses. It is level when the mass on one side is equal to the mass on the other side.

250 g

Write the masses needed to balance the scales. Choose from the masses below.

1 g    5 g    10 g    50 g    100 g

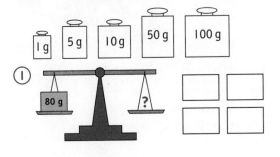

① 80 g    ?

② 65 g    ?

③ 132 g    ?

④ 165 g    ?

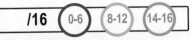

This set of scales can weigh things up to 1 kg.
This box has a mass of **650 g.**

Read the scales and write the mass of each item.

⑤ _____ g

⑥ _____ g

⑦ _____ g

⑧ _____ g

## Problem Solving

AC9M4N08

## Multiply or divide?

Solve these problems by doing multiplication or division. Show your working out.

① The baker packed 9 boxes with 24 cakes in each box. How many cakes did he pack?

_____

② Tina's school is having a concert. They have set out all the chairs in the hall. There are 85 chairs altogether, with 5 chairs in each row. How many rows of chairs are there?

_____

TERM 2 MATHS

# Grammar & Punctuation

AC9E4LA11

## Adjectives

> **Adjectives** describe people, places and things. They work with the noun to build a clear picture in the mind of the reader.
> *Examples:*
> The **round**, **red**, **juicy** apples tempted me to buy them.
> A **mysterious old** man walked by.
> We were **hungry**.

**Read the sentence and underline the adjectives. Write the noun that is being described.**

① The boys played an awesome computer game. _____

② The old, dilapidated house had stood empty for years. _____

③ The sheets had a fresh, clean smell after washing. _____

④ Our dirty shoes were left outside.
_____

⑤ Nan's old sofa was uncomfortable so she sold it. _____

⑥ The ferocious dog growled at the intruder.
_____

## Antonyms

> **Antonyms** are words **opposite** in meaning.
> The opposite or antonym of big is small.

**Match the antonyms from the box with these adjectives.**

| brave | young | ugly | poor |
|-------|-------|------|------|
| loose | true | fresh | |

⑦ beautiful _____

⑧ tight _____

⑨ false _____

⑩ old _____

⑪ stale _____

⑫ rich _____

⑬ fearful _____

# Phonic Knowledge & Spelling

AC9E4LY09, AC9E4LY10

## Letter teams er, ir and ur

**Say each word in the word bank. The letter teams er, ir and ur work together to make the sound 'er'.**

| alert | person | certain | service |
|-------|--------|---------|---------|
| circle | circuit | whirr | whirl |
| curb | cursor | furl | purchase |

**Choose words from the word bank to complete these sentences.**

① We had to edit our writing by putting a _____ around incorrect words.

② The wedding _____ follows a particular format.

③ When you _____ something at a shop, you should check the receipt.

④ The racing driver quit the race after one lap of the _____.

## Negative prefixes

> A **prefix** is added to the beginning of a word. When the prefixes **un–** and **in–** are added to words, they change the meaning to its opposite.
> *Examples:* happy – **un**happy  active – **in**active
> The prefixes **il–**, **im–**, **ir–**, **dis–**, **de–** and **non–** also change the words to mean the opposite.

**Choose the correct prefix to change these words to their opposites. Write the new word.**

⑤ personal:  **im–**  **un–**
_____

⑥ allergic:  **un–**  **non–**
_____

⑦ furl:  **in–**  **un–**
_____

⑧ certain:  **in–**  **un–**
_____

TERM 2 ENGLISH

## Changing the Rules: Nelson Mandela

**Informative text** – Biography
**Author** – Frances Mackay

Nelson Mandela was born on 18 July 1918 in South Africa. He ended up spending 27 years of his life in prison in order to be free in his own country.

In South Africa, during the time that Nelson was growing up, black people made up most of the population but they were not allowed to vote or have any say in how their country was run. The country was ruled by **apartheid** laws that denied black people many of the rights that white people had.

Like many other black people, Nelson wanted to change this so he joined a group called the African National Congress (ANC) which campaigned against these laws. During the 1950s and 1960s there were riots and strikes by black people and a lot of people were killed and arrested. Nelson was arrested many times and, in 1964, he was sentenced to life in prison for his role in the campaign against the government.

Nelson never gave up hope of freedom all the time he was in prison. People in South Africa and all around the world continued to campaign for equal rights for black people. Finally, in 1990, Nelson Mandela was released. Millions of people watched on television as this brave man proudly walked free.

Four years later, South Africa held its first one-person, one-vote elections and Nelson Mandela was voted the country's first black president.

Nelson was awarded the Nobel Peace Prize for the work he did in removing apartheid.

**TERM 2 ENGLISH**

Write or circle the correct answers.

① **What was apartheid?**

a the name of the government in South Africa

b rules and laws that prevented black people having the same rights as white people

② **What do the letters ANC stand for?**

_____

**Find words in the text that have these meanings:**

③ the number of people in a place:

p_____

④ carried out a plan of action:

c_____

⑤ violent protests: r_____

⑥ the right to do what you want:

f_____

⑦ **How old was Nelson Mandela when he was sentenced to life in prison?**

a 27

b We are not told.

c 46

⑧ **Thinking about why Mandela was imprisoned, mark any reasons that are true.**

a He was trying to help the government maintain apartheid.

b He wanted equal rights for black people.

c He was a proud man.

⑨ **What is another word for denied?**

a refused        b gave        c allowed

⑩ **In what year was Mandela elected the first black president of South Africa?**

_____

Score 2 points for each correct answer!

**SCORE** /20  (0-8)  (10-14)  (16-20)

### My Book Review

Title _____

Author _____

Rating ☆☆☆☆☆

Comment _____

_____

# Number & Algebra

AC9M4N05, AC9M4N06

## Multiplying tens

The easy way to multiply a number by 10 is to **add a zero** to the end of the number.

$6 \times 10 = 60$
$60 \times 10 = 600$
$600 \times 10 = 6000$

Look what happens when you multiply by tens:
$6 \times 70$

Multiply $6 \times 7 (= 42)$, then add a zero.
$= 420$

You are actually multiplying 6 lots of 7 tens. That's **42 tens**, which is 420.

**Write the answers.**

① $5 \times 50 =$ _____
② $6 \times 80 =$ _____
③ $7 \times 40 =$ _____
④ $9 \times 40 =$ _____
⑤ $6 \times 60 =$ _____
⑥ $8 \times 50 =$ _____

## Splitting numbers to multiply

When you multiply larger numbers, you can **split the larger number** to make it easier.

$5 \times 48$

$40 \quad 8$    Split the 48 into 40 and 8.
Then multiply each number by 5.

$5 \times 48 = 5 \times (40 + 8)$
$\qquad = (5 \times 40) + (5 \times 8)$
$\qquad = 200 + 40$
$\qquad = 240$

**Split the larger numbers into tens and ones and multiply. Show your working out.**

⑦ $6 \times 49$

_____
_____
_____

⑧ $4 \times 68$

_____
_____
_____
_____

⑨ $5 \times 76$

_____
_____
_____

⑩ $7 \times 59$

_____
_____
_____

⑪ $8 \times 87$

_____
_____
_____

⑫ $9 \times 43$

_____
_____
_____

## Splitting numbers to divide

You can use the **split method** to divide.

$88 \div 4$

$80 \quad 8$
$= (80 \div 4) + (8 \div 4)$
$= 20 + 2$
$= 22$

**Use the split method to divide. Show your working out.**

⑬ $84 \div 4$

_____
_____
_____

⑭ $96 \div 3$

_____
_____
_____

⑮ $63 \div 3$

_____
_____
_____

Score 2 points for each correct answer! **SCORE** **/30**

TARGETING HOMEWORK 4 © PASCAL PRESS ISBN 9781925726466

## Statistics & Probability

*There are no statistics & probability activities in this unit.*

## Measurement & Space

AC9M4M02

## Comparing shapes

Look at this shape.

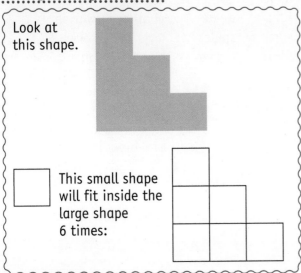

☐ This small shape will fit inside the large shape 6 times:

**How many of the small shapes will fit inside the large shapes?**

① ____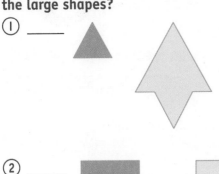

② ____

③ ____

④ ____

**Circle the small shapes you need to make the large shape.**

⑤

⑥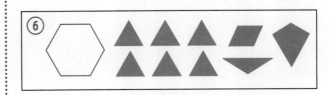

⑦

⑧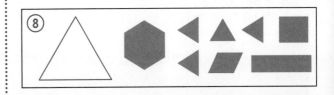

Score 2 points for each correct answer! **SCORE** /16 0-6 8-12 14-16

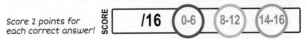

## Problem Solving

AC9M4SP01

### Make an egg!

Trace the shapes. Cut them out.

Use all the shapes to make an egg!

How many other shapes can you make? ____

# Grammar & Punctuation

AC9E4LY06

## Comparing adjectives

> **Adjectives** can show how people, animals or things **compare** with each other.
>
> You add **–er** to compare **two** things:
>
> *Example:* That knife is <u>sharp</u>, but this knife is **sharper**.
>
> You add **–est** to compare **more than two** things:
>
> *Examples:* The first dog is <u>big</u>.
> The second dog is **bigger**.
> The third dog is the **biggest**.

**Add –er and –est to these adjectives. Think about the spelling rules!**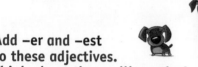

|  |  | –er | –est |
|---|---|---|---|
| ① | tall | _____ | _____ |
| ② | fat | _____ | _____ |
| ③ | happy | _____ | _____ |

**Complete these sentences by adding –er or -est to the adjectives.**

④ Jayne's hair is long, but Suzie's hair is long_____.

⑤ Wednesday was the wet_____ day of the week.

⑥ My baby sister is noisy but I am noisy_____!

## Irregular comparing adjectives

> Some **comparing adjectives** use special words.
>
> *Examples:*
> | good | better | best |
> |---|---|---|
> | bad | worse | worst |
> | many | more | most |
> | little | less | least |

**Write good, better or best to complete the sentences.**

⑦ Mum is a _____ cook, but Dad is _____.

⑧ That is the _____ film I have ever seen.

**Write bad, worse or worst to complete the sentences.**

⑨ That game was the _____ match of the season.

⑩ I had a _____ headache and now it is _____.

# Phonic Knowledge & Spelling

AC9E4LY09, AC9E4LY10

## Letter team er

**Say each word in the word bank. They all end in the letter team –er. Listen to the sound the two letters make at the end of the word.**

| anger | gather | enter | clever |
|---|---|---|---|
| finger | ginger | panther | whisper |
| super | spider | lever | cover |
| poster | corner | climber | order |

**Choose words from the word bank to complete these sentences.**

① Mum had to put an extra bandage on my _____ to protect it.

② "There's a great big _____ in the bath!" yelled Tina.

**Write compound words by choosing a word from the box.**

| bread | web | nail |
|---|---|---|

③ finger_____

④ ginger_____

⑤ spider_____

## Jobs ending in –er

> The letter team **–er** can be used to name a person's work or hobby.
>
> *Example:* bricklay**er**: a person who lays bricks

**Name the following. Remember your spelling rules.**

⑥ a person who sings:

_____

⑦ a person who farms:

_____

## Adjectives ending in –y

> When an adjective ends in –y, change it to 'i' before adding –er and –est.
>
> *Example:* bus**y**, bus**ier**, bus**iest**

**Add –er and –est to this adjective.**

|  |  | –er | –est |
|---|---|---|---|
| ⑧ | easy | _____ | _____ |
| ⑨ | angry | _____ | _____ |
| ⑩ | funny | _____ | _____ |

Persuasive text – Advertisement
Author – Frances Mackay

### NEW!

From the makers of the highly-acclaimed ROBO-MATIC I the smarter, quieter, more energy-efficient ROBO-MATIC II!

YES – EVERYONE is talking about it!

You too will be amazed at the exciting NEW FUNCTIONS this superlative HOME ROBOT can perform.

It cleans!
It vacuums!
It polishes!
It shops!
It gardens!
It cooks!
How have you lived without it?

Nothing could be more exciting than being the proud owner of ROBO-MATIC II.

You will be the envy of all your neighbours.

What are you waiting for?

DON'T DELAY – BUY TODAY!

THE **WORLD'S MOST ADVANCED TECHNOLOGY** at an **UNBELIEVABLE PRICE!**

The **smarter, smaller, more powerful, less expensive** ROBO-MATIC will astound you with its performance.

It will charm and entertain you.

It will **save you hours and hours of time** and will free you up to spend more time with your family.

**SPECIAL INTRODUCTORY OFFER!**

This will absolutely be the best decision you will ever make.

Call us now
1800 111 222

TOMO MACHINES & CO
TOPSHELF TECHNOLOGY PARK, BIGTOWN

**TERM 2 ENGLISH**

---

Write or circle the correct answers.

① **What is the name of the company that has manufactured the robot?**

_____

② **Why did the creator of the advert use capital letters and bold colours?**

a to look pretty

b to attract the attention of the reader

c to design the advert quickly

③ **Who is the advertisement aimed at?**

a children     b robot makers     c families

④ **What is another word for superlative?**

a outstanding     b poor     c unexceptional

⑤ **What three qualities make the ROBO-MATIC II better than the first model?**

_____

_____

⑥ **Write five comparing adjectives in the advertisement.**

_____

_____

_____

Score 2 points for each correct answer!   SCORE   **/12**   0-4   6-8   10-12

**My Book Review**

Title _____

Author _____

Rating ☆☆☆☆☆

Comment _____

# Number & Algebra

AC9M4N03, AC9M4N04

## Mixed numerals and improper fractions

> **Mixed numerals** have a whole number part and a fraction part.
>
>
>
> This is one and one-third or $1\frac{1}{3}$.
>
> There is one whole number ($\frac{3}{3}$) and one third.
>
>
>
> This is three and three-quarters or $3\frac{3}{4}$.
>
> There are three whole numbers ($\frac{4}{4}$) and three quarters.

**Write the mixed numerals.**

*Example:*

$2\frac{1}{2}$

① _____

② _____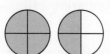

③ _____

④ _____

⑤ _____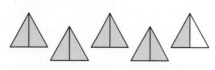

⑥ _____

---

This **number line** shows counting in quarters or fourths.

When we count in **fractions**, we can continue counting in quarters: $\frac{5}{4}, \frac{6}{4}, \frac{7}{4}, \frac{8}{4}$.

These are called **improper fractions**.

We can also count in **mixed numerals**: $1\frac{1}{4}, 1\frac{2}{4}, 1\frac{3}{4}, 2$.

**Write the improper fractions as whole or mixed numerals.**

⑦ $\frac{6}{4}$ = _____   ⑩ $\frac{9}{4}$ = _____

⑧ $\frac{12}{4}$ = _____   ⑪ $\frac{7}{4}$ = _____

⑨ $\frac{11}{4}$ = _____   ⑫ $\frac{8}{4}$ = _____

| | |
|---|---|
| 0 | $\frac{0}{4}$ |
| | $\frac{1}{4}$ |
| | $\frac{2}{4}$ |
| | $\frac{3}{4}$ |
| 1 | $\frac{4}{4}$ |
| $1\frac{1}{4}$ | $\frac{5}{4}$ |
| $1\frac{2}{4}$ | $\frac{6}{4}$ |
| $1\frac{3}{4}$ | $\frac{7}{4}$ |
| 2 | $\frac{8}{4}$ |
| $2\frac{1}{4}$ | $\frac{9}{4}$ |
| $2\frac{2}{4}$ | $\frac{10}{4}$ |
| $2\frac{3}{4}$ | $\frac{11}{4}$ |
| 0 | $\frac{12}{4}$ |

*Score 2 points for each correct answer!*

SCORE **/24**  (0-10) (12-18) (20-24)

---

# Statistics & Probability

AC9M4P01

## Things that affect events happening

> Sometimes, something can happen that affects the chances of something else happening.
>
> For example, if you ride a bike for the first time, there is a chance that you might fall off.
>
> But sometimes, the chance of something happening cannot be affected by another event.
>
> For example, if your favourite colour is blue, this will not affect the chances of you winning a running race. If Dan can swim, it will not affect the chances of him learning to drive a car.

**Which event cannot make any difference to the chances of the first event happening? Circle the correct answers.**

① Yesterday, the teacher told off Thomas for making a mess in the art area.

   **a** Thomas didn't go to school yesterday.

   **b** Thomas' favourite sport is football.

② Emma fixed the puncture in her bike's tyre.

   **a** Emma learnt to ride last year.

   **b** Emma's dad taught her how to mend a puncture.

③ Tomorrow, Jake will fall and hurt his knee at the park.

   **a** Jake's best friend is Paul.

   **b** Jake's mum is planning a surprise outing for him tomorrow.

④ Mum discovered she had run out of potatoes.

   **a** It was a lovely sunny day.

   **b** Mum decided she would cook some chips.

⑤ Tomorrow, Dad will find his lost car keys.

   **a** Dad looks for his keys.

   **b** Dad cooked spaghetti for tea.

⑥ Tomorrow, we will go to the beach and have a swim.

   **a** Our neighbour is a champion swimmer.

   **b** The forecast for tomorrow is for thunder, lightning and rain.

⑦ Tonight, I will watch my favourite TV program at 7 pm.

   **a** My favourite TV program is Sneaky Peaky.

   **b** Tonight, my bus was late and I arrived home at 8 pm.

⑧ Georgie made an apple pie for her nan.

   **a** Georgie loves baking.

   **b** Georgie's nan likes watching tennis.

*Score 2 points for each correct answer!* SCORE **/16** ( 0-6 ) ( 8-12 ) ( 14-16 )

## Measurement & Space

AC9M4M01

## Capacity

> **Capacity** is the **amount** a container can hold. When we measure capacity, we use millilitres and litres.

**How much liquid is in these containers? Write your answers in mL.**

① _____     ② _____

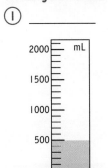

③ _____     ④ _____

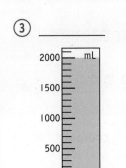
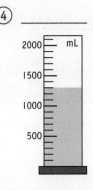

**Solve these word problems. Show your working out.**

⑤ Michael drinks 2 litres of water every day. How much does he drink in a week?

_____

⑥ A medicine cup holds 10 mL. How many medicine cups can you fill from a 250 mL bottle of cough medicine?

_____

⑦ A bucket holds 2 litres of water. How many buckets of water will it take to fill a 100-litre water tank?

_____

*Score 2 points for each correct answer!* SCORE **/14** ( 0-4 ) ( 6-10 ) ( 12-14 )

## Problem Solving

AC9M4N04

### Fraction maze

**Find a way through the maze by counting in quarters.**

**Start at $\frac{1}{4}$ and end at $4\frac{3}{4}$.**

You can move across, up, down and diagonally. You cannot move or count backwards.

| | | | | | | | | |
|---|---|---|---|---|---|---|---|---|
| $\frac{1}{5}$ | $\frac{3}{6}$ | $\frac{5}{8}$ | 1 | $1\frac{3}{4}$ | $2\frac{1}{4}$ | $2\frac{2}{4}$ | $2\frac{3}{4}$ | 3 | $2\frac{1}{2}$ |
| $\frac{1}{6}$ | $\frac{2}{5}$ | $\frac{3}{5}$ | $\frac{4}{5}$ | 1 | 2 | $2\frac{3}{5}$ | 3 | 4 | $4\frac{1}{5}$ |
| $\frac{1}{4}$ | 1 | $\frac{4}{6}$ | $1\frac{2}{4}$ | $1\frac{3}{4}$ | $2\frac{3}{4}$ | $3\frac{5}{6}$ | $3\frac{1}{4}$ | $3\frac{6}{10}$ | $4\frac{5}{6}$ |
| $\frac{1}{8}$ | $\frac{2}{4}$ | $\frac{3}{8}$ | 2 | $1\frac{2}{4}$ | $2\frac{1}{4}$ | $3\frac{7}{8}$ | $3\frac{2}{4}$ | $3\frac{2}{8}$ | $4\frac{7}{8}$ |
| $\frac{1}{10}$ | $\frac{3}{4}$ | $\frac{2}{5}$ | $1\frac{1}{4}$ | $2\frac{2}{5}$ | 3 | 4 | $3\frac{3}{4}$ | $3\frac{5}{6}$ | 4 |
| $\frac{1}{4}$ | $\frac{2}{10}$ | 1 | 2 | $1\frac{2}{6}$ | $1\frac{8}{10}$ | $3\frac{6}{8}$ | $3\frac{9}{10}$ | 4 | 5 |
| $\frac{1}{8}$ | $\frac{3}{8}$ | 2 | $2\frac{1}{5}$ | 2 | $1\frac{9}{10}$ | $3\frac{1}{2}$ | $3\frac{7}{8}$ | $4\frac{1}{4}$ | $4\frac{1}{5}$ |
| $\frac{1}{4}$ | $\frac{2}{4}$ | $\frac{3}{4}$ | 1 | $1\frac{3}{4}$ | $2\frac{4}{5}$ | 3 | $3\frac{5}{6}$ | $4\frac{2}{4}$ | 4 |
| $\frac{1}{3}$ | $\frac{2}{3}$ | 1 | $2\frac{1}{4}$ | 3 | $3\frac{1}{4}$ | $3\frac{3}{5}$ | 4 | $4\frac{1}{4}$ | $4\frac{3}{4}$ |

# Grammar & Punctuation

AC9E4LY06

## Using adjectives with more, most, less and least

> **Adjectives** that end in a suffix **compare** by using the words **more** or **most**, and **less** or **least**.
>
> *Examples:*
>
>   careful, more careful, most careful
>   valuable, less valuable, least valuable
>
> **NOTE:** words that end in the suffix **–y** do not follow this rule.

## Adjectives with more and most

> Use **more** with adjectives that compare two things.
>
> Use **most** with adjectives that compare more than two things.

**Circle the correct form of comparing adjectives in each sentence.**

① This is the (more delicious / most delicious) cake I have ever eaten.

② That diamond ring is (more beautiful / most beautiful) than this one.

③ Running is a (more physical / most physical) hobby than knitting.

## Adjectives with less and least

> Use **less** with adjectives that compare two things.
>
> Use **least** with adjectives that compare more than two things.

**Circle the correct form of comparing adjectives in each sentence.**

④ The apple is (less sweet / least sweet) than the banana.

⑤ This is the (less useful / least useful) of all my carpentry tools.

⑥ Silver is (less precious / least precious) than gold.

# Phonic Knowledge & Spelling

AC9E4LY09, AC9E4LY10

## Letter team ea

Say each word in the word bank. They all contain the letter team **ea** that works together to make the **short 'e'** sound.

| | | | |
|---|---|---|---|
| bread | spread | thread | ahead |
| death | breath | ready | heavy |
| weather | leather | healthy | wealthy |
| sweat | threat | measure | treasure |

**Choose words from the word bank to complete these sentences.**

① Too much sugar is not _____ for you.

② My shoe is made from _____.

③ "What else happened in the stormy _____?" asked Tom.

④ I would rather _____ jam on my toast than marmalade.

**Complete the rhyming words.**

⑤ bread   ah _ _ _     redh _ _ _     thr _ _ _

⑥ ready   st _ _ _ _     unst _ _ _ _     alr _ _ _ _

**Make compound words using bread as the first word. The first one has been done for you.**

   board   _____breadboard_____

⑦ basket   _____

⑧ line   _____

⑨ fruit   _____

**Circle how many syllables are in each word.**

⑩ headstrong     1   2   3

⑪ breakfast     1   2   3

⑫ deafening     1   2   3

*Score 2 points for each correct answer!* **SCORE**  /12 (0-4) (6-8) (10-12)

*Score 2 points for each correct answer!* **SCORE** /24 (0-10) (12-18) (20-24)

**Informative text** – Report
**Author** – Lisa Thompson and Sharon Dalgleish

## A Picture Code that was Hard to Crack

The ancient Egyptians didn't just leave giant pyramids and mummies behind them. They also left a mystery. When their writing was first discovered, no one could figure out how to read it. Hieroglyphs (HIGH-ro-gliffs) are mostly made of pictures of natural or man-made objects. Hieroglyphic writing is one of the oldest forms of writing in the world. It was used from about 3200 BC to AD 394.

### A Stone Key to Hieroglyphs

In 1799, the Rosetta stone was found in Rosetta, Egypt. It had the same message written on it in Egyptian hieroglyphs and in Greek. Since the code breakers could read Greek, they knew they had found the key to the hieroglyphic code. But many scientists struggled for years to match each Greek letter with a hieroglyph. Then in 1822, Jean-François Champollion cracked the code. How did he do it? He realised that some hieroglyphs stood for sounds, some for syllables and some for ideas.

### How to Read Egyptian Hieroglyphs

Hieroglyphs were mostly written in rows from right to left, or in columns from top to bottom. But sometimes, if it looked better, they were written from left to right. To tell which way to read hieroglyphic writing, look at the direction the animals or people are facing. They always face towards the beginning of the line.

Source: *Break that Code*, Brainwaves, Blake Education.

TERM 2 ENGLISH

---

Write or circle the correct answers.

1. **What does mummies mean in this text?**
   a mothers    b dead bodies wrapped in cloth

2. **Why has the author written (HIGH-ro-gliffs) in brackets?**

   _____

3. **What are hieroglyphs?**
   a a secret code
   b a place in ancient Egypt
   c an ancient Egyptian writing using pictures

4. **What object was found that helped to solve the mystery of hieroglyphic writing?**
   a a mummy
   b some Greek writing
   c the Rosetta stone

5. **How many years after the Rosetta stone was found was the hieroglyphic writing finally solved?**
   a 23 years
   b We are not told.
   c many years

6. **Which is the odd word?**
   a unknown          c puzzle
   b known            d mystery

7. **The word opposite in meaning to ancient is:**
   a modern.
   b old.
   c archaic.

Score 2 points for each correct answer! SCORE **/14**  (0-4)  (6-10)  (12-14)

### My Book Review

Title _____

Author _____

Rating ☆☆☆☆☆

Comment _____

_____

# Number & Algebra

AC9M4N09

## Looking for patterns

Patterns can help us to work things out.

The table shows how many parts are needed to make this party hat.

Can you see any patterns?

| Number of hats | | | | | | |
|---|---|---|---|---|---|---|
| | 1 | 2 | 3 | 4 | 5 | 6 |
| Stars | 6 | 12 | 18 | 24 | 30 | 36 |
| Green dots | 8 | 16 | 24 | 32 | 40 | 48 |
| Green strips | 1 | 2 | 3 | 4 | 5 | 6 |
| Yellow strips | 1 | 2 | 3 | 4 | 5 | 6 |

Sam's mum has a business making birthday cakes. She has asked Sam to help her work out how many decorations she needs to make her latest cake design.

① **Complete the table.**

| Number of cakes | | | | | | |
|---|---|---|---|---|---|---|
| | 1 | 2 | 3 | 4 | 5 | 6 |
| Large hearts | 2 | 4 | | | | |
| Small hearts | 6 | 12 | | | 30 | |
| Bows | 2 | 4 | | 8 | | |
| Cream beads | 10 | 20 | | | | 60 |

**In the table above, colour the following multiplication patterns.**

② Colour the 2 times table in red.

③ Colour the 6 times table in blue.

④ Colour the 10 times table in green.

⑤ **Sam made a table to work out the cost of the decorations. Complete the table.**

| Cost ($ each) | Number of cakes | | | | | |
|---|---|---|---|---|---|---|
| | 1 | 2 | 3 | 4 | 5 | 6 |
| Large hearts | 5 | 10 | | | | |
| Small hearts | 2 | 4 | | | 10 | |
| Bows | 7 | 14 | 21 | | | |
| Cream beads | 0.05 | 0.10 | | | | |

**The total cost for decorating one cake is $14.05. Calculate these costs.**

⑥ The total cost of decorating 2 cakes

_____

⑦ The total cost of decorating 5 cakes

_____

⑧ The total cost of decorating 6 cakes

_____

Score 2 points for each correct answer!

SCORE /16  0-6  8-12  14-16

# Statistics & Probability

*There are no statistics & probability activities in this unit.*

# Measurement & Space

AC9M4M01

## Temperature

Temperature is a measure of how cold or hot things are. We use a thermometer to measure temperature in **degrees Celsius (°C)**.

**Record the temperature shown on each thermometer. The scale is different on each one, so look carefully!**

① _____    ③ _____

② _____    ④ _____

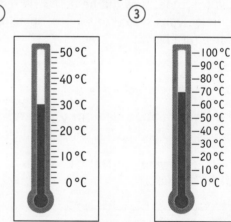

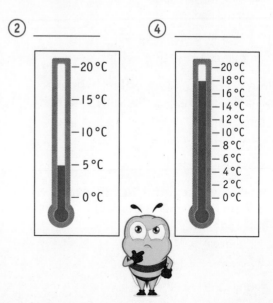

⑤ _____  ⑥ _____

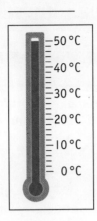

**Colour the thermometers to match the temperatures.**

⑦ 60 °C     ⑩ 45 °C

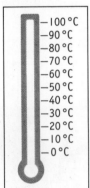

⑧ 15 °C     ⑪ 85 °C

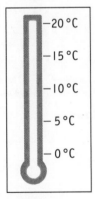
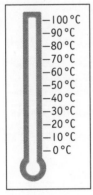

⑨ 6 °C      ⑫ 150 °C

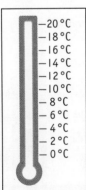
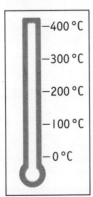

This table records changes in temperature. Complete the table by calculating the end temperature.

| | Start temperature | Change: Up = + Down = − | End temperature |
|---|---|---|---|
| | 15 °C | + 10 °C | 25 °C |
| ⑬ | 35 °C | − 8 °C | |
| ⑭ | 5 °C | + 16 °C | |
| ⑮ | 40 °C | + 21 °C | |
| ⑯ | 100 °C | − 56 °C | |
| ⑰ | 32 °C | − 12 °C | |

Score 2 points for each correct answer!  **SCORE**  /34  (0-14)  (16-28)  (30-34)

## Problem Solving

AC9M4A01

### How many ways?

How many ways can you make 15 by adding 3 of these numbers?

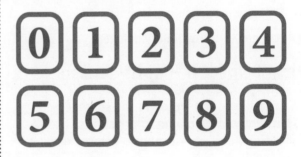

*Example:* 1 + 5 + 9

_____
_____
_____
_____
_____
_____
_____
_____
_____

# Grammar & Punctuation

AC9E4LA07, AC9E4LA12

## Direct speech – speech marks, commas, capital letters

Writers tell us what people say to each other by using **speech marks (quotation marks)**. The speech marks ("...") go at the beginning and end of what was said. The first spoken word always has a **capital letter**. A **comma** marks off the spoken words from the rest of the sentence.

*Examples:* Riley said, "That's a great idea."

"That's a great idea," said Riley.

**NOTE:** If the sentence has a **question mark (?)** or an **exclamation mark (!)**, you do not use a comma.

**Add the missing capital letters, speech marks and commas where necessary.**

① look out! yelled the shop assistant.

② Max said dogs are my favourite type of pet.

③ you are so funny laughed Jake.

## Direct speech – split sentences

When the **spoken words** in the sentence are **split**, you put a **comma** after the first chunk of speech, and you also put a **comma** after the speaking verb.

*Example:*

"Please hurry up," Mum **said**, "or we'll be late."

The spoken words, "Please hurry up or we'll be late", have been wrapped around the speaking verb. The first part of the spoken sentence begins with a **capital letter**, but the second part does not because it is a continuation of the same sentence.

**Add the missing speech marks and commas where necessary.**

④ Suddenly said Max the door swung open.

⑤ When she arrives said Eli we'll surprise her.

⑥ Once laughed Emma I put a spider in Tom's shoe!

*Score 2 points for each correct answer!* **SCORE** /12 (0-4) (6-8) (10-12)

# Phonic Knowledge & Spelling

AC9E4LY10

## Words with a soft 'g' sound

Say each word in the word bank. The letters **ge** and **dge** make a soft 'g' sound. It sounds like 'j' in the words **jump** and **jog**.

| | | | |
|---|---|---|---|
| gel | gem | cage | page |
| hinge | fringe | range | strange |
| edge | hedge | judge | trudge |
| badge | bridge | ridge | dodge |

**Choose words from the word bank to complete these sentences.**

① The _____ was too low for the boat to pass underneath.

② I only use a small amount of hair _____ to do my hair.

③ I didn't know which way to turn to _____ the ball.

## Adding –ed and –ing

**Remember!** When a word ends in **e**, you usually drop the **e** before adding **–ing**. When you add **–ed**, you just add **d** because the word already has the **e**.

**Add –ed and –ing to these words.**

|  | –ed | –ing |
|---|---|---|
| ④ judge | | |
| ⑤ change | | |

**Match the word beginnings from the box with their endings to make compound words.**

| bird | draw | hedge | gem | dodge |
|---|---|---|---|---|

⑥ _____bridge

⑦ _____hog

⑧ _____cage

⑨ _____stone

⑩ _____ball

*Score 2 points for each correct answer!* **SCORE** /20 (0-8) (10-12) (14-20)

TARGETING HOMEWORK 4 © PASCAL PRESS ISBN 9781925726466

**TERM 2 ENGLISH**

## Taste of Thailand – Meh's Kitchen

**Imaginative text** – Narrative
**Author** – Lisa Thompson
**Illustrator** – Brenda Cantell

*Lulu and Ben have been asked to help the chef, Meh Dang, prepare a banquet for the Queen's party at the Grand Palace. Meh, Lulu and Ben have just arrived at the palace.*

The Grand Palace was more than grand. It was by far the most amazing building Ben and Lulu had ever seen. Murals lined the walls. Sculptures of Buddhist gods stood in the gardens and at the entrances. Gold leaf and mirror tiles lined the walls making incredible patterns.

"Why are the roofs shaped like that?" asked Ben on their way to the kitchen. The pointy roofs had spiky shapes at every corner.

"To keep bad spirits off the building," explained Meh.

They reached the kitchen and Meh laid out the shopping. She checked through the ingredients and a look of horror came over her face.

"Oh my goodness! The prawns! How could I have forgotten?" She looked at the clock on the wall. "There is no time to go back and get them and prepare the rest of the dinner." Tears welled in her eyes. "What am I to do? How can I make *goong den* without prawns?"

Lulu whispered to Ben, "I'll stay here and help Meh. You can use your SWAT wristband to go back to the market."

Ben nodded. "It's OK, Meh. I'll get the prawns and be back before you know it."

He walked behind a pillar to count himself out.

"Three ... two ... one."

Click.

Source: *Taste of Thailand*, SWAT series, Blake Education.

---

**Write or circle the correct answers.**

1. **Another word for murals is:**

   a plants.   b paintings.   c people.

2. **Why did the roof of the palace have spiky shapes on every corner?**

   _____

   _____

3. **Which is the odd word?**

   a amazing          c fantastic

   b ordinary         d incredible

4. **What is the main ingredient of the dish goong den?**

   a We are not told.      b prawns

5. **Why did Ben go behind a pillar to use the wristband?**

   _____

   _____

6. **Ben uses his SWAT wristband to get back to the market. What do you think this wristband helps him to do?**

   a tell the time

   b buy things without any money

   c magically travel very quickly

*Score 2 points for each correct answer!*   SCORE  /12   ( 0-4 )  ( 6-8 )  ( 10-12 )

### My Book Review

Title _____

Author _____

Rating ☆ ☆ ☆ ☆ ☆

Comment _____

_____

# Number & Algebra

AC9M4A01

## Equivalent number sentences

> Number sentences or equations are **equivalent**. Equivalent means that one side of the number sentence equals the other side.
>
> *Example:*  13 + 15 = ☐ – 2
>
> 13 + 15 is 28, so the other side must equal 28 too. If you add 2 to 28, you get **30**.

**Complete these equivalent number sentences.**

① 24 + 8 = ☐ – 8

② 12 + ☐ = 10 + 10

③ 100 – 50 = 25 + ☐

④ 50 – 20 = 100 – ☐

⑤ 36 – 6 = ☐ – 30

⑥ 45 + 10 = 50 + ☐

⑦ 28 – ☐ = 30 – 9

## Solving number stories

> *Example:*  Dan gave away 12 of his toy cars. He had 18 left. How many cars did he have to begin with?
>
> You can work this out by writing one of these number sentences:
>
> ☐ – 12 = 18  *or*  12 + 18 = ☐
>
> Answer = **30**

**Write number sentences for these problems. Calculate the answers.**

⑧ At 10 o'clock there were 80 people at the school fair. By 11 o'clock another 25 had arrived. How many people were at the fair at 11 o'clock?

_____

⑨ What number can be taken from 45 so that the answer is the same as 25 plus 12?

_____

⑩ Maree needs 12 more beads to finish making her bracelet. The bracelet will have a total of 60 beads. How many beads does the bracelet have already?

_____

⑪ When a number is added to 35, the answer is the same as 40 plus 10. What is the number?

_____

Score 2 points for each correct answer!

SCORE

/22   ( 0-8 )  ( 10-16 )  ( 18-22 )

# Statistics & Probability

AC9M4ST01

## Milly's TV survey results

> Milly carried out a survey of the students in her class. These are the questions she asked:
>
> 1 **Do you watch TV every day?**
>    yes   no
>
> 2 **How often do you watch TV with your family?**
>    never     sometimes     always
>
> 3 **How many hours of TV per day do you usually watch?**
>    0  1  2  3  4  5  6  7  8

Here are the results of Milly's survey.

**Do You Watch TV Every Day?**

| Yes | ⊦⊦⊦⊦ ⊦⊦⊦⊦ ⊦⊦⊦⊦ ⊦⊦⊦⊦ ||| |
|-----|-------------------------|
| No  | |||| |

**How Often Do You Watch TV With Your Family?**

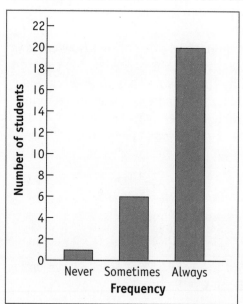

**How Many Hours of TV per Day Do You Usually Watch?**

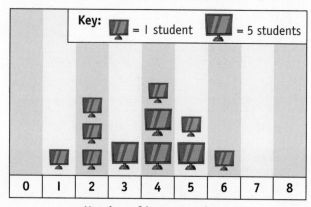

| 0 | 1 | 2 | 3 | 4 | 5 | 6 | 7 | 8 |
|---|---|---|---|---|---|---|---|---|

**Number of hours per day**

**Use Milly's results to answer the questions. Write or circle the correct answers.**

1. How many students were included in the survey? _____

2. For which question did Milly use a column graph to show her results? Circle the answer.

   a  1        b  2        c  3

3. How many students always watch TV with their family? _____

4. How many students watch TV every day? _____

5. How many students watch TV for 4 hours a day? _____

6. How many students watch TV for 5 hours a day? _____

7. How many students never watch TV with their family? _____

8. What is the most common number of hours of TV watched per day? _____

Score 2 points for each correct answer! **SCORE** /16   0-6   8-12   14-16

## Measurement & Space

AC9M4M02

### Area

> **Area** is the amount of space inside a shape.
>
> This shape has an area of 12 squares.
>
> Each square is **1 cm × 1 cm**. We call this **1 cm²** (1 square centimetre).
>
> There are 12 one centimetre squares in this shape, so we write this as **12 cm²** or **12 square centimetres.**

**Write the area of these shapes in words and in cm².**

1. Area = _____ square centimetres or _____ cm²

2. Area = _____ square centimetres or _____ cm²

UNIT **UNIT 15**

3. Area = _____ square centimetres or _____ cm²

**Write the answers to the questions about shapes 1 to 3 above.**

4. Which shape has the largest area? _____

5. Which two shapes have a combined area of 24 cm²? _____

6. Which shape is 2 cm wide and 7 cm long? _____

7. What are the dimensions of shape 3? _____ wide × _____ long.

8. What is the difference in area between shape 1 and shape 2? _____

Score 2 points for each correct answer! **SCORE** /16   0-6   8-12   14-16

## Problem Solving

AC9M4M02

### Carpet conundrum

Jesse's mum wants to put new carpet in Jesse's bedroom. This is a picture of Jesse's room. Each square is 1 metre × 1 metre (1 m²).

The **blue** squares show the area that is to be carpeted.

**Work out the following:**

1. How many square metres of carpet do they need? _____

2. If the carpet costs $40 per square metre, how much will the carpet cost? _____

3. If the underlay costs $20 per square metre, how much will the underlay cost? _____

4. The carpet fitter charges $50 an hour to lay the carpet. It will take 2 hours to fit. How much will this cost? _____

5. What is the total cost of laying the carpet in Jesse's room? _____

TARGETING HOMEWORK 4 © PASCAL PRESS ISBN 9781925726466

**65**

# Grammar & Punctuation

AC9E4LA07, AC9E4LA12

## Direct and reported speech

We can record what a speaker says in a text in two ways:

1 **Direct speech**: We **repeat** the words spoken by the speaker.
*Example:* "I am going to visit Nan tomorrow," said Maria.

2 **Reported speech**: We **report** the words spoken by the speaker.
*Example:* Maria said that she was going to visit her nan tomorrow.

**Speech marks** (or quotation marks) are **not required** in reported speech.

To write reported speech, we usually change the spoken words to **past tense**.

*Examples:*

"I <u>am writing</u> a story," said Jack.
present tense (direct speech)

Jack said that he <u>was writing</u> a story.
past tense (reported speech)

**Rewrite these sentences as reported speech.**

1 "Lunch is ready," said Mum.
Mum said _____

2 He said, "I am learning French."
He said _____

**Write what these people are saying as reported speech. The first one has been done for you.**

*Example:*

 That's an excellent idea!

The businessman said <u>that it was an excellent idea</u>.

3  I'm not sure.

She said that _____
_____

4  I am going into town.

Sara said that _____
_____

*Score 2 points for each correct answer!*

SCORE **/8** ( 0-2 ) ( 4-6 ) ( 8 )

# Phonic Knowledge & Spelling

AC9E4LY09, AC9E4LY10

## Letter teams ie and ei

**Say each word in the word bank. In these words, the letter teams ie and ei make a long 'e' sound.**

| chief | thief | grief | believe |
| shield | field | niece | pierce |
| ceiling | deceit | receive | receipt |

**Choose words from the word bank to complete these sentences.**

1 A _____ stole the cash box from the community hall.

2 We walked by the hockey _____.

## Spelling rule – i before e, except after c

We usually write **i** before **e**, but when this sound follows the letter **c**, we change the order to **ei**. This gives the **c** a soft sound.

**NOTE:** some words do not follow this rule.

*Examples:* weir, weird, seize, vein, foreign, protein, their, sovereign, height

**Complete these words by adding ie or ei.**

3 rec____ve

4 c____ling

## Spelling rule – plural of words that end in f, ff and fe

For many of the words that end in **f** and **fe**, change the **f** and **fe** to **v** before adding **–es**.

*Examples:* wolf, wolves   life, lives

For words that end in **ff**, you just add **s**.

*Examples:* cliff, cliffs   bluff, bluffs

**NOTE:** There are many exceptions to these rules!

*Examples:* roof, roofs   chief, chiefs
hoof, hoofs (or hooves)
scarf, scarfs (or scarves)

**Write the plural of these words.**

5 knife _____

6 giraffe _____

7 wife _____

8 belief _____

*Score 2 points for each correct answer!*

SCORE **/16** ( 0-6 ) ( 8-12 ) ( 14-16 )

# A Ship Out to Sea

**Imaginative text** – Narrative
**Author** – Christopher Stitt
**Illustrator** – Jan D'Silva

Toby stood on the cliffs with his grandfather, Skip, looking out over the crashing sea.

"Will there be a storm?" Toby asked.

"No doubt. I'd better go up and turn the light on."

Toby loved spending his school holidays with his grandparents. They were lighthouse keepers and lived in a house at the bottom of the lighthouse.

Toby breathed in the wet, salty air. "You can smell a storm, can't you?"

"Sure can. You take after your old grandfather." He put his hand on Toby's shoulder. "Coming to help turn the light on?"

"In a minute."

Skip headed for the lighthouse. "Don't be long. Those clouds are about to release a huge downpour."

Toby stood alone on the cliff. The wind was blowing his hair wildly. The salt air made his face tingle. He watched the seagulls ride the wind, not beating their wings – just gliding. Free.

Toby noticed something out to sea. It was a ship, an old-fashioned ship, with sails and rigging. It was kind of hazy and hard to see. He stared harder. It was almost see-through.

"I'll have to tell Grandad. Maybe I can get a better look through the telescope."

Toby ran to the lighthouse and up the one hundred and thirty-five steps. "There's a ship out there!" puffed Toby. "I need the telescope."

"A ship you say?" Skip handed Toby the telescope. "I wonder who it is?"

Toby looked out across the sea. He pointed the telescope at the exact place where he had seen the ship. The ship had disappeared.

Source: *Isabella*, Sparklers, Blake Education.

**Write or circle the correct answers**

1. 'Looking out over the crashing sea', tells us that the sea was:

    a calm.

    b stormy.

    c blue.

2. What is a **lighthouse keeper**?

    a someone who likes lighthouses

    b someone whose job it is to manage a lighthouse

    c someone who lives in a lighthouse

**Which words in the text have these meanings?**

3. a heavy fall of rain: _____

4. misty: _____

5. completely accurate: _____

6. What is a **telescope**?

    a an instrument for seeing things in the distance more closely

    b an instrument for lighting the lighthouse

*Score 2 points for each correct answer!* **SCORE** /12 ( 0-4 ) ( 6-8 ) ( 10-12 )

### My Book Review

Title _____

Author _____

Rating ☆☆☆☆☆

Comment _____

_____

# Number & Algebra

AC9M4N01, AC9M4N03

## Decimal fractions: tenths

This shape is divided into **ten equal parts** or **tenths**. Each part is equal to one-tenth or $\frac{1}{10}$.

| $\frac{1}{10}$ | $\frac{1}{10}$ | $\frac{1}{10}$ | $\frac{1}{10}$ | $\frac{1}{10}$ | $\frac{1}{10}$ | $\frac{1}{10}$ | $\frac{1}{10}$ | $\frac{1}{10}$ | $\frac{1}{10}$ |

We can write one-tenth like this: **0.1**

The dot is a decimal point. It separates the ones from the tenths. The 0 tells us there are zero ones and the 1 tells us there is one tenth.

To read this number, say: **zero point one**.

**Complete the table.**

| | Words | Fraction | Decimal |
|---|---|---|---|
| | one-tenth | $\frac{1}{10}$ | 0.1 |
| | two-tenths | $\frac{2}{10}$ | 0.2 |
| ① | three-tenths | | |
| ② | four-tenths | | |
| ③ | five-tenths | | |
| ④ | six-tenths | | |
| ⑤ | seven-tenths | | |
| ⑥ | eight-tenths | | |
| ⑦ | nine-tenths | | |
| | ten-tenths | $\frac{10}{10}$ | 1.0 |

Look at these **decimal fractions**:

**0.9    1.8    2.4    1.9    3.6    0.5**

**0.5** is the smallest.
It is equal to zero ones and five tenths.

**3.6** is the largest.
It is equal to three ones and six tenths.

**Write these decimal fractions in order from smallest to largest.**

⑧ 0.8    1.7    0.5    2.4    1.9

_____

⑨ 1.6    2.3    1.8    2.2    2.0

_____

⑩ 0.3    2.8    0.1    2.5    0.8

_____

⑪ 4.5    3.2    5.6    2.7    5.0

_____

## Counting in decimal fractions

These **number lines** count in fractions and decimal fractions.

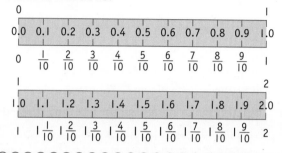

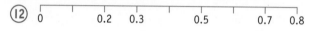

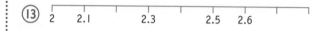

**Write the missing numbers.**

⑫ 0    0.2  0.3    0.5    0.7  0.8

⑬ 2  2.1    2.3    2.5  2.6

⑭ 3.5  3.6    3.9  4.0    4.2

## Decimal fractions: hundredths

If a shape is divided into **100 equal parts**, each part is one hundredth or $\frac{1}{100}$. Here, $\frac{1}{100}$ is coloured blue. 0.01 is the same as $\frac{1}{100}$.

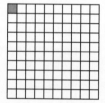

**Complete the table.**

| | Words | Fraction | Decimal |
|---|---|---|---|
| | one-hundredth | $\frac{1}{100}$ | 0.01 |
| | two-hundredths | $\frac{2}{100}$ | 0.02 |
| | three-hundredths | $\frac{3}{100}$ | 0.03 |
| ⑮ | four-hundredths | | |
| ⑯ | five-hundredths | | |
| ⑰ | six-hundredths | | |
| ⑱ | seven-hundredths | | |
| ⑲ | eight-hundredths | | |
| ⑳ | nine-hundredths | | |
| | ten-hundredths | $\frac{10}{100}$ | 0.10 |
| | fifteen-hundredths | $\frac{15}{100}$ | 0.15 |
| ㉑ | twenty-four hundredths | | |

Score 2 points for each correct answer!

SCORE **/42**  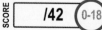 (0-18)  (20-36) (38-42)

TARGETING HOMEWORK 4 © PASCAL PRESS ISBN 9781925726466

## Statistics & Probability

*There are no statistics & probability activities in this unit.*

## Measurement & Space

AC9M4SP02

## Measuring distance on a map

A **scale** is used to show distance on the map.

Here is a map of Mainton and its surrounding towns. The scale on the map is **I cm = I km.**

This means that every I centimetre that you measure on the map is equal to I kilometre on the ground.

The red lines on the map represent roads.

**Mainton and its Surrounding Towns**

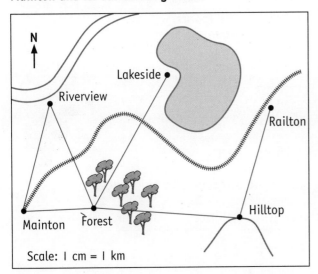

Scale: I cm = I km

**What is the distance between these places in kilometres (km)? Use a ruler.**

① Riverview to Forest _____ km

② Forest to Hilltop _____ km

③ Hilltop to Railton _____ km

④ Riverview to Mainton _____ km

⑤ Mainton to Forest _____ km

⑥ Forest to Lakeside _____ km

**Write the correct answers.**

⑦ How far would you travel if you drove from Riverview to Forest and then on to Hilltop?

_____

⑧ How far would you travel if you walked from Mainton to Forest and then from Forest to Lakeside?

_____

⑨ A bus travelled from Lakeside to Forest and then on to Hilltop. How far did it travel?

_____

⑩ A new road is going to be built in a straight line from Riverview to Hilltop. What is the length of the new road?

_____

*Score 2 points for each correct answer!* | SCORE | **/20** | 0-8 | 10-14 | 16-20

**TERM 2 MATHS**

## Problem Solving

AC9M4A01

## What do the symbols equal?

The sum of the symbols in each row has been worked out for you.

**What is the value of each symbol?**

| ◆ | ★ | ★ | ☺ | 16 |
| ☺ | ◆ | ◆ | ◆ | 14 |
| ★ | ◆ | ☺ | ★ | 16 |
| ☺ | ☺ | ☺ | ☺ | 20 |
| 17 | 15 | 17 | 17 | |

◆ = ☐   ★ = ☐   ☺ = ☐

**Make up your own symbol sentence below.**

## Grammar & Punctuation

**Replace the nouns in bold with a pronoun. Rewrite the sentence.**

① Max wanted to go swimming so **Max** asked his mum if **Max** could go.

_____

_____

_____

**Circle the correct pronoun in this sentence.**

② Please take (I   me) to the beach with you.

**Underline the noun or noun group that the pronoun in bold is referring to.**

③ Yesterday, I went to see my friend. **She** is really nice.

**Circle the possessive pronouns. Underline what they 'own'.**

④ The red bike is mine, but the blue bike is hers.

**Rewrite this sentence to avoid unnecessary repetition.**

⑤ Are those books your books or our books?

_____

_____

**Read this sentence and underline the adjectives. Write the noun that is being described.**

⑥ The old, dilapidated fence finally fell down.

_____

**Add –er and –est to these adjectives. Think about the spelling rules!**

|        | –er         | –est        |
|--------|-------------|-------------|
| ⑦ tall | _____ | _____ |
| ⑧ thin | _____ | _____ |
| ⑨ happy | _____ | _____ |

**Choose the correct form of comparing adjectives in this sentence.**

⑩ This is the (more delicious / most delicious) meal I have ever eaten.

**Rewrite this sentence. Put in the capital letters, speech marks and commas where necessary.**

⑪ watch out! yelled the police officer.

_____

_____

**Rewrite this sentence as reported speech.**

⑫ "I am going fishing today," said Tom.

Tom said _____

_____

Score 2 points for each correct answer! SCORE  **/24**  (0-10)  (12-18)  (20-24)

## Phonic Knowledge & Spelling

**Circle the correct homophone in this sentence.**

① Dad had to (paws   pause) the DVD.

**Add the correct ending. Choose from –s, –ed, –ing or –er. Remember the rules!**

② These prawn_____ are just what I need for my recipe.

③ Jackie was ignore_____ me so I nudge_____ her in the arm.

**Write the plurals of these words.**

④ class   _____

⑤ waltz   _____

⑥ task   _____

⑦ fox   _____

**Match the antonyms of these adjectives.**

| beautiful   rich   fearful   old |
|---|

⑧ brave   _____

⑨ young   _____

⑩ ugly   _____

⑪ poor   _____

**Choose the correct prefix to change these words to their opposites. Write the new word.**

⑫ personal:   im-   un-

_____

⑬ certain:   un-   in-

_____

**Circle how many syllables in these words.**

⑭ breakfast   1   2   3

⑮ unpleasant   1   2   3

**Complete the rhyming words.**

⑯ healthy   w _ _ _ _ _ _   st _ _ _ _ _ _

**Add –ed and –ing to these words. Write the words.**

|         | –ed         | –ing        |
|---------|-------------|-------------|
| ⑰ judge | _____ | _____ |
| ⑱ change | _____ | _____ |

TARGETING HOMEWORK 4 © PASCAL PRESS ISBN 9781925726466

**Complete these words with ie or ei.**

(19) f___ld

(20) rec___ve

(21) s___ge

**Write the plural of these words.**

(22) life _____

(23) giraffe _____

(24) thief _____

(25) chief _____

Score 2 points for each correct answer! | SCORE **/50** (0-22) (24-44) (46-50)

Informative text
**Author** – Ian Rohr

## Far-flung Fleas

A flea is only about the size of a pin head. But when it comes to jumping high, the flea is leaps and bounds ahead of us.

Fleas are parasites that live on other animals. They jump from animal to animal looking for food. Fleas don't have wings but they do have rubbery pads in their back legs. These are squashed up tightly like springs, until the flea wants to jump. Then, with a trigger-click, the pads are released and the flea rockets 30 centimetres into the air. In proportion to its size, the force required for a flea to do its flip is 20 times more than the force needed to launch a rocket into space! And fleas don't stop after just one jump! They can make these incredible jumps 600 times an hour.

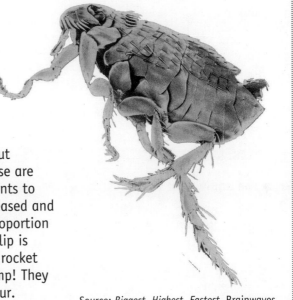

Source: *Biggest, Highest, Fastest*, Brainwaves, Blake Education.

**Write or circle the correct answers.**

(1) **What does the phrase when it comes to jumping high, the flea is leaps and bounds ahead of us mean?**

a The flea is jumping in front of us.

b The flea is much better at jumping high than humans.

c The flea can leap and bound.

(2) **What is a parasite?**

a a tiny bug

b a type of flea

c a plant or animal that gets its food from another living thing by living on or inside it

(3) **What do fleas have that enables them to jump really high?**

_____

_____

(4) **Which word in the text means let go?**

_____

(5) **Which word in the text means the amount of one thing compared to another?**

a required    b proportion    c incredible

(6) **Which one of these is the odd word out?**

a compressed        c squashed

b flattened          d loosened

(7) **Which word in the text is another word for power?**

_____

(8) **How high can a flea jump?**

_____

(9) **How many legs does a flea have?** _____

(10) **Can humans jump with the same force as a flea?**

_____

Score 2 points for each correct answer! | SCORE **/20** (0-8) (10-14) (16-20)

## Number & Algebra

① Use the split method to add these numbers. Show your working out.

648 + 337

_____

_____

_____

_____

_____

**Complete these multiplications and divisions.**

② 4 × 6 = _____

③ 6 × _____ = 24

④ 24 ÷ 4 = _____

⑤ 24 ÷ _____ = 6

⑥ 3 × 7 = _____

⑦ _____ × 3 = 21

⑧ 21 ÷ 3 = _____

⑨ 21 ÷ _____ = 7

**Write the next numbers in these sequences.**

⑩ 12, 18, 24, 30, _____, _____, _____, _____

⑪ 40, 48, 56, 64, _____, _____, _____, _____

**Write the equivalent fractions.**

⑫

$$\frac{4}{12} = \boxed{\phantom{0}}$$

⑬

$$\frac{1}{5} = \boxed{\phantom{0}}$$

⑭ Use the split method to multiply these numbers. Show your working out.

6 × 48

_____

_____

_____

_____

**Write these improper fractions as whole or mixed numerals.**

⑮ $\frac{5}{4}$ = _____

⑯ $\frac{7}{4}$ = _____

⑰ $\frac{9}{4}$ = _____

⑱ $\frac{12}{4}$ = _____

**Complete these equivalent number sentences.**

⑲ 36 + 8 = ___ − 8

⑳ 12 + ___ = 30 + 10

㉑ 100 − 25 = 50 + ___

㉒ 50 − 16 = 100 − ___

㉓ Write an equivalent number sentence to help you solve this problem.

What number can be taken from 55 so that the answer is the same as 25 plus 15?

_____

㉔ Write these decimal fractions in order from smallest to largest.

0.2    2.7    0.5    2.4    1.9

_____

Score 2 points for each correct answer! | SCORE | **/48** | 0-22 | 24-42 | 44-48

## Statistics & Probability

Jackson carried out a survey of the students in his class. These are the questions he asked:

1. Do you play sport?
2. What sport do you play?
3. How many hours each week do you practise your sport?

Here are the results of Jackson's survey:

**Do You Play Sport?**

| Yes | ＼＼＼＼ ＼＼＼＼ ＼＼＼＼ ＼＼＼＼ ＼＼＼＼ |
|-----|-----------------------------------|
| No  | ＼＼＼＼ ||| |

**What Sport Do You Play?**

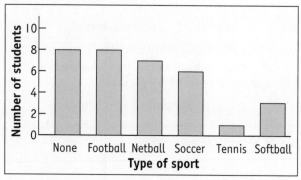

**How Many Hours Do You Practise Your Sport Each Week?**

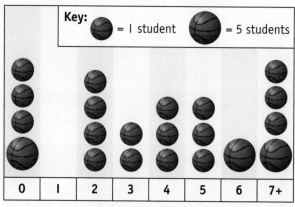

Key:  = 1 student   = 5 students

Number of hours per week

TARGETING HOMEWORK 4 © PASCAL PRESS ISBN 9781925726466

## Use Jackson's results to answer the questions. Write or circle the correct answers.

① How many students were included in the survey? _____

② For which question did Jackson use a column graph to show his results?

    **a** 1     **b** 2     **c** 3

③ How many students play a sport? _____

④ How many students play no sport? _____

⑤ What is the most popular sport played?

    _____

⑥ What is the least popular sport?

    _____

⑦ How many students spend 5 hours a week practising their sport? _____

⑧ How many students spend over 7 hours a week practising their sport? _____

⑨ What type of graph did Jackson use to record the results of question 3?

    _____

Score 2 points for each correct answer! **SCORE /18** (0-6) (8-14) (16-18)

## Measurement & Space

**Convert these measurements.**

① 60 mm = _____ cm

② 4 metres = _____ cm

③ 5000 m = _____ km

④ 7 cm = _____ mm

**Convert these times.**

⑤ 3 minutes = _____ seconds

⑥ 5 minutes = _____ seconds

⑦ 2 hours = _____ minutes

⑧ 4 hours = _____ minutes

⑨ 120 seconds = _____ minutes

⑩ 180 minutes = _____ hours

**Read the scales and write the mass.**

⑪ _____ g      ⑫ _____ g

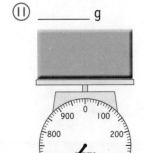 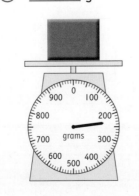

## How much liquid is in these containers?

⑬ _____ mL      ⑭ _____ mL

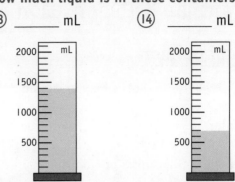

## Colour the thermometers to show the temperatures.

⑮ 12 °C      ⑯ 35 °C

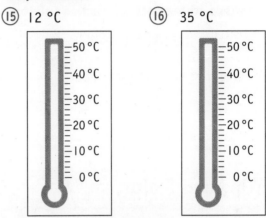

## Write the area of each shape.

⑰

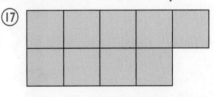

Area = ___ square centimetres or ___ cm²

⑱

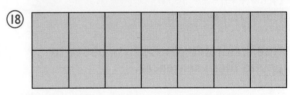

Area = ___ square centimetres or ___ cm²

## Use the scale on the map and a ruler to answer the questions.

**Redtown and its Surrounding Towns**

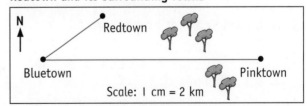

Scale: 1 cm = 2 km

**What is the distance between:**

⑲ Bluetown and Redtown? _____ km

⑳ Bluetown and Pinktown? _____ km

㉑ **What is the direct distance from Redtown to Pinktown?** _____ km

Score 2 points for each correct answer! **SCORE /42** (0-18) (20-36) (38-42)

# Grammar & Punctuation

AC9E4LA02

## Fact and opinion

> A **fact** is something that is **true** or can be proven.
>
> An **opinion** is your **feelings** or how someone else feels about a topic.
>
> **Fact:** Paris is the capital of France.
>
> **Opinion:** I think the traffic in Paris is terrible.

**Write if these statements are fact or opinion.**

1. We visited the museum yesterday.

   _____

2. I believe that cats make better pets than dogs.

   _____

3. Deciduous trees lose their leaves in winter.

   _____

## Thinking and feeling verbs

> When we write, or talk, about our **thoughts** and **feelings**, we can use certain words and phrases to express our opinion.
>
> *Examples:*
> I think    I believe    I feel
> In my opinion    My favourite
> The best    It's my belief
> I strongly believe    I am convinced
> In my view    It seems to me that
> I tend to think that

**Choose a suitable phrase from above to complete these sentences.**

4. _____ colour is blue.
5. _____ that honesty is always best.
6. _____ movie ever made was Star Wars.

**Circle the feeling that best fits each statement.**

7. I think today was the best day of my life.
   **a** sad    **b** happy

8. I am convinced that the man is innocent.
   **a** confident    **b** unsure

9. I am convinced that there will be trouble.
   **a** worried    **b** hopeful

# Phonic Knowledge & Spelling

AC9E4LY09, AC9E4LY10

## Words ending in –et, –en and –le

**Say each word in the word bank. They all have two syllables.**

| ticket | cricket | rocket | bucket |
|--------|---------|--------|--------|
| chicken | thicken | written | kitchen |
| juggle | wriggle | shuffle | dazzle |
| rumble | tremble | angle | ankle |

**Choose words from the word bank to complete these sentences.**

1. Do you know how to _____ three tennis balls?

2. This evening, Dad is making a _____ pie for dinner.

3. I caught the fish as it tried to _____ out of the net.

**Write the words from the word bank that match these clues.**

4. to make something thicker:
   _____

5. to shake gently:
   _____

6. to make a deep heavy sound:
   _____

7. to drag your feet as you walk:
   _____

**Build the words by adding the ending of the example word.**

8. dazzle    pu _ _ _ _    no _ _ _ _    dri _ _ _ _
9. shuffle    sni _ _ _ _    ru _ _ _ _    ra _ _ _ _
10. rumble    crum _ _ _    nib _ _ _    bob _ _ _

**Add the endings –ed, –ing and –er to these words.**

11. juggle    _____

    _____    _____

    _____

12. thicken

13. tumble

    _____

    _____

Score 2 points for each correct answer!    SCORE /18    0-6    8-14    16-18

Score 2 points for each correct answer!    SCORE /26    0-10    12-20    22-26

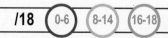
TARGETING HOMEWORK 4 © PASCAL PRESS ISBN 9781925726466

## Should Our Convicts be Sent to New South Wales?

**Persuasive text** – Discussion
**Author** – Merryn Whitfield
**Illustrator** – Philip Rice

*Transcript of a speech given by William Huskisson, member for Morpeth, to the British Parliament in 1796.*

Thieves, forgers, petty criminals — why wouldn't we want to rid fair England of these lowly convicts and send them to the distant colonies? There are many benefits of transportation and these surely outweigh the negatives.

Firstly, our London gaols are overcrowded as it is. The convicts are unhealthy and spread disease. If we continue to transport them, we will free up space and these unpleasant health issues will be easier to manage.

Another important reason in favour of transportation is money. The large number of convicts in prison here is costing the government far too much. If we send the wretches to the new colony, they will have to farm their own food and look after themselves. They will be out of our sight and out of our pockets!

Finally, the threat of transportation may prevent the underclass from committing petty crimes. If they go to gaol here, they simply return home when released and they are free to break the law again. But if they are transported, there is no chance of them ever raising enough money to pay their way back to Mother England.

On the other hand, there are some bleeding hearts who believe that we should not transport our convicts overseas.

Some believe that, as proper English men and women, they should serve their punishment in England and not in some distant heathen land. "We should not send our problems overseas," says one woman. "No matter what their crime, they are still of English blood and should be treated with respect."

Others believe that for some small crimes, transportation is too harsh a penalty. The months of travel across the seas are dangerous, with the constant threat of illness and shipwreck, and such a punishment may not always fit the crime.

So should our convicts be transported to the new colony? This is not an easy question to answer, as both sides are very vocal. However, for the future of our nation, I believe that transporting our criminals to New South Wales is the only possible solution.

Source: *Writing Centres: Persuasive Texts*, Middle Primary, Blake Education.

TERM 3 ENGLISH

**Write or circle the correct answers.**

① **What is a transcript?**

a a written version     b a translation

② **What are the three reasons William Huskisson gives for sending convicts to Australia?**

a stop disease, keep them out of sight, punish them

b overcrowded gaols, cheaper to transport them, may prevent criminals from committing crimes again

③ **Which is the odd word?**

a petty    b small    c major    d minor

④ **What does bleeding hearts mean?**

a people who are considered to be soft-hearted and kind

b people who are considered to be hard-hearted and cruel

**Are these statements from the text fact (F) or opinion (0)?**

⑤ Our London gaols are overcrowded. ____

⑥ We should not send our problems overseas. ____

Score 2 points for each correct answer!   SCORE   /12   0-4   6-8   10-12

### My Book Review

Title _____

Author _____

Rating ☆☆☆☆☆

Comment _____

_____

# Number & Algebra

AC9M4N02

## Odd and even numbers

> **Even** numbers end in 0, 2, 4, 6 or 8.
> **Odd** numbers end in 1, 3, 5, 7 or 9.
> **Rules**
> • odd number + odd number = even number
> • even number + even number = even number
> • odd number + even number = odd number

**Investigate these statements and write true or false.**

① If you double any odd number, the answer is always an even number. _____

② If you double any even number, the answer is always an even number. _____

③ The sum of three odd numbers is always an even number. _____

④ The sum of two odd numbers and one even number is always an even number. _____

⑤ The sum of two even numbers and one odd number is always an even number. _____

**Use what you found out to decide if the sums will be odd or even, without working out the answers.**

⑥ 156 + 156      **a** odd    **b** even

⑦ 403 + 609 + 800      **a** odd    **b** even

⑧ 720 + 1000 + 533      **a** odd    **b** even

⑨ 539 + 253 + 125      **a** odd    **b** even

⑩ 933 + 933      **a** odd    **b** even

> **Rules**
> • even – even = even    • even × even = even
> • even – odd = odd    • even × odd = even
> • odd – odd = even    • odd × odd = odd

**Use the rules to decide if the answers will be odd or even, without working out the answer.**

⑪ 4563 – 2375      **a** odd    **b** even

⑫ 546 × 321      **a** odd    **b** even

⑬ 2000 – 630      **a** odd    **b** even

⑭ 655 × 787      **a** odd    **b** even

⑮ 782 – 453      **a** odd    **b** even

⑯ 1258 × 1356      **a** odd    **b** even

# Statistics & Probability

AC9M4ST02

## Survey results

> Greg carried out a survey of the students in his class. He asked them to choose which food they liked best: pizza, roast chicken, hamburger, spaghetti or fish and chips.
>
> Here is the graph he drew to show his results.

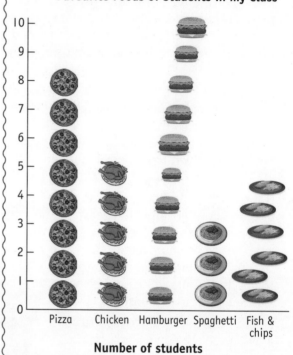

**Favourite Foods of Students in my Class**

Number of students

**Answer the questions about Greg's graph.**

① How do you think he collected the information?

_____
_____
_____
_____

② How many students prefer hamburgers? _____

③ How many students prefer pizza? _____

④ What is the total number of students surveyed? _____

**List three things that are wrong with Greg's graph.**

⑤ _____

⑥ _____

⑦ _____

⑧ Use the information in Greg's graph to make a column graph.

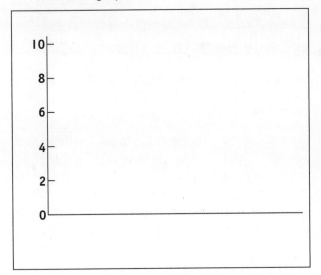

Score 2 points for each correct answer! **SCORE** /16 (0-6) (8-12) (14-16)

## Measurement & Space

AC9M4SP02

## Following directions

This is a map of where Sara lives. She lives at 16 Walker Street – marked **X**.

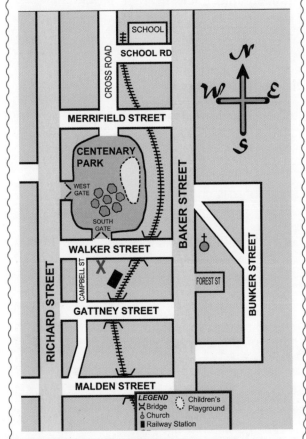

**Use the map to answer the questions.**

There are three ways that Sara can walk to school. Complete the directions for the three different ways.

① Sara crosses over Walker Street, heading north into _____ _____. She walks through the park and comes out through _____ Gate. She crosses over _____ Street, walks up _____ Road and turns _____ into School Road.

② Sara turns left, heading west. She turns right into _____ Street and walks north up to Merrifield Street where she turns _____. She turns _____ into Cross Road and then _____ into School Road.

③ Sara turns right, heading _____. She turns left into _____ Street and walks north. She then turns _____ into School Road.

There are 5 railway bridges on the map. Name the 5 streets that the bridges cross.

④ _____
⑤ _____
⑥ _____
⑦ _____
⑧ _____

⑨ **Find the church. It is on the corner of which two streets?**

_____
_____

Score 2 points for each correct answer! **SCORE** /18 (0-6) (8-14) (16-18)

## Problem Solving

AC9M4N06

### Crack the safe!

Solve these problems to get the numbers to crack open the safe.

① 63 ÷ 7 = _____
② double 7 minus eight = _____
③ $\frac{1}{4}$ of 100 subtract 20 = _____
④ (2 × 2) + (2 × 2) = _____
⑤ There are 60 chickens and 53 run away. How many are left? _____
⑥ How many hours in 180 minutes? _____

## Grammar & Punctuation

AC9E4LA04

### Compound sentences

> A simple sentence has a subject and a verb.
>
> A **compound sentence** is two simple sentences joined together by a **joining word** such as **or, and, but** and **so**. Each sentence has a subject and a verb.
>
> I like swimming and I also like running.
> subject  verb     joining subject verb
>                    word

**Join these sentences together by choosing or, and, but or so.**

① We didn't have enough money _____ we couldn't buy a pizza.

② I chased after Susan _____ I couldn't catch up with her.

③ Jed loves strawberries _____ he also loves raspberries.

④ Do you want some cake _____ do you want a biscuit?

### Compound sentences – subjects

> Each part of a **compound sentence** has a **subject**. Sometimes it is the same and sometimes it is different.
>
> Jayne bought some bread **but** she forgot to buy some milk. (same subject)
>
> Su swept the floor **and** Max cleaned the windows. (different subject)

**Underline the subjects in these sentences and write if the subjects are the same or different.**

⑤ Jackie prefers netball **but** Milly prefers soccer. _____

⑥ Mum bought some wool **so** she can knit me a jumper. _____

⑦ Dad mowed the lawn **and** I picked up the grass. _____

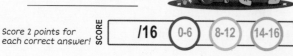

⑧ Mia used to have a bike **but** her mother sold it. _____

Score 2 points for each correct answer!  SCORE /16  0-6  8-12  14-16

## Phonic Knowledge & Spelling

AC9E4LY09, AC9E4LY10

### Two-syllable words – the first syllable ends in a vowel

Say each word in the word bank. They all have two syllables. The first syllable of each word ends in a vowel.

| begin | ruby | bacon | radar | station |
|-------|------|-------|-------|---------|
| siren | final | program | able | table |
| stable | fable | rifle | trifle | bridle |

Choose words from the word bank to complete these sentences.

① Are you sure you are _____ to help on Saturday?

② The fence post wasn't _____ so it had to be cemented in.

③ The sign at the front of the railway _____ was difficult to read.

④ A _____ is my favourite kind of gem stone.

### Homographs

> **Homographs** are words that have the same spelling but sound different and have different meanings.

Match the words in the box to their two different meanings.

| trifle | stable | rifle | kind |

⑤ not likely to fall over; a building for horses: _____

⑥ to ransack and rob; a type of gun: _____

⑦ a thing of little value; a type of dessert: _____

⑧ a group of the same things; helpful: _____

Build the words by adding the beginning or ending of the example word.

⑨ able    c _ _ _ _    t _ _ _ _    st _ _ _ _

⑩ station    _ _ _ ble    _ _ _ ple    _ _ _ men

Score 2 points for each correct answer!  SCORE /20  0-8  10-14  16-20

## The Science of Cycling

**Informative text** – Report
**Author** – Lisa Nicol

Science can describe everyday activities, such as riding a bicycle.

Riding is all about forces. A force is a push or pull that changes the speed, direction or shape of something. Forces happen when energy is used.

Friction is a force that happens when objects touch each other. Friction holds back the movement of an object, slowing it down. There is friction between a bicycle's tyres and the road. If you stop pedalling — that is, stop applying a force to move forwards — the bicycle will eventually stop due to friction. Pumping up the tyres reduces the amount of rubber touching the road. This reduces friction.

The brakes on a bicycle also use friction. When you press the brake levers, pads grip the rim of the wheel. This creates friction and slows the bicycle down.

Drag also resists forward motion. This is the friction of the air pulling on the cyclist. Some cyclists wear **streamlined** clothing to reduce drag.

Riding a bicycle converts energy from one form (energy in the food you eat) into another form (movement, also known as kinetic energy). Bicycling is very **efficient**. It takes less energy to bicycle one kilometre than it does to walk one kilometre.

Source: *Science + You*, Go Facts, Blake Education.

**Write or circle the correct answers.**

① **Explain what a force is.**

_____

_____

② **What does friction do to a moving object?**

a speeds it up

b slows it down

c moves it forwards

③ **Name two ways to reduce friction when cycling.**

_____

_____

④ **Which is the odd word?**

a increase

b reduce

c decrease

d lower

⑤ **What is the meaning of streamlined?**

a a type of bicycle

b a type of clothing

c something designed to give little resistance to the flow of air or water

⑥ **What is kinetic energy?**

_____

_____

### My Book Review

Title _____

Author _____

Rating ☆☆☆☆☆

Comment _____

*Score 2 points for each correct answer!*

SCORE **/12** ( 0-4 ) ( 6-8 ) ( 10-12 )

**TERM 3 ENGLISH**

# Number & Algebra

AC9M4N09

## Number patterns

Use the rules to fill in the blanks in these number patterns.

① **Rule: + 6**

78, 84, 90, _____, _____, _____

② **Rule: + 7**

126, 133, _____, _____, _____, 161

③ **Rule: – 6**

1200, 1194, 1188, _____, _____, _____

④ **Rule: + 8**

1250, 1258, 1266, _____, _____, _____

⑤ **Rule: – 8**

3000, _____, _____, _____, 2968

⑥ **Rule: + 10**

1320, 1330, 1340, _____, _____, _____

⑦ **Rule: + 9**

2000, 2009, 2018, _____, _____, _____

Complete these number patterns. Write the rule.

⑧ **Rule: ____**

890, 899, 908, _____, _____, _____

⑨ **Rule: ____**

5000, 4990, 4980, _____, _____, _____

⑩ **Rule: ____**

12 100, 12 106, 12 112, _____,

_____, _____

⑪ **Rule: ____**

800, 793, 786, _____, _____, _____

⑫ **Rule: ____**

5030, 5040, 5050, _____, _____,

_____

⑬–⑯ Join the boxes that have the same answers.

| double 9 | one sixth of 36 |
|---|---|

| 140 divided by 10 | (7 × 10) + 2 |
|---|---|

| the product of 9 and 8 |
|---|

| half of 28 | 9 lots of 2 | 36 ÷ 6 |
|---|---|---|

Fill in the boxes. For some, more than one answer is possible.

⑰ ☐ × ☐ = 36

⑱ ☐ × ☐ = 50

⑲ ☐ × ☐ = 100

⑳ ☐ × ☐ = 56

㉑ ☐ × ☐ = 40

㉒ ☐ × ☐ = 80

㉓ ☐ ÷ ☐ = 7

㉔ ☐ ÷ ☐ = 6

Score 2 points for each correct answer!

SCORE  **/48**  ( 0-22 ) ( 24-42 ) ( 44-48 )

# Statistics & Probability

*There are no statistics & probability activities in this unit.*

# Measurement & Space

AC9M4M03

## am and pm time

**am** means before midday.
**pm** means after midday.

Write **am** or **pm** to complete these statements.

① I woke up at 7:00 ____ to get ready for school.

② At school, we eat lunch at 12:30 ____.

③ I always go to bed at 9:00 ____.

④ After school, I watch TV until 6:00 ____.

⑤ On Saturday, our football match begins at 2:00 ____.

⑥ Yesterday morning, we watched a play at 10:00 ____.

## How much time has passed?

If you start watching a play at 5:30 pm and it ends at 7:00 pm, how long does the play go for? The play lasts for 1½ hours.

To work this out, start at 5:30 and add 30 minutes to take the time to 6:00 pm.

Then add one more hour to take the time to 7:00 pm.

The play lasts one hour and 30 minutes, or 1½ hours.

**How much time has passed between these times? Write the correct answers.**

⑦ 4:00 pm and 5:00 pm

_____

⑧ 2:30 pm and 4:00 pm

_____

⑨ 6:30 pm and 10:30 pm

_____

⑩ 8:15 pm and 9:15 pm

_____

⑪ 9:45 pm and 10:30 pm

_____

⑫ 4:00 am and 6:00 am

_____

⑬ 5:30 am and 6:30 am

_____

⑭ 7:15 am and 8:30 am

_____

⑮ 10:45 am and 11:30 am

_____

⑯ 11:15 am and 12 noon

_____

**Solve these word problems.**

⑰ Mum drove to my nan's house. She left at 2:30 pm. The drive took 1½ hours. At what time did she arrive at my nan's?

_____

⑱ I ordered a pizza at 5:15 pm. They told me to come back in half an hour. At what time was the pizza ready to collect?

_____

⑲ My dad started cleaning his car at 9:30 am. He finished cleaning it at 11:00 am. How long did it take him to clean the car?

_____

⑳ The bus timetable told us the next bus would arrive in 45 minutes. It was 2:30 pm. At what time should the bus arrive?

_____

## Reminder notes

Maxine asked her husband, Dan, to do the chores last Saturday. She left him a big pile of reminder notes!

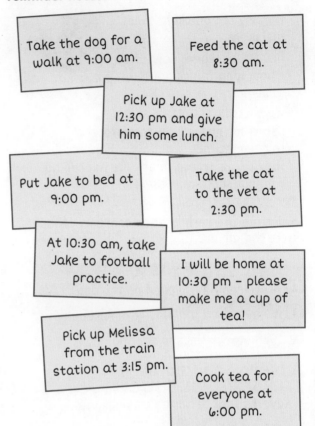

Take the dog for a walk at 9:00 am.

Feed the cat at 8:30 am.

Pick up Jake at 12:30 pm and give him some lunch.

Put Jake to bed at 9:00 pm.

Take the cat to the vet at 2:30 pm.

At 10:30 am, take Jake to football practice.

I will be home at 10:30 pm – please make me a cup of tea!

Pick up Melissa from the train station at 3:15 pm.

Cook tea for everyone at 6:00 pm.

**Complete the chart to help Dan work out what he has to do.**

| Time | Task |
| --- | --- |
|  |  |
|  |  |
|  |  |
|  |  |
|  |  |
|  |  |
|  |  |
|  |  |
|  |  |
|  |  |
|  |  |

TERM 3 MATHS

# Grammar & Punctuation

AC9E4LA08

## Adverbs

> **Adverbs** tell us more about verbs.
>
> They tell us **how** something is happening:
>
> *Example:*
> The boy ran **quickly** down the street.
>
> They tell us **when, how often** or **how long** things are happening:
>
> *Examples:*
> I start my new school **tomorrow**.
> Tom **sometimes** goes to the park.
> They tell us **where** things are happening.
> Put your shoes over **there**.

**Underline the verb in each sentence, then circle the adverb.**

1. Jason drank his coffee silently.
2. I accidentally stepped on the dog's tail.
3. We bought a birthday cake yesterday.
4. Dad always sings in the shower.

## Adverbs ending in –ly

> **Adverbs** that tell us **how** things are happening often end in **–ly**.
>
> *Examples:* softly, loudly, anxiously, sadly, brightly

**Add –ly to these adjectives to make them adverbs. Remember the 'y' rule! If the word ends in y, change the y to i before adding the ending.**

5. brave _____
6. regular _____
7. cruel _____
8. noisy _____
9. hungry _____
10. busy _____

**Choose the best adverb to complete the sentences.**

11. Ted plays football (loudly  sadly  regularly).
12. The stars twinkled (brightly  fondly  cruelly) in the sky.

# Phonic Knowledge & Spelling

AC9E4LY10

## Words that end in –y

**Say each word in the word bank. They all end in –y.**

| family | beauty | city | monkey |
|--------|--------|------|--------|
| library | sturdy | busy | dirty |
| apply | reply | rely | deny |
| carry | study | obey | annoy |

**Choose words from the word bank to complete these sentences.**

1. At the zoo, I saw a _____ eating a banana.
2. If you ask politely, you should receive a polite _____.
3. My _____ likes to grow lemons.

## Plurals of words that end in –y

> When a word ends in **y** after a vowel (–ay, –ey, –oy or –uy), just add **–s** to make the plural (more than one).
>
> *Examples:*  boy, boy**s**   tray, tray**s**
>                      trolle**y**, trolle**ys**
>
> When a word ends in **y** after a consonant, change the **y** into **i** and add **–es** to make the plural.
>
> *Examples:*  lorry, lorr**ies**   pony, pon**ies**
>                      spy, sp**ies**

**Write the plural of these words.**

4. monkey _____
5. city _____
6. library _____
7. journey _____
8. turkey _____
9. family _____

**Add the endings –er, –est and –ly to these words. Remember! Change the y to i before adding the ending.**

10. busy                         11. sturdy

_____               _____
_____               _____
_____               _____

*Score 2 points for each correct answer!*  SCORE  /24  (0-10) (12-18) (20-24)

*Score 2 points for each correct answer!*  SCORE  /22  (0-8) (10-16) (18-22)

## Emilio and the Volcano

**Imaginative text** – Narrative
**Author** – Patricia Bernard

*Emilio and his friend, Manuel, live in the village of San Domingo in the Philippines, on the slopes of Mount Mayon, a volcano. Emilio is at home with his sister, Belle. He is threading frangipani flowers onto a long thread for a flower festival. Manuel has called to the house to see Emilio.*

The boys went out onto the veranda. Rising before them was Mount Mayon, considered to be one of the most beautiful volcanoes in the world because of its near perfect cone shape.

Mayon erupted regularly — when it did, the nearby villages reaped the rewards. Tourists flocked to the area to see the eruption. Local men worked as guides to lead foreign climbers as close as they could get to the lava flows. Local women used the shape of the volcano in their crocheting and needlework, which they sold as souvenirs.

Mount Mayon was usually a peaceful pyramid silhouetted against a blue sky. But not today. Plumes of steam spurted from its summit.

Manuel looked worried. "I hope it doesn't explode with boiling mud the way it did last year. That was scary."

"It won't," Emilio assured him. "That was a big eruption, so it will be years before another big one. Now it's just letting off steam."

"My mother says the dogs know what's going on," Manuel said. "She's taking a big white cross up to the church. If that doesn't stop the eruption, she's leaving at the first sign of lava. She said you and Belle should come to our house if you're worried."

"Will do," said Emilio and returned to his flower threading.

Emilio sat on the veranda and watched the summit of Mount Mayon glow brighter and brighter as the evening wore on. All the village dogs were barking. Emilio's mother had not returned, so Emilio put his sister to bed. She was sound asleep and Emilio was dozing when a truck pulled up outside the house.

"Evacuation! Evacuation!" a voice declared through a loudspeaker. "There is an eruption. Everyone out! Trucks are waiting. The village is being evacuated."

Source: *Emilio and the Volcano*, Sparklers, Blake Education.

**TERM 3 ENGLISH**

---

**Write or circle the correct answers.**

① **Where does Emilio live?**

_____

② **Why is Mount Mayon considered to be 'one of the most beautiful volcanoes in the world'?**

_____

③ **What does eruption mean in this text?**

a a skin rash

b the ejection of molten rock from a volcano

c a mountain

④ **Which is the odd word?**

a side   b summit   c peak   d top

*Score 2 points for each correct answer!*

**SCORE** /14   (0-4)   (6-10)   (12-14)

**Find words in the text that have these meanings.**

⑤ made someone feel sure: a_____

⑥ molten rock: l_____

⑦ clouds: p_____

### My Book Review

Title _____

Author _____

Rating ☆☆☆☆☆

Comment _____

_____

# Number & Algebra

AC9M4A02

## Multiplying numbers: doubling

> When we double a number, we multiply it by 2.
>
> *Example:* double 9
> = 9 × 2
> = 18
>
> When we double larger numbers, we can **split the number** to make it easier.
>
> *Example:* double 56
>
> Split 56 into 50 and 6.
> Then multiply 50 by 2 and multiply 6 by 2:
> 50 × 2 = 100    6 × 2 = 12
>
> Add 100 and 12: 100 + 12 = **112**

**Calculate these doubles by using the split method. Show your working out.**

① double 47

_____

_____

② double 59

_____

③ double 64

_____

_____

> When you **double hundreds**, you can use the same split method.
>
> *Example:* double 184
> 100 × 2 = 200    80 × 2 = 160    4 × 2 = 8
> 200 + 160 + 8 = 368

**Calculate these doubles by using the split method. Show your working out.**

④ double 153

_____

_____

⑤ double 458

_____

_____

## Dividing numbers: halving

> When you halve a number, you are dividing by 2.
>
> *Example:* half of 20
> = 20 ÷ 2
> = 10

> You can use the **split method** to halve numbers too.
>
> *Example:* half of 486
> 400 ÷ 2 = 200    80 ÷ 2 = 40    6 ÷ 2 = 3
> 200 + 40 + 3 = 243

**Calculate these halves by using the split method. Show your working out.**

⑥ half of 264

_____

_____

⑦ half of 428

_____

⑧ half of 642

_____

_____

Score 2 points for each correct answer!  **SCORE** **/16** ( 0-6 ) ( 8-12 ) ( 14-16 )

# Statistics & Probability

AC9M4ST02

## Evaluating results

> Tom carried out a survey of the colours of the cars that passed his school in one hour last Thursday.
>
> Here is a picture graph of his results.
>
> **Colour of Cars that Passed our School in One Hour**
>
>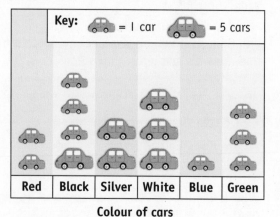

**Answer the questions about Tom's graph.**

① How many cars passed Tom's school in one hour? _____

② Which colour was seen the most?

_____

③ Which colour was seen the least?

_____

④ How many more white cars drove past than black cars? _____

TARGETING HOMEWORK 4 © PASCAL PRESS ISBN 9781925726466

⑤ What other three ways could Tom represent his results?

_____

_____

_____

⑥ Which way do you think is most effective? Why?

_____

_____

⑦ Write two more questions that could be answered by Tom's graph.

_____

_____

_____

_____

*Score 2 points for each correct answer!* **SCORE** /14 ( 0-4 ) ( 6-10 ) ( 12-14 )

## Measurement & Space

AC9M4N05, AC9M4M01

## Grams and kilograms

We can use **decimals** to convert grams into kilograms.

*Examples:*
  1000 g = 1.0 kg
  1100 g = 1.1 kg
  1200 g = 1.2 kg
  1300 g = 1.3 kg

Can you see the pattern? We are **dividing by 1000**, because there are 1000 grams in 1 kilogram.

To divide by 1000, move the decimal point 3 places to the left: 1.000.

**Convert the grams into kilograms.**

① 1500 g = _____ kg
② 1600 g = _____ kg
③ 1800 g = _____ kg
④ 2400 g = _____ kg
⑤ 3500 g = _____ kg
⑥ 5700 g = _____ kg

Look at these conversions of **kilograms to grams**. Can you see the pattern?

*Examples:*   5.6 kg = 5600 g
    1.5 kg = 1500 g
    3.2 kg = 3200 g

**Convert these kilograms into grams.**

⑦ 1.6 kg = _____ g
⑧ 2.3 kg = _____ g
⑨ 4.5 kg = _____ g

⑩ 5.8 kg = _____ g
⑪ 6.4 kg = _____ g
⑫ 8.9 kg = _____ g

*Example:*
  4500 g = 4.5 kg

**Read the scales. Write the mass in grams and kilograms.**

⑬ _____ kg
= _____ g

⑮ _____ kg
= _____ g

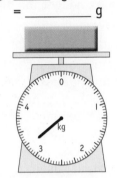

⑭ _____ kg
= _____ g

⑯ _____ kg
= _____ g

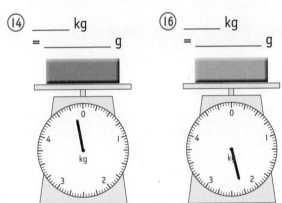

*Score 2 points for each correct answer!* **SCORE** /32 ( 0-14 ) ( 16-26 ) ( 28-32 )

## Problem Solving

AC9M4N08

## Zoo dilemmas

① An elephant, a giraffe and a hippo have a total mass of 7700 kg.

• The hippo has a mass of 2000 kg.

• The elephant has a mass 2.5 times the mass of the hippo.

What is the mass of the giraffe?

_____

_____

② The hippo is moved to a new zoo and loses 45 kg. What is the mass of the hippo in the new zoo?

_____

# Grammar & Punctuation

AC9E4LA08

## Adverbial phrases and prepositions

> **Adverbial phrases** say **how**, **where**, **when** and **why** things happen.
>
> *Examples:*
>
> She swept the floor <u>with an old broom</u>. **how**
> We met <u>by the train station</u>. **where**
> <u>At eight o'clock</u>, we started walking. **when**
> Jack bought the flowers <u>for his mother</u>. **why**
>
> Adverbial phrases usually begin with a **preposition**.
>
> Prepositions include: about, above, across, after, almost, at, before, behind, below, by, down, during, except, for, from, in, near, of, off, on, over, past, since, through, till, to, under, until, up, upon, with

**Underline the adverbial phrase in each sentence. Then write if it answers how, where, when or why.**

1. Our friends will arrive in half an hour.
   _____

2. The snake slithered through the tall grass.
   _____

3. My brother can run almost as fast as I can.
   _____

4. I made a cake for my sister's birthday.
   _____

**Match a main clause with an adverbial phrase from the box so the sentences make sense.**

| | |
|---|---|
| with a soft cloth | for my cat |
| on the other side of the street | |
| in the afternoon | in the forest |

5. We saw a rabbit _____
   _____.

6. The police car stopped _____
   _____.

7. We finally arrived home _____
   _____.

8. Mum cleaned the table _____
   _____.

# Phonic Knowledge & Spelling

AC9E4LY09, AC9E4LY10, AC9E4LY11

## Words that begin with a silent k or w

**Say each word in the word bank. They each have either a silent k or a silent w in them.**

| | | | |
|---|---|---|---|
| knob | knot | knit | knock |
| know | knife | kneel | knelt |
| wring | wrong | wrist | wreck |
| write | wrote | answer | sword |

**Choose words from the word bank to complete these sentences.**

1. The mighty _____ wore a suit of armour and carried a _____.

2. I meant to ring Mum but I rang the _____ number.

3. When I _____, I tend to _____ the wool!

## Alliterations

> An **alliteration** is a sentence where most of the words begin with the same letter or sound.
>
> *Examples:*
>
> The knock-kneed knight knocked his knuckles on the knotty knocker.
>
> Rob wrapped the wrinkled wrapper round the wrecked wreath.

4. **Write your own alliteration using words that begin with a silent k or a silent w.**
   _____
   _____

## Homophones

> **Homophones** are words that sound the same but have different spellings and meanings.

**Choose the correct word to complete each sentence.**

5. Do you (no  know) how to speak French?

6. I (rung  wrung) the cloth out until it was dry.

## South America

**Informative text** – Report
**Author** – Frances Mackay

South America is a **continent** which lies 16 087 kilometres from Australia. It has an area of 17 840 000 square kilometres compared with Australia which has an area of 7 692 000 square kilometres.

South America is made up of 12 countries: Argentina, Bolivia, Brazil, Chile, Colombia, Ecuador, Guyana, Paraguay, Peru, Suriname, Uruguay and Venezuela. It also includes French Guiana, which is part of France and the Falkland Islands which is a British Overseas Territory (something that is disputed by Argentina).

The islands of Aruba, Bonaire and Curacao (part of the Netherlands), Trinidad and Tobago and Panama may also be considered to be part of South America.

South America has many natural wonders of the world:

- World's highest waterfall
  – Angel Falls in Venezuela
- World's largest river by volume
  – Amazon River
- World's largest rainforest
  – Amazon Rainforest
- World's longest mountain range
  – The Andes
- World's driest non-polar region
  – Atacama Desert
- World's highest lake
  – Lake Titicaca

Brazil is the largest country in South America, taking up almost half of the continent's land and population. Suriname is the smallest country.

The highest mountain in South America is Aconcagua (6962 m).

Spanish is the main language spoken in South America. In Brazil, people speak Portuguese and in Suriname they speak Dutch. Quechua is the most common indigenous language and many people speak English as a second language.

**TERM 3 ENGLISH**

---

Write or circle the correct answer.

① **What is a continent?**

a a large country

b We are not told.

c one of the main areas of land in the world

② **Which two oceans lie on either side of South America?**

_____

_____

③ **Approximately how many times larger than Australia is South America?**

a 2½ times

b 10 times

c 5 times

④ **What does disputed mean?**

a agreed      b disagreed      c belonged

Score 2 points for each correct answer!

SCORE /8      0-2   4-6   8

**My Book Review**

Title _____

Author _____

Rating ☆☆☆☆☆

Comment _____

_____

# Number & Algebra

AC9M4N03

## Improper fractions and mixed numbers

In an **improper fraction**, the **numerator** (the number on top of the fraction) is larger than the **denominator** (the number on the bottom of the fraction).

$\frac{7}{4}$ ← numerator
    ← denominator

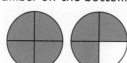

We can write this as a **mixed number**.
Ask: How many wholes are there? 1.
Then ask: How many parts are there? 3.
So: $\frac{7}{4} = 1\frac{3}{4}$

**Write the improper fraction and mixed number for each diagram.**

① _____  ② _____

③ _____  ④ _____

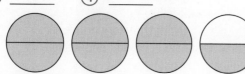

⑤ _____  ⑥ _____

⑦ _____  ⑧ _____

## Changing mixed numbers to improper fractions

$2\frac{1}{2} = \frac{?}{2}$

**Step 1:** Multiply the whole number by the denominator. **2 × 2 = 4**

**Step 2:** Add the answer to the numerator.
    **4 + 1 = 5**

**Step 3:** Put that number as the numerator. The denominator always stays the same.

**Answer:** $\frac{5}{2}$

**Convert these mixed numbers to improper fractions.**

⑨ $2\frac{3}{4} = \frac{\Box}{4}$   ⑪ $4\frac{1}{2} = \frac{\Box}{2}$   ⑬ $2\frac{5}{6} = \frac{\Box}{6}$

⑩ $3\frac{1}{3} = \frac{\Box}{3}$   ⑫ $5\frac{3}{5} = \frac{\Box}{5}$   ⑭ $4\frac{3}{4} = \frac{\Box}{4}$

## Changing improper fractions to mixed numbers

$\frac{7}{3} = ?$

**Divide** the numerator by the denominator.
7 ÷ 3 = 2 and 1 left over ($\frac{1}{3}$ left over)
Answer: $2\frac{1}{3}$

**Convert these improper fractions to mixed numbers.**

⑮ $\frac{5}{4}$ = _____   ⑱ $\frac{8}{3}$ = _____

⑯ $\frac{7}{5}$ = _____   ⑲ $\frac{5}{2}$ = _____

⑰ $\frac{6}{4}$ = _____   ⑳ $\frac{9}{5}$ = _____

Score 2 points for each correct answer!   SCORE   /40   0-18   20-34   36-40

# Statistics & Probability

*There are no statistics & probability activities in this unit.*

# Measurement & Space

AC9M4M04

## Right angles

An **angle** that is like a **quarter turn** is a **right angle**.

quarter turn

right angle

These angles are **smaller** or less than a **right angle**:

The angles are **larger** or greater than a **right angle**:

TARGETING HOMEWORK 4 © PASCAL PRESS ISBN 9781925726466

Are these angles equal to a right angle, less than a right angle or greater than a right angle? Write **equal, less than** or **greater than**.

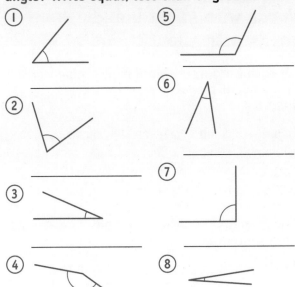

① ____

⑤ ____

② ____

⑥ ____

③ ____

⑦ ____

④ ____

⑧ ____

Write the letter of the right angle. There is one right angle in each shape.

⑨ ____

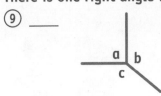

⑩ ____

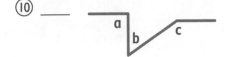

⑪ ____

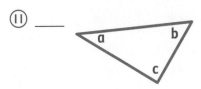

⑫ ____

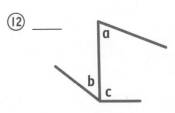

⑬ ____

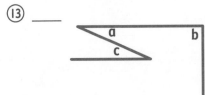

⑭ ____

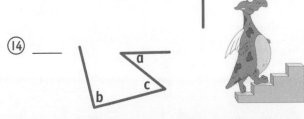

## Mystic Rose

A mystic rose is formed by joining dots that are equally spaced around a circle. Each dot is joined to every other dot on the circle.

Here is the mystic rose for 4 dots:

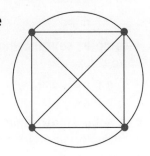

① Use a ruler to draw the mystic roses for 2, 3, 5 and 6 dots.

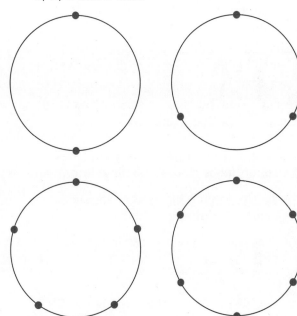

② Complete the table.

| Dots | Lines |
|------|-------|
| 2 | 1 |
| 3 | |
| 4 | 6 |
| 5 | |
| 6 | |

③ What do you notice about the number of dots and the number of lines?

_____

_____

TERM 3 MATHS

# Grammar & Punctuation

AC9E4LA06

## Complex sentences

A **clause** is a group of words with a subject and a verb.

*Example:* Jess likes ice-cream.

      subject   verb

A **complex sentence** has two or more clauses:

• a **main clause**, which contains the main idea

• a **subordinate clause**, which adds more information about the main idea.

*Example:*   main clause    subordinate clause

Jess likes ice-cream <u>because it tastes so creamy</u>.

The **subordinate clause** can come at the beginning of the sentence:

*Example:*   subordinate clause     main clause

<u>When he had finished washing up</u>, Dad watched TV.

A main clause makes sense on its own, but a subordinate clause does not.

**Is the underlined clause the main clause or the subordinate clause? Circle your answer.**

① <u>We like to go walking</u> when it's sunny.
  main   subordinate

② <u>Jake was excited</u> because it was his birthday.
  main   subordinate

③ Here is your book <u>which you left at my house</u>.
  main   subordinate

**Circle the correct subordinate clause that matches with the main clause.**

④ When she had finished breakfast,
  **a** Alex went for a walk.
  **b** and cleaned the house.

⑤ Lions are carnivorous mammals
  **a** lions live in a pride.
  **b** that live in Africa.

*Score 2 points for each correct answer!*   SCORE   **/10**   0-2   4-8   10

---

# Phonic Knowledge & Spelling

AC9E4LY10

## Words with silent b and words with silent t

Say each word in the word bank. Some words have a **silent b** and some words have a **silent t.**

| limb | comb | numb | dumb |
|------|------|------|------|
| thumb | climb | debt | doubt |
| listen | glisten | fasten | hasten |
| whistle | nestle | wrestle | rustle |

Choose words from the word bank to complete these sentences.

① He cut his _____ trying to _____ through the smashed window.

② The baby _____ tried to _____ against the mother sheep.

③ The pirate wore a false _____ to replace his missing leg.

④ Is it true that we should talk less and _____ more?

Add **–ing** to these words. Remember your spelling rules!

         **–ing**

⑤ nestle _____

⑥ comb _____

⑦ rustle _____

⑧ listen _____

Make compound words by writing a word from the box on each line.

| bomb | jamb | nail | comb |
|------|------|------|------|

⑨ thumb_____

⑩ honey_____

⑪ fire_____

⑫ door_____

*Score 2 points for each correct answer!*   SCORE   **/24**   0-10   12-18   20-24

TARGETING HOMEWORK 4 © PASCAL PRESS ISBN 9781925726466

# Daniel Radcliffe, aka Harry Potter

**Informative text** – Biography
**Author** – Lisa Thompson

Daniel Radcliffe was born on 23 July 1989 in Queen Charlotte's Hospital, London, England. At the age of 11, after several **auditions**, Daniel was chosen to play the lead role in the first, big-budget film of author J.K. Rowling's *Harry Potter* books.

Overnight, Daniel became an international film star, bringing Harry Potter to life on screen.

At the age of nine, Daniel made his television **debut**, acting in an adaptation of the Charles Dickens novel *David Copperfield*.

Daniel's friend suggested he audition for the role of David Copperfield, for a "bit of fun". Daniel didn't expect to get the part because there were thousands of boys trying for it, so he was surprised when he was successful.

"I never expected to actually get the part." — Daniel.

After *David Copperfield*, Daniel took a small part in a film called *The Tailor of Panama*. In the film, he played the part of Mark Pendel and his mother in the film was played by American actor Jamie Lee Curtis.

At the time, there was a huge talent search underway to find the actor to play the role of Harry Potter. While taking a break from filming *The Tailor of Panama* one day, Jamie Lee Curtis saw something in Daniel and remarked to Daniel's mother, "He could be Harry Potter."

The director of the first Harry Potter film, *Harry Potter and the Philosopher's Stone*, was Chris Columbus. He had seen *David Copperfield* and wanted Daniel to audition. But Daniel's parents were reluctant for him to go through the tough auditioning process, only to be disappointed if he didn't get the role.

Then one evening in a theatre, the producer of the film, David Heyman, spotted Daniel and his family in the audience. David knew Daniel's father and introduced himself to Daniel. The next morning, David called Daniel's parents to persuade them to let Daniel audition. But they had already changed their minds — Daniel auditioned for the role of Harry and topped the long list of boys vying for the part.

Source: *Stars of Harry Potter*, Brainwaves, Blake Education.

**TERM 3 ENGLISH**

---

**Write or circle the correct answers.**

① **What is an audition?**

a a performance

b a test to see if a person is suitable to act in a play or film

c a person who watches a film

② **Which words in the text tell you that the first Harry Potter film cost a lot of money to make?**

_____

**List the three films or TV series the text mentions that Daniel acted in — in order from first to third.**

③ _____

④ _____

⑤ _____

**Are these statements fact or opinion?**

⑥ "I never expected to actually get the part."

_____

⑦ In the film, he played the part of Mark Pendel. _____

⑧ **What does vying mean?**

a wishing   b acting   c competing

**My Book Review**

Title _____

Author _____

Rating ☆☆☆☆☆

Comment _____

_____

*Score 2 points for each correct answer!*

SCORE /16   0-6   8-12   14-16

# Number & Algebra

AC9M4N03

## Fractions and decimals

We can write a **fraction** as a **decimal**.

$\frac{1}{10} = 0.1$

ones place — tenths place

This is equal to **zero** ones and **one** tenth.

Complete the table.

| Diagram | Fraction | Decimal |
|---|---|---|
| 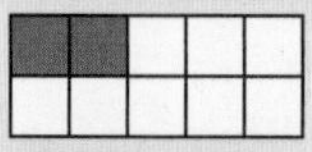 | $\frac{2}{10}$ | 0.2 |
| ① 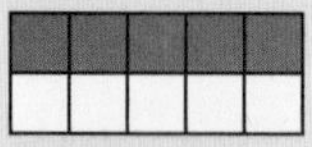 | | |
| ② 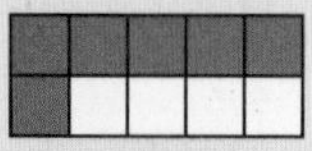 | | |
| ③ 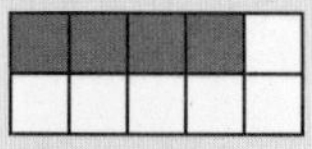 | | |
| ④ 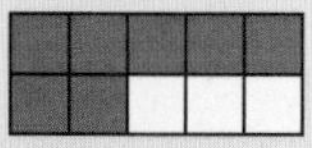 | | |
| ⑤ 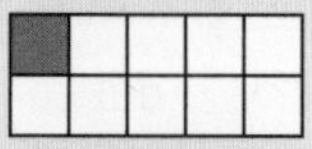 | | |
| ⑥ 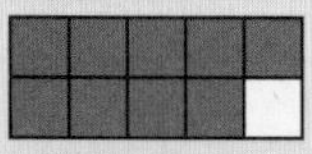 | | |
| ⑦ 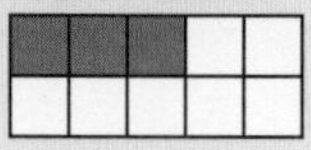 | | |

TERM 3 MATHS

**0.01** is equal to **zero** ones, **zero** tenths and **one** hundredth:

$\frac{1}{100} = 0.01$

ones place — tenths place — hundredths place

A **whole** can be divided into **10 equal parts** (tenths). Each **tenth** can be divided into **10 equal parts** (hundredths).

**one whole**

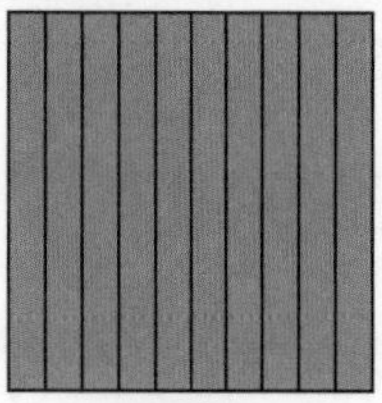

**tenths**

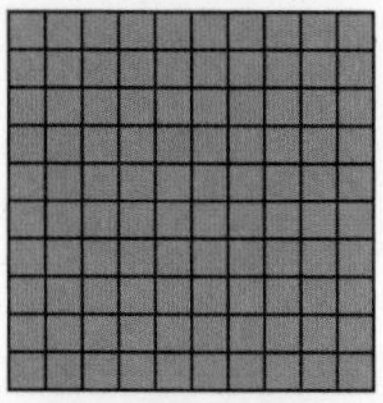

**hundredths**

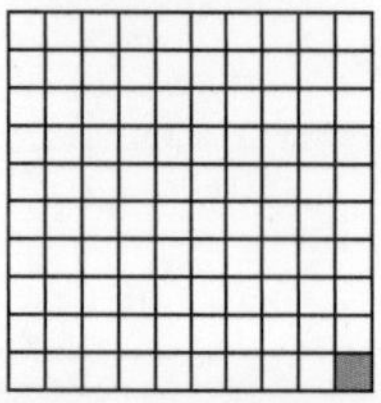

**one hundredth**

*Examples:* $\frac{9}{100} = 0.09$   $\frac{24}{100} = 0.24$   $\frac{65}{100} = 0.65$

Complete the table.

| Diagram | Fraction | Decimal |
|---|---|---|
| 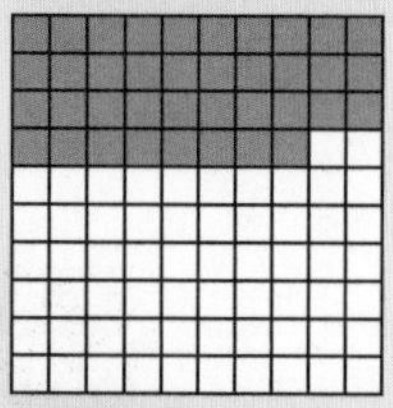 | $\frac{38}{100}$ | 0.38 |
| ⑧ 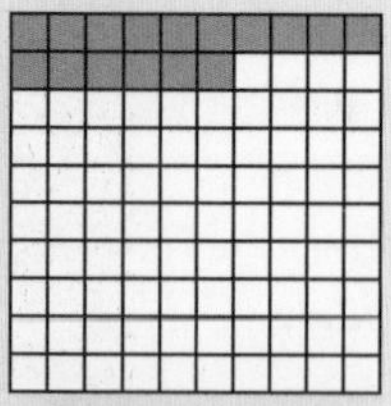 | | |
| ⑨ 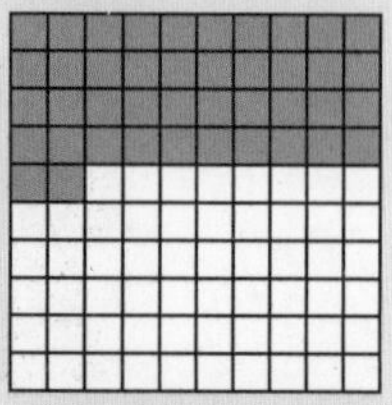 | | |
| ⑩ 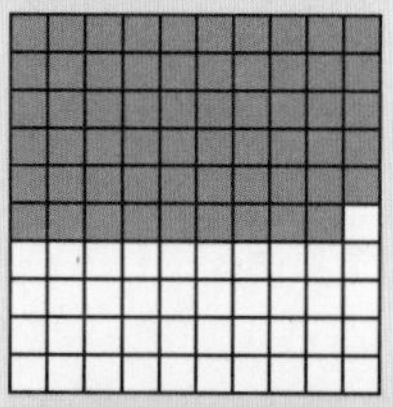 | | |
| ⑪ 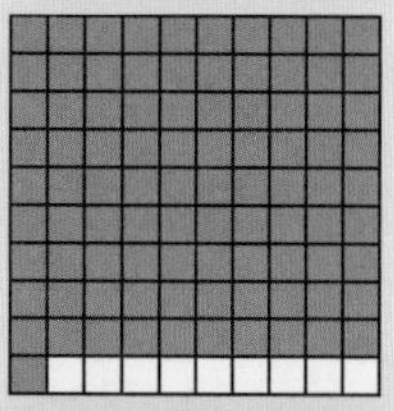 | | |
| ⑫ 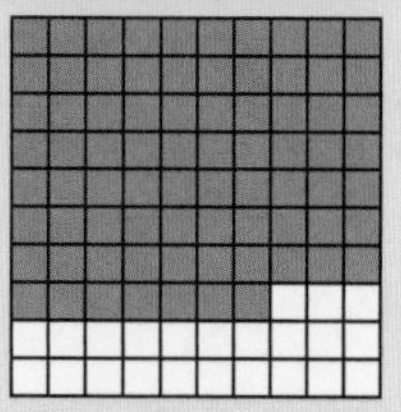 | | |

*Score 2 points for each correct answer!*

**SCORE** /24  (0-10) (12-18) (20-24)

## Statistics & Probability

AC9M4P01

### Chance events

**Are these true or false? Circle the correct answer.**

① Mike and Sam are playing a game with a die. Mike throws a six. Sam has a 1 in 6 chance of throwing a six too.

  **a** true    **b** false

② Sarah's mum is expecting a baby. Because she already had a girl, this baby will definitely be a boy.

  **a** true    **b** false

TARGETING HOMEWORK 4 © PASCAL PRESS ISBN 9781925726466

③ There are 6 marbles in a bag: 3 blue ones, 2 red ones and 1 green one. Without looking, Max pulls a blue marble out of the bag. For his next turn, Max has a greater chance of pulling out a blue or red marble than a green one.

**a** true    **b** false

**Use the word bank to complete the sentences.**

| closed | summer | cold | adult | off | tails |

④ If the television is on, it cannot be
_____.

⑤ If a coin lands on heads, it cannot show _____.

⑥ If it is hot outside, it cannot be _____ outside.

⑦ If Grant is a child, he cannot be an _____.

⑧ If it is winter, it cannot be _____.

⑨ If the window is open, it cannot be _____.

⑩ **Colour the jelly beans red, blue and green so that you are more likely to pick out a red jelly bean than a blue or a green one.**

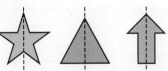

*Score 2 points for each correct answer!*  SCORE  **/20**  0-8  10-14  16-20

## Measurement & Space

AC9M4SP03

## Symmetrical shapes

A shape that can be folded in **half** so that one side fits **exactly** on top of the other side has a **line of symmetry**.
*Examples*:

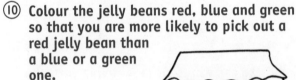

**Do these shapes have a correct line of symmetry? Circle the correct answer.**

①
**a** yes    **b** no

④
**a** yes    **b** no

②
**a** yes    **b** no

⑤
**a** yes    **b** no

③
**a** yes    **b** no

⑥
**a** yes    **b** no

Some shapes have more than one line of symmetry.
*Examples*:

**Do these shapes have two correct lines of symmetry? Circle the correct answer.**

⑦
**a** yes    **b** no

⑨
**a** yes    **b** no

⑧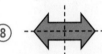
**a** yes    **b** no

⑩
**a** yes    **b** no

**Complete these shapes so that the dotted line is a correct line of symmetry.**

⑪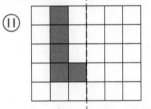

⑫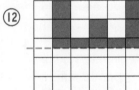

*Score 2 points for each correct answer!*  SCORE  **/24**  0-10  12-18  20-24

## Problem Solving

AC9M4N03

**Which would you rather have? Circle the larger amount.**

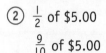

① $\frac{6}{10}$ of a chocolate bar
0.4 of a chocolate bar

② $\frac{1}{2}$ of $5.00
$\frac{9}{10}$ of $5.00

④ 0.7 of a cake
$\frac{3}{10}$ of a cake

③ 0.45 of a pizza
0.85 of a pizza

⑤ 0.80 of a pie
$\frac{5}{100}$ of a pie

# Grammar & Punctuation

AC9E4LA04

## Text connectives

> **Text connectives** are words and phrases that **join ideas together** throughout text. They guide readers from one sentence to the next and from one paragraph to the next. They are used to place information or events in order. They are used to show time passing and settings changing.
>
> *Examples:* although, however, therefore, consequently, later, until, then, so, as a result, meanwhile, afterwards, on the other hand, firstly, after lunch, later that day

**Choose the most suitable connective for these sentences.**

① (As soon as   Until) we got home, we went to bed.

② (However   Later that day) we visited the museum.

③ (Firstly   Consequently), gather all the ingredients.

**Underline all the connectives in these paragraphs. There are nine to be found!**

④–⑫ Last week, we went to visit my grandma who lives in a small apartment by the beach. Although she is happy to live alone, she loves to have visitors and enjoys baking cakes for us when we visit.

We left home at 9 o'clock and we should have arrived at Grandma's by 10, but things just didn't happen that way. Firstly, there were roadworks and we had to wait twenty minutes before we could move on. Then, we had to pull in to buy petrol and that was when Mum discovered she'd come without the gift we had bought for Grandma. So, we had to go to the flower shop to buy some flowers.

We all clambered back into the car. Unfortunately, the car wouldn't start and Dad had to phone for a tow truck.

An hour later, the truck arrived to take us to the repair garage. We all had to sit at the garage for hours before the car was fixed. Consequently, it was 3 o'clock by the time we arrived at grandma's, but I really enjoyed those cakes when we finally ate them!

# Phonic Knowledge & Spelling

AC9E4LY09, AC9E4LY10

## Letter teams oi and oy

**Say each word in the word bank. They contain the letter teams oi or oy which make the same sound.**

| spoil | hoist | moist | voice |
|-------|-------|-------|-------|
| choice | avoid | point | appoint |
| enjoy | employ | annoy | destroy |
| loyal | royal | oyster | voyage |

**Choose words from the word bank to complete these sentences.**

① We had to save up to go on our _____ across the sea.

② It was almost time to _____ the new team captain.

③ There was an _____ shell among our collection.

**Complete the words so they rhyme with the example.**

④ spoil   c _ _ _   b _ _ _   t _ _ _

⑤ enjoy   dec _ _   ann _ _   ah _ _

**Match the words in the box to their meanings.**

| moist | appoint | avoid | hoist |
|-------|---------|-------|-------|

⑥ to keep yourself away from something:
_____

⑦ to lift something heavy with ropes:
_____

⑧ to choose someone for a job:
_____

⑨ slightly damp:
_____

## Mama and Papa Decide

**Imaginative text** – Narrative
**Author** – Patricia Bernard, **Illustrator** – Jarrod Prince

*Aiko lives in Japan with her family. She wants to learn traditional Japanese stick and sword fighting like her brother, Haru. But her mother thinks it's not ladylike. Aiko has to go to tea making and flower arranging classes instead. She decides to be deliberately clumsy in her classes so she won't have to go to them anymore. One day, she visits a fortune teller who tells her, "Your wish will come true if you know when to make the right move."*

The next day after school, Haru insisted they go straight home. Aiko saw her father's shoes outside when they got there — he was home early.

Aiko and Haru found their parents waiting for them in the traditional dining room.

"Neither the tea ceremony teacher nor the flower arranging teacher want you in their classes!" burst out Mama, the moment Aiko knelt at the table. "They say you are clumsy. Aiko are you doing it on purpose?"

There was silence. Aiko remembered what the fortune teller had said about the right move.

"Mama, if I could learn stick and sword fighting," she said, "I am sure I would become graceful. And then maybe I could return to flower arranging and tea ceremony school later."

"She isn't clumsy when she fights," added Haru.

Papa frowned. "Is that so?"

"I like stick and sword fighting much more than flower arranging and tea ceremonies, Papa," whispered Aiko. "But if I could learn fighting, like Haru does, I would try much harder not to be clumsy."

"Really?" said Papa. "How much harder?"

"A thousand times harder," smiled Aiko.

Papa whispered to Mama. Mama shook her head. Papa whispered some more.

Finally Mama frowned. "Aiko, if we let you take fighting lessons, do you promise not to be clumsy in flower arranging and tea ceremony school?"

Aiko was so happy that all she could do was nod. Haru answered for his sister. "She promises."

Source: *The Paper Wish*, Sparklers, Blake Education.

---

**Write or circle the correct answers.**

① **What does traditional mean?**

a new

b old-fashioned

c a long-established custom or way of life

② **Which is the odd word?**

a intentionally      c knowingly

b deliberately       d unintentionally

③ **What could be a reason for Aiko's mother not wanting her to do stick and sword fighting?**

a She wants to be mean to Aiko.

b It is normally something that only boys do.

c She doesn't want her to go to classes after school.

④ **Circle all the phrases that are connectives showing the passing of time.**

a There was silence.

b The next day after school

c Finally

d And then

e Aiko was so happy

### My Book Review

Title _____

Author _____

Rating ☆☆☆☆☆

Comment _____

_____

Score 2 points for each correct answer!    **SCORE** /8    0-2    4-6    8

TERM 3 ENGLISH

# Number & Algebra

AC9M4N07

## Shopping

In Australia, the smallest amount of money you can spend is five cents. This means you need to know how to **round** a number up or down.

When rounding money, always look at the **cent place value**.

If the cent place value is:

- **1** or **2** then you **round down** to the nearest dollar
- **3** or **4** then you **round up** to 5 cents
- **6** or **7** then you **round down** to 5 cents
- **8** or **9** then you **round up** to 10 cents

*Examples*:

$1.01 and $1.02: round down to $1.00

$1.03 and $1.04: round up to $1.05

$1.06 and $1.07: round down to $1.05

$1.08 and $1.09: round up to $1.10

**Answer the questions about the pet shop.**

$8.98
$19.99
$18.89
$3.55
$6.09
$0.15 each
$2.49
$5.64

① How much change from $5 if you buy one lead?

_____

② How much change from $10 if you buy flea spray?

_____

③ How much change from $5 if you buy a ball and two dog biscuits

_____

④ How much would a dog bowl and a pet carrier cost?

_____

⑤ Which two items would cost you $25 to buy?

_____

_____

⑥ Jake has $10 to spend. He wants to buy three things for his dog. He already has enough dog biscuits. What else can he buy?

_____

⑦ How many dog biscuits can you buy for $1.50?

_____

⑧ The pet carrier normally sells for $25. How much money would you save if you bought it today?

_____

⑨ Which costs more: two dog bowls or three flea sprays?

_____

⑩ The pet shop owner will sell the bird cage to you for $5 less than the price. How much would you pay?

_____

*Score 2 points for each correct answer!*  SCORE  **/20**  (0-8) (10-14) (16-20)

# Statistics & Probability

AC9M4ST02

## Temperature graph

This is a **line graph** showing the **maximum temperature** recorded for each day in a week.

Temperature (°C) vs Days of the week (Sun, Mon, Tue, Wed, Thu, Fri, Sat)

Sun 25, Mon 28, Tue 26, Wed 22, Thu 19, Fri 23, Sat 27

TERM 3 MATHS

To read the temperature for **Saturday**, find Saturday on the bottom of the graph. Follow the line up to the dot. Then read across to the temperature scale.

The temperature reached on Saturday was **27 °C.**

**Use the graph to answer the questions. Write or circle the correct answers.**

① What temperature did it reach on Wednesday?

_____

② What temperature did it reach on Sunday?

_____

③ Which day had the highest temperature?

_____

④ Which day had the lowest temperature?

_____

⑤ What do you think maximum temperature refers to?

    **a** The lowest temperature recorded that day.

    **b** The highest temperature recorded that day.

⑥ How many degrees cooler was it on Thursday than Monday?

_____

⑦ How many degrees hotter was it on Saturday than Wednesday?

_____

⑧ Use the graph to complete the table.

| | Sun | Mon | Tue | Wed | Thu | Fri | Sat |
|---|---|---|---|---|---|---|---|
| Max. temp. (°C) | | | | | | | |

## Measurement & Space

*There are no measurement & space activities in this unit.*

## Temperature word problems

**Solve these problems.**

① The temperature in Sydney is 25 °C. The temperature in Brisbane is 6 degrees warmer than Sydney. The temperature in Melbourne is 8 degrees cooler than Brisbane. What is the temperature in Brisbane and Melbourne?

Brisbane: _____

Melbourne: _____

② The weather for Saturday was predicted to be 18 °C. It turned out to be 7 degrees warmer on the day. What was the actual temperature on Saturday?

_____

③ Mum baked a cake at 180 °C. Just before it was cooked, she turned the oven down by 60 degrees. What was the new oven temperature?

_____

④ The lowest temperature overnight was 9 °C. During the day, the temperature peaked at 26 °C. By how many degrees did the temperature rise during the day?

_____

⑤ The weather for Sunday was predicted to be 24 °C, but a cool change reduced the maximum expected by 9 degrees Celsius. What was the actual temperature on Sunday?

_____

⑥ When Tracy left Sydney, the temperature was 29 °C. When she arrived in London, the temperature was only 8 °C. What was the difference in temperature between Sydney and London?

_____

## Grammar & Punctuation

AC9E4LY06

### Possessive nouns

Some nouns show **ownership**. These are called **possessive nouns**. An **apostrophe (')** is used to show who the owner is.

For a singular noun owner, add **'s**:

*Examples:*

Melanie (singular noun)   Melanie**'s** book
dog    the dog**'s** bowl
girl    the girl**'s** phone

Most plural nouns already end in **s**, so just add an **apostrophe (')**:

*Examples:*

students (plural noun)   the student**s'** desks
girls        the girl**s'** dormitory
monkeys   the monkey**s'** cage

**Rewrite each underlined noun to make it possessive. The first one has been done for you.**

<u>Sam</u> sister is younger than he is.   Sam's

① The <u>baby</u> bottle was empty.

_____

② I can't find <u>Dad</u> key anywhere.

_____

③ The <u>horses</u> bodies were strong.

_____

④ The <u>artists</u> paintings were on display.

_____

**Rewrite each sentence to include a possessive noun. The first one has been done for you.**

He painted the house of my neighbour.
<u>He painted my neighbour's house.</u>

⑤ I washed the car of my dad.

_____

⑥ The shoes of Emily were new.

_____

## Phonic Knowledge & Spelling

AC9E4LY09, AC9E4LY10, AC9E4LY11

### Letter teams air, are and ear

Say each word in the word bank. They contain the letter teams **air**, **are** or **ear** that all make the same 'air' sound.

| pair | lair | repair | dairy | fairy |
| bare | scare | parent | prepare | compare |
| wear | bear | pear | tear | swear |

**Choose words from the word bank to complete these sentences.**

① We tasted each other's pizza to _____ the taste.

② Dad had to _____ an apron when he cooked the steak.

③ I cut up a _____ to add to the fruit salad.

### Homophones

Homophones are words that sound the same but have different spellings and meanings.

**Choose the correct word to complete each sentence.**

④ I had my (hare   hair) cut really short.

⑤ It is rude to (stair   stare) at people.

⑥ Our school held a (fare   fair) to raise money.

⑦ Mum didn't know which dress to (wear   ware) to the party.

⑧ I had my (hare   hair) cut really short.

⑨ My brother has a real (flare   flair) for drawing.

⑩ It is rude to (stair   stare) at people.

⑪ A huge brown (bear   bare) came out of the cave.

⑫ Our school held a (fare   fair) to raise money.

**Add hair to the beginning of these words to make compound words.**

⑬ _____brush   ⑮ _____style

⑭ _____dresser   ⑯ _____piece

## Government Barking Up the Wrong Tree

Persuasive text – Editorial
Author – Merryn Whitfield

What would you do if one day you were told you couldn't have a haircut? It's your hair; you own it, why not get it cut?

Well this is the situation facing many south-western hinterland farmers. They've recently been told by the government that they can't cut down trees that they own that are on their land. It's almost unbelievable!

During the past 25 years, our population has increased by more than 30%. As our population grows, so does our need for basic foods such as fruit, vegetables, meats and grains. Yet the farmers who need to grow the food and herd the cattle need pastureland. They need land that is cleared of trees and can be irrigated and ploughed, or you and I don't eat.

Why is this happening, you may ask? Well it all has to do with climate change. In order to reduce the nation's carbon footprint, the government has decided to create so-called 'carbon sinks'. This is where large forested areas are used to absorb carbon dioxide from the atmosphere.

A noble idea indeed, but why destroy a farmer's livelihood? As Bill Ah-Bong, a hinterland farmer, said last week,

"If this continues, I'll be ruined. I will have no choice but to leave my farm and try to get a job somewhere else. It's terrible."

Despite the fact that our farmers can no longer farm their own land, our demand for food is maintained. So we will be forced to import fruit, vegetables and meat from other countries, sending our hard-earned money overseas. This does not seem like a very clever idea.

**So what should we do?** For a start, the government should pay farmers for the use of their land as a carbon sink. Also, encourage all landowners to regenerate poor quality land to help offset climate change, rather than using good quality agricultural land. **We need to use our heads!**

Nic Wheatly, Editor, *The Daily Harvest*

Source: *Writing Centres: Persuasive Texts*, Middle Primary, Blake Education.

TERM 3 ENGLISH

---

**Write or circle the correct answers.**

1. **What is the purpose of the editorial? Why was it written?**

   a to alert people to the government's decision of keeping farmland trees as carbon sinks

   b to explain what carbon sinks are

   c to warn people not to cut down trees

2. **What is a carbon sink?**

   a an open-air bathroom

   b a large area of forest that will be kept to absorb carbon dioxide from the atmosphere

   c something caused by climate change

**Are these statements fact or opinion?**

3. During the past 25 years, our population has increased by more than 30%.

   _____

4. A noble idea indeed ... _____

5. **Which is the odd word?**

   a encourage          c urge

   b persuade           d discourage

**Which words in the text have these meanings?**

6. A layer of gases surrounding the earth:

   a_____

7. To revive or restore an area:

   re_____

---

**My Book Review**

Title _____

Author _____

Rating ☆ ☆ ☆ ☆ ☆

Comment _____

_____

---

# Number & Algebra

AC9M4N02, AC9M4A02

## Number patterns

Use this 100-square to find number patterns.

| 1 | 2 | 3 | 4 | 5 | 6 | 7 | 8 | 9 | 10 |
|---|---|---|---|---|---|---|---|---|---|
| 11 | 12 | 13 | 14 | 15 | 16 | 17 | 18 | 19 | 20 |
| 21 | 22 | 23 | 24 | 25 | 26 | 27 | 28 | 29 | 30 |
| 31 | 32 | 33 | 34 | 35 | 36 | 37 | 38 | 39 | 40 |
| 41 | 42 | 43 | 44 | 45 | 46 | 47 | 48 | 49 | 50 |
| 51 | 52 | 53 | 54 | 55 | 56 | 57 | 58 | 59 | 60 |
| 61 | 62 | 63 | 64 | 65 | 66 | 67 | 68 | 69 | 70 |
| 71 | 72 | 73 | 74 | 75 | 76 | 77 | 78 | 79 | 80 |
| 81 | 82 | 83 | 84 | 85 | 86 | 87 | 88 | 89 | 90 |
| 91 | 92 | 93 | 94 | 95 | 96 | 97 | 98 | 99 | 100 |

① **5 times table:**
   Start at 5 and count in fives. Colour the numbers red.

② What do you notice about the pattern?

   _____

   _____

③ **9 times table:**
   Start at 9 and count in nines. Colour the numbers blue.

④ What do you notice about the pattern?

   _____

   _____

⑤ **8 times table:**
   Start at 8 and count in eights. Colour the numbers green.

⑥ Which numbers are multiples of 8 and 10?

   _____

⑦ Start at 3 and count in tens. Colour the numbers yellow.

⑧ What do you notice about the pattern?

   _____

   _____

⑨ Start at 7 and count in tens. Colour the numbers pink.

⑩ What do you notice about the pattern?

   _____

   _____

## Odd and even numbers

Circle the even numbers.

⑪  56        83        92        33

⑫  125       349       360       782

⑬  1346      2355      3978      4001

⑭  24 500    36 789    89 202    124 567

**True or false? Circle the correct answer.**

⑮ There are ten odd numbers between 80 and 100.
   a  true        b  false

⑯ 4385 is an even number that is written as four thousand, three hundred and eighty-five.
   a  true        b  false

⑰ The smallest even number you can make from the digits 4, 8 and 2 is 284.
   a  true        b  false

⑱ 3508 is an even number that is exactly 100 larger than 3408.
   a  true        b  false

⑲ All even numbers end in 8.
   a  true        b  false

⑳ Some odd numbers end in 7.
   a  true        b  false

**Write <, > or = to make these statements true.**

Remember, < means 'less than' and > means 'greater than'.

㉑ an even number plus an even number [ ] an even number

㉒ the next odd number after 59 [ ] the next even number after 58

㉓ the difference between 824 and 712 [ ] 120 − 8

㉔ the next even number after 800 [ ] the next odd number after 803

Score 2 points for each correct answer!   SCORE   /48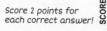

TARGETING HOMEWORK 4 © PASCAL PRESS ISBN 9781925726466

## Statistics & Probability

AC9M4ST02

### Column graph with multiple values

Jai carried out a survey of the students in his class. He wanted to find out if boys and girls preferred different types of holidays.

Here are Jai's results, presented in a table:

| Holiday | Boys | Girls |
|---|---|---|
| Camping | 8 | 4 |
| Caravan or touring | 2 | 3 |
| Hotel or resort | 5 | 10 |
| Staying with family or friends | 2 | 4 |
| Activity or adventure | 15 | 10 |

Jai used the results from his survey to create a column graph. Instead of making one graph for boys and one graph for girls, he made a graph showing the results for both.

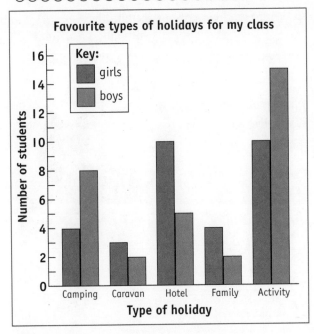

Favourite types of holidays for my class

**Use the table and graph to answer the questions.**

① What was the favourite type of holiday for boys?

_____

② What were the least favourite types of holiday for boys?

_____

_____

③ What were the favourite types of holidays for girls?

_____

_____

④ What was the least favourite type of holiday for girls?

_____

⑤ What was the total number of students Jai surveyed?

_____

⑥ What was the least favourite type of holiday for both girls and boys?

_____

⑦ How many boys preferred hotel holidays?

_____

⑧ How many girls preferred to stay with family and friends?

_____

Score 2 points for each correct answer!  SCORE  /16  ( 0-6 )  ( 8-12 )  ( 14-16 )

## Measurement & Space

*There are no measurement & space activities in this unit.*

## Problem Solving

AC9M4A02

### Multiplication wheels

**Complete the multiplication fact wheels.**

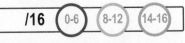

TERM 3 MATHS

# Grammar & Punctuation

AC9E4LY06

## Noun groups – determiners

**Remember!** A noun group is a chunk of words built around a noun.

A **determiner** is part of a noun group. Its job is to point out (determine) the noun.

*Examples:* **his** book, **that** house, **every** flower

Determiners include: the, a, an, this, that, these, those, some, every, each, any, my, your, hers, his, its, our, their, whose, what, which, one, two, three

**Underline the determiners in these noun groups.**

① my new bike

② every tall building

③ the dog's kennel

④ that girl's hat

⑤ your red car

⑥ an old friend

⑦ some yellow roses

⑧ their baby daughter

## Classifiers

A **classifier** is placed before the main noun to say what type it is.

*Examples:* that **tomato** sauce, the **soccer** ball, some **pineapple** juice

**Match the classifiers in the box to the most suitable nouns. All the items belong in the kitchen.**

| carving | frying | wooden | oven |
| mixing | vegetable | cutting | |
| ice-cream | microwave | measuring | |

⑨ _____ glove

⑩ _____ scoop

⑪ _____ knife

⑫ _____ peeler

⑬ _____ oven

⑭ _____ board

⑮ _____ cup

⑯ _____ pan

⑰ _____ bowl

⑱ _____ spoon

Score 2 points for each correct answer! **SCORE** **/36** (0-16) (18-30) (32-36)

# Phonic Knowledge & Spelling

AC9E4LY09, AC9E4LY10

## Prefixes: a– and al–

Say each word in the word bank. The prefix **a–** at the beginning of a word sounds like 'uh'. When we add **all** to the beginning of a word, we drop one l.

**Example: All ways = always.**

| ago | again | afraid | ahead |
| along | aloud | alert | alike |
| alive | alone | amaze | amuse |
| always | already | alright | almost |
| almighty | also | although | altogether |

**Choose words from the word bank to complete these sentences.**

① I _____ ask if I can have another scoop of ice-cream.

② I do not know whether to be _____ of big dogs or not.

③ Mum said we can either run on _____ or walk with them.

④ Neither my brother nor myself like reading _____ .

**Add all– to these words. Write the new word.**

⑤ _____ways

⑥ _____though

⑦ _____right

⑧ _____ready

⑨ _____together

⑩ _____mighty

⑪ _____most

⑫ _____so

**Build the words and write new words. Remember your spelling rules!**

⑬ un + afraid = _____

⑭ alert + ness = _____

⑮ amaze + ment = _____

⑯ amuse + ing = _____

⑰ amaze + ing = _____

⑱ alert + ed = _____

Score 2 points for each correct answer! **SCORE** **/36** (0-16) (18-30) (32-36)

TARGETING HOMEWORK 4 © PASCAL PRESS ISBN 9781925726466

# The Macassans

**Informative text** – Report
**Author** – Frances Mackay and Neil Johnson

Some of the first people to visit Australia were the Macassans. They were fishermen from Sulawesi (now called Indonesia) who sailed to Northern Australia in small dugout canoes called *perahu* or *prau*. They came every year to fish for *trepang* (sea cucumber). Some people think they may have travelled to Australia as early as the 1500s.

The Macassans set up camps on the shores of Northern Australia, where they boiled and then smoked the trepang in large pots to preserve them. The Macassans stayed in Australia for many months until they had enough trepang to take back home to trade with the Chinese.

The local Aboriginal peoples, the Yolngu, worked with the Macassans and some even sailed back to Indonesia with them. The Macassans and the Yolngu did not always get along and sometimes fought, but usually things were peaceful between the two groups.

The Macassans traded metal knives, blades and axes — as well as smoking pipes and fish hooks — in return for tortoiseshell and pearl shell. The metal tools made cutting things

such as wood and food much easier for the Yolngu. The Yolngu also liked the Macassans' dugout canoes, so they copied the design to make their own.

The visits of the Macassans are remembered by local Aboriginal peoples in their stories, songs, dances and paintings. Some Macassan words are still used today in Aboriginal languages along the north east. Some examples include *rupiah* (money), *jama* (work) and *balanda* (white person). The Macassans also planted tamarind trees, which still grow in some parts of Northern Australia.

Source: *Australian History Centres*, Middle Primary, Blake Education.

**TERM 3 ENGLISH**

---

**Write or circle the correct answers.**

① **Where did the Macassans come from?**

_____

**Which words in the text have these meanings?**

② small dugout canoes: p_____

③ sea cucumber: t_____

④ Aboriginal peoples of Northern Australia: Y_____

⑤ to keep something in good condition: p_____

**Are these statements true or false?**

⑥ The Macassans came to Australia from Indonesia. _____

⑦ The Macassans always fought with the Yolngu. _____

⑧ Trepangs were boiled and smoked to preserve them. _____

⑨ The Macassans and Yolngu did not trade with each other. _____

⑩ **Which is the odd word?**

a untroubled          c calm

b unfriendly          d peaceful

⑪ **Describe how the Macassans and Yolngu helped each other.**

_____

_____

Score 2 points for each correct answer!  **SCORE** **/22**

**My Book Review**

Title _____

Author _____

Rating ☆☆☆☆☆

Comment _____

_____

# Number & Algebra

AC9M4N05

## Solving word problems

**Write the correct number sentence from the box below each word problem. Then calculate the answer.**

| | |
|---|---|
| 4 × 9 = ____ | 8 × 4 = ____ |
| 40 ÷ 5 = ____ | 8 × 10 = ____ |
| 88 ÷ 2 = ____ | 32 ÷ 4 = ____ |
| 6 × 9 = ____ | 50 × 4 = ____ |

① How many toy cars does Paul have if he has 6 times as many as Sam, who has 9 cars?

_____

② Ross sorted his 40 sports cards evenly into 5 containers. How many cards in each container?

_____

③ There are 8 rows of chairs with 10 chairs in each row. How many chairs altogether?

_____

④ Max bought 32 cupcakes for his birthday. He ate one-quarter of them. How many did he eat?

_____

⑤ 50 horses trotted past the guard on duty. How many horse legs trotted past?

_____

⑥ $\frac{1}{2}$ of the 88 party balloons blew away. How many balloons were left?

_____

⑦ How many cousins does Jude have if she has 4 times as many as Sara who has 9 cousins?

_____

⑧ How many sides are there in 8 squares?

_____

Score 2 points for each correct answer!  **SCORE** **/16**   0-6   8-12   14-16

## Statistics & Probability

*There are no statistics & probability activities in this unit.*

---

# Measurement & Space

AC9M4SP03

## Symmetrical patterns

A shape that can be folded in **half** so that one side fits **exactly** on top of the other side has a **line of symmetry**.
*Examples*:

These patterns are **symmetrical**. The colours and shapes on one side of the line are an exact reflection of the colours and shapes on the other side of the line.

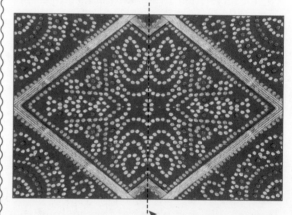

↙ lines of symmetry

**Colour the pattern to make it symmetrical.**

①

↙ line of symmetry

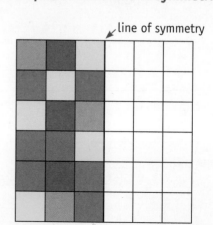

②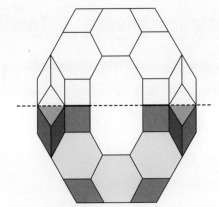

**Colour the patterns so they have one line of symmetry. Draw in the line of symmetry.**

③

④

## Problem Solving

AC9M4SP03

### Coloured squares puzzle

**This square has red, blue, green and yellow tiles. The tiles are placed so that no tiles of the same colour touch each other.**

**Colour this square in a different way, using the same colours and the same rule.**

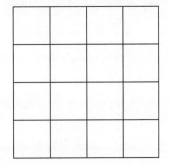

TERM 3 MATHS

# Grammar & Punctuation

**Write if these statements are fact or opinion.**

① I prefer ice-cream to gelato. _____

② We went to an ice cream parlour last Wednesday. _____

**Circle the word that shows how this person was feeling.**

③ I strongly believe that what you did was very wrong. (angry   happy)

**Join these sentences together by choosing or, and, but or so.**

④ We don't have any money _____ we can't go to the cinema.

⑤ I chased after Ryan _____ I couldn't catch up with him.

**Underline the verb, then circle the adverb.**

⑥ Maggie sang a song softly.

**Underline the adverbial phrase, then write if it answers how, where, when or why.**

⑦ The concert will commence in one hour.

_____

⑧ The horse galloped through the lush forest.

_____

**Circle whether the underlined clause is the main clause or the subordinate clause.**

⑨ After finishing the race, Riley had a cold drink.   main   subordinate

⑩ My legs were aching after the uphill run. main   subordinate

**Choose the most suitable connective for this sentence.**

⑪ (Therefore / Although) I like movies, I prefer reading.

**Rewrite the underlined noun to make it possessive.**

⑫ Tom brother is older than he is. _____

**Circle the determiners in these noun groups.**

⑬ my new shoes         ⑯ that boy's bike

⑭ every house

⑮ the dog's lead

**Rewrite this sentence to include a possessive noun.**

⑰ The hutch of the rabbits needs cleaning.

_____

_____

# Phonic Knowledge & Spelling

**Add the endings by writing the words.**

① juggle

_____ (–ed)

_____ (–ing)

_____ (–er)

**Write the plural of these words.**

② donkey   _____

③ city   _____

**Add the endings by writing the words.**

④ busy

_____ (–er)

_____ (–est)

_____ (–ly)

**Choose the correct word to complete this sentence.**

⑤ Do you (no   know) how to knit a scarf?

**Complete the rhyming words.**

⑥ spoil   c _ _ _   b _ _ _   t _ _ _

**Make compound words by writing a word from the box.**

brush   chair   castle

⑦ wheel_____

⑧ hair_____

⑨ sand_____

**Add all to these words. Write the new words.**

⑩ all + most = _____

⑪ all + together = _____

**Match a word from the box to its two different meanings.**

bridle   kind   stable

⑫ not likely to fall over; building for horses:

_____

⑬ to show anger; headgear on a horse:

_____

⑭ a group of things the same; helpful:

_____

**Choose the correct homophone to complete this sentence.**

⑮ What shoes should I (wear   ware)?

**Imaginative text** – Narrative
**Author** – Frances Mackay

## Gran's Garden

When Sam came home from school, Gran was working in the garden.

"How many rows have you put in?" she asked.

"Twelve, so far," Gran replied.

"Well, we won't run out of potatoes this year, will we?" Sam said. "Have you got your pea sticks yet?"

"No, I'm planting a new kind that don't need sticks. The same goes for the beans."

Sam picked up the seed catalogue. "Cauliflower, carrots, brussel sprouts, onions and lettuce. I'm surprised you've got room."

"I haven't," said Gran. "I never grow onions and none of you like brussel sprouts."

"That's true! I'll go and change and give you a hand," said Sam.

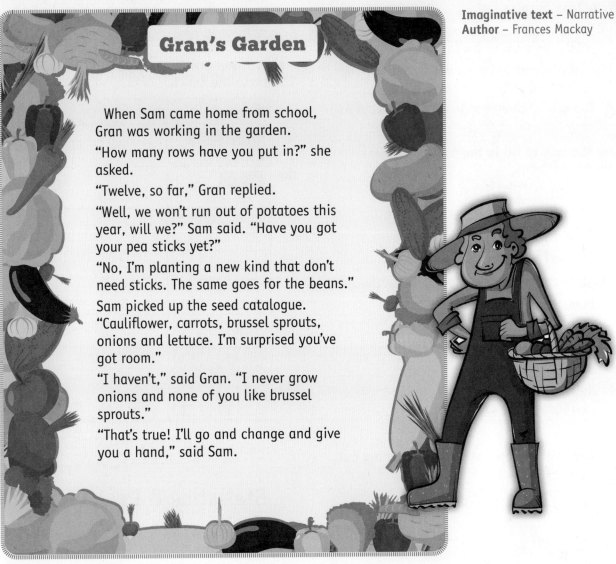

TERM 3 ENGLISH

---

**Write or circle the correct answers.**

① **Was this a Saturday?**

_____

② **What was Gran planting when Sam arrived?**

_____

③ **Was Sam a girl or a boy?**

_____

④ **Which is the odd word?**

  a  list

  b  catalogue

  c  packet

  d  record

⑤ **Did they have plenty of potatoes last year?**

_____

⑥ **List the vegetables that Gran was growing this year.**

_____

_____

⑦ **What sort of peas will Gran grow this year?**

_____

⑧ **Will the beans need sticks this year?**

_____

⑨ **Did Sam like brussel sprouts?**

_____

⑩ **What was Sam going to do next?**

_____

*Score 2 points for each correct answer!*

SCORE | **/20** | 0-8 | 10-14 | 16-20

# Number & Algebra

**Write true or false.**

① If you double any odd number, the answer is always an even number. _____

② If you double any even number, the answer is always an even number. _____

③ The sum of three odd numbers is always an even number. _____

**Use the rule to fill in the blanks in these number patterns.**

④ **Rule: + 7**

126, 133, _____, _____, _____, 161

⑤ **Rule: − 8**

1200, 1192, 1184, _____, _____, _____

**Complete the number patterns. Write the rule.**

⑥ **Rule:** ____

881, 890, 899, _____, _____, _____

⑦ **Rule:** ____

5000, 4995, 4990, _____, _____, _____

⑧ **Rule:** ____

12 100, 12 106, 12 112, _____,

_____, _____

**Use the split method. Show your working out.**

⑨ double 36

_____

_____

⑩ half of 482

_____

_____

**Write the mixed number and improper fraction for this fraction diagram.**

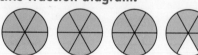

⑪ _____    ⑫ _____

**Convert these mixed numbers to improper fractions.**

⑬ $1\frac{3}{4} = \dfrac{\boxed{\phantom{0}}}{4}$     ⑭ $2\frac{2}{3} = \dfrac{\boxed{\phantom{0}}}{3}$

**Write the answers.**

⑮ How much change from $5 if you buy a pencil for $3.55? _____

⑯ How much change from $10 if you buy a book for $8.99? _____

⑰ How much change from $5 if you buy two cakes that cost $0.12 each? _____

⑱ Write a number sentence to solve this word problem.

How many football cards does Ryan have if he has 10 times as many as Jack who has 12 football cards?

_____

**Complete the chart.**

| Diagram | Fraction | Decimal |
|---|---|---|
| ⑲ | | |
| ⑳ | | |
| ㉑ | | |
| ㉒ | | |

*Score 2 points for each correct answer!* **SCORE** /44  (0-20)  (22-38)  (40-44)

# Statistics & Probability

**Are these true or false? Circle the correct answer.**

① There are 6 marbles in a bag: 3 red ones, 2 blue ones and 1 orange one. Without looking, Max pulls a blue marble out of the bag. For his next turn, Max has a greater chance of pulling out a blue or red marble than an orange one.

a true    b false

② Maddy's pet chicken has laid two eggs. The first one hatched was a boy chicken, so the next one will definitely be a girl chicken.

a true    b false

**Write the correct word from the brackets to complete the sentences.**

③ If the lamp is on, it cannot be _____. (on / off)

④ If a coin lands on tails, it cannot land on _____. (tails / heads)

⑤ If the door is open, it cannot be _____. (open / closed)

TARGETING HOMEWORK 4 © PASCAL PRESS ISBN 9781925726466

⑥ If it is cold outside, it cannot be
_____ outside.
(hot / cold)

Tom did a survey to find out the favourite pets of the students in Year 4. Use his graph to answer the questions.

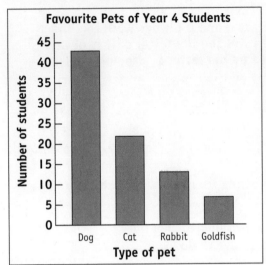

Favourite Pets of Year 4 Students

⑦ Which pet was the favourite overall?
_____

⑧ Which pet was the least popular?
_____

⑨ How many students prefer dogs as pets?
_____

⑩ How many students prefer cats? _____

⑪ How many more students prefer rabbits than goldfish? _____

Score 2 points for each correct answer!

SCORE **/22** ( 0-8 ) ( 10-16 ) ( 18-22 )

## Measurement & Space

**Write am or pm.**

① I get up at 7:30 ____ to get ready for school.

② On Sunday, we eat lunch at 12:30 ____.

③ After school, I start watching TV at 6:30 ____.

**Write how much time has passed between the two times.**

④ 2:00 pm and 5:00 pm _____

⑤ 1:30 pm and 3:00 pm _____

⑥ 11:15 am and 12 noon _____

⑦ **Solve this time problem.**

I ordered a pizza at 6:15 pm. They told me to come back in half an hour. At what time was the pizza ready to collect?

_____

**Convert these measurements in grams into kilograms.**

⑧ 1300 g = _____ kg

⑨ 2500 g = _____ kg

⑩ 3300 g = _____ kg

**Convert these measurements in kilograms into grams.**

⑪ 2.8 kg = _____ g

⑫ 5.5 kg = _____ g

⑬ 1.4 kg = _____ g

**Read the scales. Write the mass in kilograms and grams.**

⑭ _____ kg

⑮ _____ g

**Are these angles equal to a right angle, less than a right angle or greater than a right angle? Write equal, less than or greater than.**

⑯
_____

⑱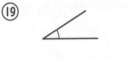
_____

⑰ 
_____

⑲ 
_____

**Write the area of each shape.**

⑳ _____ cm²

㉒ _____ cm²

㉑ _____ cm²

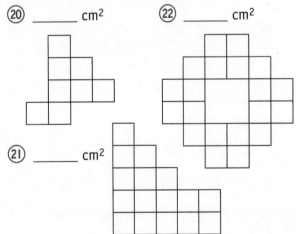

㉓ **Colour this pattern to make it symmetrical.**

line of symmetry

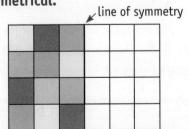

Score 2 points for each correct answer!

SCORE **/46** ( 0-20 ) ( 22-40 ) ( 42-46 )

# Grammar & Punctuation

AC9E4LY06

## Collective nouns

> **Collective nouns** are names given to groups of people, animals and things.
>
> *Examples:*
>
> a **pride** of lions
> a **bunch** of flowers
> a **school** of fish

**Match the collective nouns in the box to these groups.**

| crew | pack | bunch | swarm | galaxy |

① stars _____

② keys _____

③ wolves _____

④ sailors _____

⑤ bees _____

## Collective nouns with singular and plural verbs

> When the members of a group are all doing the same thing at the same time, the **collective noun** is followed by a **singular verb**.
>
> *Examples:* The class **is** singing a song.
> Our family **has** dinner at 6 pm.
>
> When the members of the group are behaving individually, the **collective noun** is followed by a **plural verb**.
>
> *Examples:*
>
> The class **are** practising their lines for the play.
>
> Our family **have** dinner at different times.

**Choose the correct verb to complete each sentence.**

⑥ That school of fish (was   were) huge.

⑦ The class (has   have) created some poems.

⑧ A herd of elephants (is   are) running towards us.

⑨ A colony of ants (is   are) in our garden.

# Phonic Knowledge & Spelling

AC9E4LY10

## Words with gu and qu

Say each word in the word bank. In the letter team **gu**, the **u** is silent and is always followed by a vowel. Example: **guard**

The letters **q** and **u** always work together — when you see the letter **q**, it is always followed by the letter **u**. Example: **quick**

| guard | guess | guest | guilty |
| guitar | guide | disguise | penguin |
| quick | quite | quiet | query |
| queue | squeal | squash | mosquito |

**Choose words from the word bank to complete these sentences.**

① I am learning to play the _____ and I have to do exams.

② It only takes a second for a _____ to bite you!

③ The thief wore a _____ during the burglary.

**Add guard to the end of these words to make compound words.**

④ mouth_____

⑤ coast_____

⑥ safe_____

⑦ life_____

**Some words look similar but have different meanings. Take care with these tricky words! Match a word from the box to its meaning.**

| quiet | quite | dairy | diary | desert | dessert |

⑧ a barren place: _____

⑨ a daily account: _____

⑩ a place where cows are milked: _____

⑪ no noise: _____

⑫ sweet food eaten at the end of a meal: _____

⑬ completely: _____

Score 2 points for each correct answer! SCORE /18 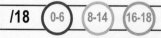 0-6  8-14  16-18

Score 2 points for each correct answer! SCORE /26 0-10  12-20  22-26

TARGETING HOMEWORK 4 © PASCAL PRESS ISBN 9781925726466

**Imaginative text** – Narrative
**Author** – Jeni Jones
**Illustrator** – Craig Smith

## The Rever Family

Ariel Rever came from a long line of almost famous bikers. There was Great Uncle Pillion, who had the first motorbike taxi service. Unfortunately, he lost more passengers than he delivered. Then there was Grandad Throttle. He almost made it into the Guinness Book of Records for 'The most speeding tickets issued to a motorbike rider'. Now ... Ariel's father was away from home a lot being the 'Dare Devil Rider' in Roady's Travelling Circus.

Ariel lived with her two big brothers, Norton and Harley. They had large round bellies, skull rings on their fingers, studs in their ears and tattoos all over.

When Harley got the tattoo on his arm, the tattooist was a learner.

Harley's tattoo read - Real men ride bi

   kes

   Cars are for wim

   ps

Norton decided to wait until the tattooist got a bit better.

He finally had tattooed a list of his favourite bikes.

   Indian
   Matchless
   BSA
   AJS
   Triumph
   Trident
   Yamaha

On their hands were tattooed the words left and right.

Norton and Harley both wore old leathers that creaked when they moved. The well-worn cracks in the leather looked like road maps. When they rode their motorbikes, dark sunglasses covered their beady eyes. Dull, black helmets covered their shaved, misshapen heads. So, apart from their tattoos, you couldn't tell them apart.

When they weren't out showing-off on their fabulous, shiny motorbikes, they spent their time down at the clubhouse. Their sister, Ariel, spent most of her time covered in grease, at home in the garage.

Source: *Ariel*, Sparklers, Blake Education.

**Write or circle the correct answers.**

① **Why did the author use motorbike words as people's names in the story?**

  a because she likes motorbikes

  b to add humour to the story

  c because she couldn't think of any other names

② **List the people in Ariel's family.**

  _____

  _____

③ **Ariel's father was the 'Dare Devil Rider' in a travelling circus. This means his job was:**

  a running the circus.

  b acting as a clown.

  c doing stunts on a motorbike.

④ **What does misshapen mean?**

  a not in the right shape   b bald

⑤ **Look at the tattooed list of Norton's favourite bikes. What is funny about the list?**

  _____

  _____

*Score 2 points for each correct answer!* SCORE **/10** ( 0-2 ) ( 4-8 ) ( 10 )

**TERM 4 ENGLISH**

# Number & Algebra

AC9M4A01

## Equivalent number sentences

This is an **equivalent** or **balanced** number sentence:

$10 + 12 = 30 - 8$

To balance, both sides of the = sign must have the same answer.

| 10 + 12 | 30 – 8 |

**Write the answers to make the number sentences balance.**

①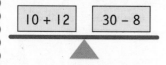
| 25 + | 30 + 10 |

②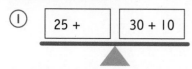
| 38 + | 58 – 18 |

③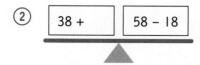
| 50 – | 17 + 3 |

④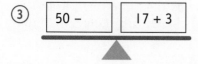
| 100 – 10 | 115 – |

**Write these word problems as number sentences. Then work out the answers.**

⑤ What number can be taken from 35 so that the answer is the same as 15 plus 12?

_____

⑥ When a number is added to 30, the answer is the same as 40 plus 10. What is the number?

_____

⑦ Take 15 away from 30 and you get the same answer as taking what from 40?

_____

⑧ What number can be added to 45 so that the answer is the same as 200 minus 100?

_____

⑨ If a number has 10 added to it, the answer will be the same as 34 + 6. What is the number?

_____

⑩ What number can be taken from 100 so that the answer is the same as double 30?

_____

Score 2 points for each correct answer! **SCORE** /20 (0-8) (10-14) (16-20)

# Statistics & Probability

AC9M4ST01

## Comparing results

Grace counted the number of cars that went past her house between 7:30 am and 8:00 am every day for a week.

Here is the graph she drew from her results.

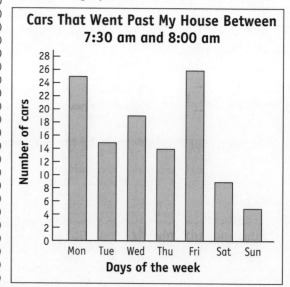

**Cars That Went Past My House Between 7:30 am and 8:00 am**

**Circle the correct answer.**

① **What were the results of Grace's survey?**

a Monday 9, Tuesday 14, Wednesday 19, Thursday 25, Friday 26, Saturday 9, Sunday 5

b Monday 26, Tuesday 15, Wednesday 19, Thursday 14, Friday 25, Saturday 14, Sunday 7

c Monday 25, Tuesday 15, Wednesday 19, Thursday 14, Friday 26, Saturday 9, Sunday 5

TARGETING HOMEWORK 4 © PASCAL PRESS ISBN 9781925726466

Grace drew different graphs to present her results. Do the graphs accurately show her results? Circle the correct answer.

② **a** yes    **b** no

**Cars That Went Past My House Between 7:30 am and 8:00 am**

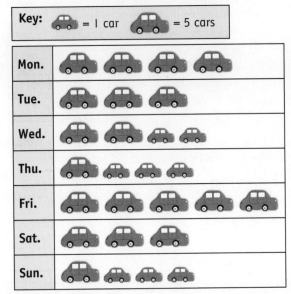

③ **a** yes    **b** no

**Cars That Went Past My House Between 7:30 am and 8:00 am**

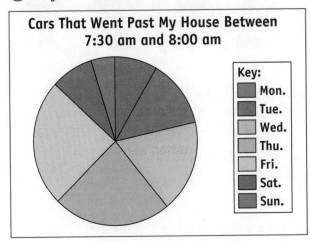

Key:
Mon.
Tue.
Wed.
Thu.
Fri.
Sat.
Sun.

Score 2 points for each correct answer!  SCORE **/6**  0  2-4  6

## Measurement & Space

AC9M4M03

### Time units

① There are _____ hours in one day.

② There are _____ minutes in half an hour.

③ There are _____ seconds in one minute.

④ To set a timer for $1\frac{1}{2}$ minutes, you would use _____ seconds.

⑤ It is 4:30 and the next bus is due at 4:37. How many minutes do you have to wait?

_____

⑥ A TV show that lasts for an hour and a quarter would be _____ minutes long.

⑦ If a 90-minute show starts at 8:10, what time will it finish?

_____

⑧ The microwave was set for 150 seconds. How many minutes is that?

_____

⑨ How many minutes in one day? You can use a calculator to work it out.

_____

⑩ If it is 2:15, what time will it be in 45 mins?

_____

⑪ In 120 minutes it will be 12:30. What time is it now?

_____

⑫ Three hours after half past ten is

_____.

⑬ How many Sundays in one fortnight? _____

⑭ If Wednesday is the 26th of March, what will be the date of the following Monday?

_____

Score 2 points for each correct answer!  SCORE **/28**  0-12  14-22  24-28

## Problem Solving

AC9M4A01

### Make it balance

- The first two scales are balanced.
- Look carefully at them.
- Work out how many triangles you need to make the scales balance on number 3.
- Draw the triangles on the scales.

**Balanced scales:**

**Balanced scales:**

**Make these scales balance.**

TERM 4 MATHS

## Grammar & Punctuation

AC9E4LA04

### Pronouns

> **Pronouns** usually **refer back** to a previous noun. This is called **pronoun reference**.
>
> *Example:* **Graham** is my brother. **He** is two years older than me.
>
> The pronoun **he** refers back to the noun **Graham**.

**Underline the nouns or noun groups that the pronouns in bold refer back to.**

① My mum likes to knit jumpers. **She** is very good at it.

② Last year, we visited London. **It** was a very busy city.

③ My cat has eight kittens. **They** are adorable.

④ My favourite food is roast lamb. **It** is delicious.

### Pronouns referring forward

> **Pronouns** can also **refer forwards** to a noun.
>
> *Example:*
> "Would **you** like some tea, **Jan**?" asked Ben.
>
> The pronoun **you** refers forward to the noun **Jan**.

**Underline the nouns the pronouns in bold refer forward to.**

⑤ "Why are **you** crying, Sarah?" asked the teacher.

⑥ "May **I** join you?" asked Tim.

⑦ "Please join **me** for lunch," said Luke to Sam.

⑧ "I will meet **you** at the shop," shouted Max to his sister.

*Score 2 points for each correct answer!* **SCORE** **/16** (0-6) (8-12) (14-16)

---

## Phonic Knowledge & Spelling

AC9E4LY09, AC9E4LY10

### Words that end in –el and –al

Say each word in the word bank. They all end in the same sound, so you need to learn whether they end in **–el** or **–al**.

| | | | |
|---|---|---|---|
| level | label | fuel | cruel |
| tunnel | gravel | model | angel |
| oval | feral | final | global |
| local | plural | medal | usual |

**Choose words from the word bank to complete these sentences.**

① The first time I went through a _____ in a train, I was scared.

② In the _____ race, I came third and I got a bronze _____.

**Build words by writing the new word. Remember your spelling rules!**

③ global + ly = _____

④ angel + ic = _____

⑤ model + ing = _____

⑥ label + ed = _____

**Sort the words into the three columns according to their endings.**

| | | | | | |
|---|---|---|---|---|---|
| model | trouble | juggle | angel | fuel | plural |
| general | cancel | final | ankle | animal | title |

⑦ –le

_____
_____
_____
_____

⑨ –el

_____
_____
_____

⑧ –al

_____
_____
_____
_____

*Score 2 points for each correct answer!* **SCORE** **/18** (0-6) (8-14) (16-18)

TARGETING HOMEWORK 4 © PASCAL PRESS ISBN 9781925726466

## Indigenous Country and Place

**Informative text** – Report
**Author** – Frances Mackay and Neil Johnson

Traditional homelands are known as 'country' to Indigenous Australians. 'Country' is not just where an Indigenous person lives. The culture of each country is different. Culture is how people who live in a certain place know how to behave, what laws to follow, what to eat, and when and where to hunt. Parts of the country are used for special ceremonies and are sacred. This means not everyone is allowed to go there. Each country has its own stories and songs about how the country was made and how to look after it. It is the duty of everyone who lives there to look after their country by caring for its plants and animals. Indigenous peoples who are separated from their country feel very sad if they are not able to go back there or it is damaged.

### Kombumerri country

The Kombumerri people's country is found in the Gold Coast region of Queensland. They speak the Yugambeh language. Before white settlement, they lived in extended family groups. They moved between several permanent camps, called *kudgen*, to find food. The camps had huts made from bark and wood and could hold up to 12 people. They would leave their hunting spears and nets in the huts for when they needed them.

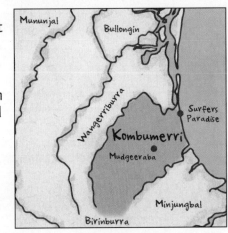

Food was plentiful in this part of Australia, so there was no need to travel very far. The Kombumerri people were skilled net makers. They ate a lot of seafood and fish from the lakes and sea, where they enjoyed swimming in the warmer months.

The Kombumerri people had regular *corroborees*, where they would decorate their bodies and sing and dance through the night around a big fire. Boys and girls also enjoyed playing *purru-purru*, which is a game like touch football. They carried and threw a rugby shaped ball made of kangaroo skin, and two teams would try and score a goal at each end of a field.

Source: *Australian History Centres*, Middle Primary, Blake Education.

---

Write or circle the correct answers.

① **What does traditional homeland mean?**
  a an old-fashioned home
  b a place where generations of people have lived
  c somewhere new to live

② **What does sacred mean?**
  a something very special that deserves respect
  b a place where no one is allowed to go

Match the Aboriginal words from the box to their meanings.

corroborees  purru-purru  kudgen

③ a game like touch football:

_____

④ permanent camps:

_____

⑤ dance ceremonies around a fire:

⑥ **Which is the odd word?**
  a plentiful    c sufficient
  b insufficient  d unlimited

⑦ **What tools did the Kombumerri people use to hunt for their food?**

_____

_____

Score 2 points for each correct answer! **SCORE** /14   (0-4) (6-10) (12-14)

### My Book Review

Title _____

Author _____

Rating ☆☆☆☆☆

Comment _____

_____

# Number & Algebra

AC9M4A02

## Multiplication and division facts

This **multiplication grid** contains the multiplication facts up to 10 × 10.

|    | 1  | 2  | 3  | 4  | 5  | 6  | 7  | 8  | 9  | 10  |
|----|----|----|----|----|----|----|----|----|----|-----|
| 1  | 1  | 2  | 3  | 4  | 5  | 6  | 7  | 8  | 9  | 10  |
| 2  | 2  | 4  | 6  | 8  | 10 | 12 | 14 | 16 | 18 | 20  |
| 3  | 3  | 6  | 9  | 12 | 15 | 18 | 21 | 24 | 27 | 30  |
| 4  | 4  | 8  | 12 | 16 | 20 | 24 | 28 | 32 | 36 | 40  |
| 5  | 5  | 10 | 15 | 20 | 25 | 30 | 35 | 40 | 45 | 50  |
| 6  | 6  | 12 | 18 | 24 | 30 | 36 | 42 | 48 | 54 | 60  |
| 7  | 7  | 14 | 21 | 28 | 35 | 42 | 49 | 56 | 63 | 70  |
| 8  | 8  | 16 | 24 | 32 | 40 | 48 | 56 | 64 | 72 | 80  |
| 9  | 9  | 18 | 27 | 36 | 45 | 54 | 63 | 72 | 81 | 90  |
| 10 | 10 | 20 | 30 | 40 | 50 | 60 | 70 | 80 | 90 | 100 |

**Write these word problems as number sentences. Then work out the answers. You can use the multiplication grid to help.**

① There are 8 rows of chairs in a hall with 9 chairs in each row. How many chairs are there altogether?

_____

② Seven people shared 35 party pies. How many pies did they have each?

_____

③ 10 dogs had their toenails clipped. How many dog paws got clipped in total?

_____

④ 9 people each donated $7 to a charity. How much money was donated altogether?

_____

⑤ 9 children equally shared 45 balloons. How many balloons did they each have?

_____

⑥ Six cooks each baked 9 cupcakes. How many cupcakes were baked in total?

_____

⑦ A monster with 8 hands grabbed 4 children in each hand. How many children did the monster grab?

_____

⑧ A centipede has 9 pairs of legs. How many legs altogether?

_____

⑨ Max had double the number of marbles as Hal who had 9 marbles. Max then bought five more. How many did he have in total?

_____

⑩ 10 people shared 100 pizza slices. How many slices did they have each?

_____

Score 2 points for each correct answer!  SCORE  /20  0-8  10-14  16-20

# Statistics & Probability

*There are no statistics & probability activities in this unit.*

# Measurement & Space

AC9M4M03

## Timetables

This is a timetable for the daily buses from Springtown to the bus station.

The timetable tells us that if the bus departs Springtown at 8:10 am, it arrives at the bus station at 8:45 am.

| Spring-town | Bus station |
|-------------|-------------|
| 8:10 am  | 8:45 am  |
| 9:30 am  | 10:05 am |
| 10:50 am | 11:25 am |
| 12:10 pm | 12:45 pm |
| 1:30 pm  | 2:05 pm  |
| 2:50 pm  | 3:25 pm  |
| 4:10 pm  | 4:45 pm  |

**Use the timetable to answer the questions.**

① You catch the bus at Springtown at 2:50 pm. What time do you arrive at the bus station?

_____

② You need to be at the bus station by 10:30 am. Which bus should you catch at Springtown?

_____

③ How long does the journey take from Springtown to the bus station?

_____

④ How long is there between one bus and the next?

_____

⑤ The 2:50 bus is 5 minutes late. What time will it arrive at the bus station?

_____

⑥ You arrive at the Springtown bus stop at 11:45 am. How long will you have to wait for the next bus?

_____

⑦ If the bus departs the bus station at 8:50 am, what time will it arrive at Springtown?

_____

**The bus company decides to alter all the bus times by 10 minutes. Complete the new bus timetable.**

| | Springtown | Bus station |
|---|---|---|
| | 8:20 am | 8:55 am |
| | 9:40 am | 10:15 am |
| ⑧ | 11:00 am | |
| ⑨ | 12:20 pm | |
| ⑩ | 1:40 pm | |
| ⑪ | 3:00 pm | |
| ⑫ | 4:20 pm | |

**Use the bus timetable above to answer the questions.**

⑬ The 1:40 pm bus is 10 minutes late. What time will it arrive at the bus station?

_____

⑭ You arrive at Springtown bus stop at 2:20 pm. How long will you need to wait for the next bus to the station?

_____

⑮ The 11:00 am bus didn't arrive at Springtown bus stop because it broke down. How long will passengers have to wait for the next bus?

_____

⑯ The 9:40 am bus was held up in a traffic jam for 10 minutes. What time did it arrive at the bus station?

_____

Score 2 points for each correct answer!

SCORE /32 (0-14) (16-26) (28-32)

## Follow the instructions

**Follow the instructions to draw and colour a picture. Use a ruler and coloured pencils or pens.**

① Start at the red dot. Draw a triangle where each side measures 6 centimetres.

② Colour the left-hand side of the triangle red.

③ Colour the right-hand side of the triangle blue.

④ Outline the triangle in black.

⑤ Draw a circle approximately 1 cm wide on each corner of the triangle.

⑥ Colour the three circles green.

⑦ Draw a semi-circle at the base of the triangle with a depth of 3 cm in the middle.

⑧ Colour the semi-circle yellow.

⑨ Draw a face on the semi-circle in black.

●

**TERM 4 MATHS**

# Grammar & Punctuation

AC9E4LA07, AC9E4LA12

## Quotation marks

You have learned that **quotation marks** (" ") can be used to show dialogue, or the exact words spoken by someone. We use **double** quotation marks for speech.

*Examples:*

Jack said, "I want to go home now."

"I want to go home now," said Jack.

**Quotation marks** can also be used to show titles, for example, the name of an episode in a television series, a chapter in a book or the name of an article in a newspaper or magazine. We use **single quotation marks** (' ') for titles.

*Examples:*

Last night, I watched the 'Crazy Monster' episode of *Monster's Creek*.

My favourite chapter in *Stars of Harry Potter* is 'Emma Watson'.

Su North's article, 'It's Time', was published in *The Herald*.

**NOTE:** The name of the television series, the name of the book and the name of the newspaper are in *italics*.

**Add the quotation marks to these sentences.**

① Julia cried out, Wait for me!

② Why didn't you come to my party? asked Peta.

③ Slow Reader is a poem in the book *Please Mrs Butler* by Allan Ahlberg.

④ Please help me with the dishes, said Mum.

**Have the quotation marks in these sentences been used correctly? Write correct or incorrect on the line.**

⑤ "Where are you going?" asked Maxine.

_____

⑥ "Paul said," I am going to be late.

_____

⑦ The first chapter in 'The Paper Wish' is called Make a Wish.

_____

⑧ Lee replied, "I am going fishing on Sunday."

_____

# Phonic Knowledge & Spelling

AC9E4LY09, AC9E4LY10, AC9E4LY11

## Letter team ough

Say each word in the word bank. They all contain the letter team **ough** but the letters make different sounds.

> **or** sound – brought, thought, sought, fought
> **off** sound – cough, trough
> **uff** sound – rough, tough, enough
> **oh** sound – dough, though, although
> **ow** sound – bough, plough, drought

**Choose words from the word bank to complete these sentences.**

① The cross-country race was really _____.

② I had to finish kneading the _____ to make the bread.

③ I had a bad _____ so I didn't go to school.

## Homophones

> **Homophones** are words that sound the same but have different spellings and meanings.

**Choose the correct homophone to complete each sentence.**

④ The (bough    bow) of the tree was bent.

⑤ A female deer is called a (doe    dough).

## Past tense

> Most words add **–ed** to make the **past tense**.
> *Example:* cough, cough**ed**
> Some words have an **irregular form** of the past tense.
> *Example:* sing, sang

**Circle the correct form of the past tense.**

⑥ I never (thinked    thought) he would do that.

⑦ Tim (bringed    brought) a cake for the party.

## Protect Your Future

Persuasive text – Exposition
Author – Merryn Whitfield

> If we hadn't made so many bad choices in the past,
> if we hadn't taken our environment for granted,
> if we hadn't polluted our atmosphere with toxic gases,
> then we wouldn't need to take such drastic action now.

Recently there has been much publicity over a system called 'Carbon Trading' with many people in the local community upset over how much it is going to cost. How can people be so narrow minded? Yes, any system to save our environment is going to cost. Nothing in life is free. *But what is the cost of inaction?*

Our climate is warming up. That is an undisputed fact. What is the cost of inaction? Farmers will have to battle longer and harsher droughts. Food will become scarce and the poorer nations will be unable to afford to feed their people.

Furthermore, our weather patterns are becoming more unpredictable. What is the cost of inaction? Our cities and towns will be battered by more frequent fierce storms. Millions of dollars will be spent on clean-up programs and the rebuilding of damaged infrastructure.

Every year we are losing our treasured and unique native wildlife. What is the cost of inaction? Since European settlement, over 200 species of mammals have become extinct and many more birds, reptiles and amphibians are on the endangered list. If we do not act, our children may never see a koala or a wombat in the wild.

If we, as a community, do not act now, no amount of money will be able to repair the damage in the future. The future benefits truly outweigh the present costs.

Source: *Writing Centres: Persuasive Texts*, Middle Primary, Blake Education.

---

**Write or circle the correct answers.**

① **Why is your in red in the title?**
   a titles are usually in colour
   b to make the title look more attractive
   c to grab the attention of the reader because it is **their** future that needs protection

**Are these statements fact or opinion? Write F or O.**

② If we do not act, our children may never see a koala or a wombat in the wild. _____

③ ... no amount of money will be able to repair the damage in the future. _____

④ Our climate is warming up. _____

⑤ The author repeats the question 'What is the cost of inaction?' several times throughout the text. What impact does this have on the reader?

_____

_____

_____

**Match the words from the box to their meanings.**

| unpredictable   unique   toxic   drastic |
|---|

⑥ unlike anything else: _____

⑦ extreme: _____

⑧ uncertain: _____

⑨ poisonous: _____

Score 2 points for each correct answer!  SCORE  **/18**  ( 0-6 ) ( 8-14 ) ( 16-18 )

### My Book Review

Title _____

Author _____

Rating ☆ ☆ ☆ ☆ ☆

Comment _____

# Number & Algebra

AC9M4N08

## Giving change: Adding on

Li and Su are selling ice-creams at the school fair. They need to know how much change to give to the people who buy things from their stall.

*Example:*

A single ice-cream cone costs $1.80.
If someone buys one single cone and gives Su and Li $5.00, how much change will they give the customer?

**You can work this out by adding on.**
Start with $1.80 (in your head) and give the customer 20 cents. This brings the amount to $2.00 ($1.80 + $0.20 = $2.00). Then give the customer $3.00 more to bring the total to $5.00.
**The total change given is $3.20.**

Use the **adding on strategy** to work out the correct change for these purchases.

| | Cost | Amount received | Change |
|---|---|---|---|
| ① | $3.60 | $5.00 | _____ |
| ② | $5.40 | $10.00 | _____ |
| ③ | $2.10 | $5.00 | _____ |
| ④ | $6.30 | $10.00 | _____ |
| ⑤ | $3.40 | $10.00 | _____ |
| ⑥ | $10.30 | $20.00 | _____ |

*Example:*

At Rav's stall, all the items cost $1.95. A customer buys three items which costs $5.85 and hands Rav a $10 note.

Rav gives the customer 15 cents first ($0.85 + $0.15 brings it up to $1.00), then a further $4.
**Total change = $4.15**

Use the **adding on strategy** to work out the correct change for these purchases.

| | Cost | Amount received | Change |
|---|---|---|---|
| ⑦ | $1.95 | $5.00 | _____ |
| ⑧ | $3.90 | $10.00 | _____ |
| ⑨ | $5.95 | $20.00 | _____ |
| ⑩ | $9.75 | $20.00 | _____ |

**TERM 4 MATHS**

# Statistics & Probability

AC9M4P01

## How likely is it?

Out of any group of events, some things are more likely to happen than others. Read this list of events:

- I will have a birthday this year. Most likely
- Our class will have an outing this year. Likely
- I will not do any writing at school this week. Least likely

**Order these events from least likely to most likely by numbering them from 1 (least likely) to 6 (most likely).**

① ☐ I will eat something today.

② ☐ I will speak to a friend this week.

③ ☐ I will get a cold this year.

④ ☐ I will eat pancakes for breakfast every day.

⑤ ☐ I will travel to London one day.

⑥ ☐ I will be a hippopotamus when I wake up tomorrow.

Some things can change how likely it is for something to happen.

*Examples:*

- If Max doesn't like ice-cream, it is most likely that he will not eat ice-cream at Tom's party.
- If the weather forecast for tomorrow is for rain and thunderstorms, it is unlikely that tomorrow's football match will go ahead.

**Read the two events. What will probably happen next? Circle the correct answer.**

⑦ • Tina and Susan will have a picnic tomorrow.
• Tina woke up with the measles.

  a The picnic will most likely be cancelled.
  b The picnic is likely to go ahead.

⑧ • Dad will take me on a bike ride tomorrow.
• Today Dad had to go away for work for a week.

  a The bike ride is likely to go ahead.
  b The bike ride is most unlikely to go ahead.

⑨ • We will be watching a play on Saturday.
 • The play is in a theatre that was flooded on Friday.

**a** It is most unlikely that we will watch the play.

**b** It is likely that we will watch the play.

## Measurement & Space

AC9M4SP01

## Shape matching

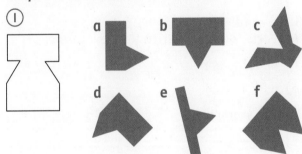

Look at this shape:

It has been made from two smaller shapes:

**Which two small shapes make up the larger shape? Circle the correct answers.**

①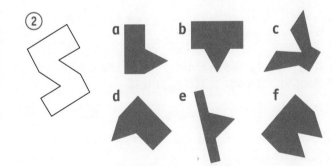

②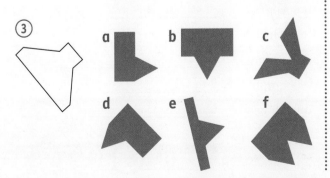

③

④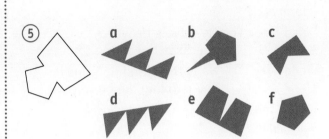

⑤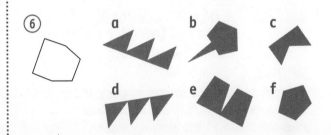

⑥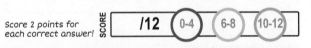

## Problem Solving

AC9M4M03

## 100 metre sprint

These are the results of the men's 100 metre race at the world championships.

Runner A – 9.8 sec          Runner D – 10.8 sec
Runner B – 11 sec           Runner E – 10.5 sec
Runner C – 10.2 sec         Runner F – 10 sec

① **Put the runners' times on the timeline. One has been done for you.**

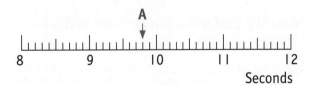

② Which runner was the fastest? _____

③ Which runner was the slowest? _____

④ How many seconds faster than the slowest runner was the fastest runner?

_____

⑤ How much slower than runner F was runner D?

_____

# Grammar & Punctuation

AC9E4LA09

## Irregular verbs in past tense

Most verbs use the same endings to show the present and past tense.

**Present tense** (happening now)
*Examples:*

| add **–s** or **–es** | He **travels** to Sydney. |
| | She **fixes** the broken toy. |
| add **–ing** | He **is travelling** to Sydney. |
| | She **is fixing** the broken toy. |

**Past tense** (happened in the past)
*Examples:*

| add **–ed** | He **travelled** to Sydney. |
| | She **fixed** the broken toy. |
| add **–ing** | He **was travelling** to Sydney. |
| | She **was fixing** the broken toy. |

Some verbs, called **irregular verbs**, have special past tense forms.

**Present tense** She **swims** in the pool.
**Past tense** She **swam** in the pool.
**Present tense** I **am singing** a song.
**Past tense** I **sang** a song.

**Match the past tense verbs in the box to their present tense form.**

| caught | laughed | began | fell |
| said | looked | hung | thought |

1. laugh _____
2. begin _____
3. think _____
4. catch _____
5. say _____
6. hang _____
7. fall _____
8. look _____

**Write the past tense form of each verb to complete the sentences.**

9. (lie) Jack _____ on the beach for an hour.

10. (eat) I _____ a huge piece of chocolate cake.

11. (find) We _____ an old newspaper in the cupboard.

12. (kneel) Jade _____ down to wash the floor.

---

# Phonic Knowledge & Spelling

AC9E4LY10

## Letter teams th, wh and ph

Say each word in the word bank. The letter teams **th, wh** and **ph** work together to make one sound. Listen to the different sounds the letter teams make in the words as you say them.

| throb | thrust | thorough | myth |
| whine | whinge | whether | whisk |
| photo | phrase | nephew | graph |

**Choose words from the word bank to complete these sentences.**

1. We visited my aunty to say hello to my new baby _____.

2. Our dog started to _____ when we said goodbye.

3. Dad usually gives the car a _____ clean every weekend.

4. My grandad showed me a _____ of him as a youth.

**Build words with graph by putting the parts together. Write the new words.**

5. photo + graph _____
6. para + graph _____
7. geo + graph + y _____
8. auto + graph _____
9. graph + ics _____
10. picto + graph _____
11. tele + graph _____

**Add –ing to these words. Write the new words. Remember your spelling rules!**

12. throb _____
13. phone _____
14. whisper _____
15. whinge _____
16. whisk _____
17. whine _____
18. graph _____
19. phrase _____

## Letters

Persuasive text – Letters
Author – Frances Mackay

**Letter A**

Store Manager
Electric Heaven
409 Main Road
Newtown

12 Fresh Street
Newtown
15 June 2018

Dear Sir or Madam,

I recently purchased a new washing machine from your store and I am extremely unhappy with its performance.

We used it for the first time yesterday and it flooded our laundry, causing considerable damage to our new floor. We followed the instructions in the manual so we are certain that the machine is at fault and that we did not use it incorrectly.

Please can you send an engineer out immediately to replace the machine and to assess our laundry for the damages we wish to be compensated for.

Yours faithfully

*Thomas Wiseman*

Mr T Wiseman

**Letter B**

12 Fresh Street
Newtown
15 June 2018

Dear Nan,

Hope this letter finds you and Pop well?

I am really hoping that you can come and see us next week. Dad bought a new washing machine and it flooded our new laundry floor. You can imagine how angry he was! Mum and I have kept away from him as much as possible because he is so grumpy! So, I am hoping you can come and calm him down a bit.

I feel really sorry for him because it took him ages to lay the new laundry floor and now it's ruined. He's written to the company he bought the machine from, hoping to get things replaced or repaired. I hope it all gets sorted soon. It's nearly time to go back to school and we haven't had a day out anywhere yet.

Please come!

Lots of love

Tammy

---

**Write or circle the correct answers.**

**Write A or B on the line. Which letter is:**

① a complaint? ___

② a request? ___

③ **How are the two writers of the letters related?**

a mother and daughter

b father and daughter

c father and grandmother

**How does the language used in each letter differ?**

④ The language used in letter A is

_____.

⑤ The language used in letter B is

_____.

**Match the words in the box to their meanings.**

| purchased  assess  compensated |

⑥ to judge / work out: _____

⑦ receive money for: _____

⑧ bought: _____

⑨ **What is the purpose of Tammy's letter?**

_____

_____

**My Book Review**

Title _____

Author _____

Rating ☆☆☆☆☆

Comment _____

*Score 2 points for each correct answer!*
SCORE **/18** 0-6 8-14 16-18

TERM 4 ENGLISH

# Number & Algebra

AC9M4A02

## Multiplication and division facts

If you know the multiplication facts, you also know the division facts.
*Examples:*

$5 × 8 = 40$   $40 ÷ 8 = 5$
$8 × 5 = 40$   $40 ÷ 5 = 8$

**Complete the fact families.**

① $9 × 2 = 18$

___ × ___ = 18
$18 ÷ 2 =$ ___
$18 ÷$ ___ = ___

② $6 × 10 = 60$

___ × ___ = 60
$60 ÷ 10 =$ ___
___ ÷ ___ = ___

③ $4 × 5 = 20$

___ × ___ = 20
$20 ÷$ ___ = ___
___ ÷ ___ = ___

④ $7 × 4 = 28$

___ × ___ = ___
___ ÷ ___ = ___
___ ÷ ___ = ___

⑤ ___ × ___ = ___
___ × ___ = ___
$72 ÷ 8 = 9$
___ ÷ ___ = ___

⑥ $6 × 3 = 18$

___ × ___ = ___
___ ÷ ___ = ___
___ ÷ ___ = ___

⑦ ___ × ___ = ___
___ × ___ = ___
$90 ÷ 10 = 9$
___ ÷ ___ = ___

⑧ $9 × 6 = 54$

___ × ___ = ___
___ ÷ ___ = ___
___ ÷ ___ = ___

⑨ $8 × 4 = 32$

___ × ___ = ___
___ ÷ ___ = ___
___ ÷ ___ = ___

⑩ ___ × ___ = ___
___ × ___ = ___
$56 ÷ 7 = 8$
___ ÷ ___ = ___

**Write the answers.**

⑪ $24 ÷ 6 =$ ☐
⑫ $3 × 5 =$ ☐
⑬ $9 × 2 =$ ☐
⑭ $10 × 5 =$ ☐
⑮ $5 ÷ 5 =$ ☐
⑯ $8 ÷ 4 =$ ☐
⑰ $3 × 7 =$ ☐
⑱ $45 ÷ 9 =$ ☐
⑲ $5 × 5 =$ ☐
⑳ $30 ÷ 5 =$ ☐
㉑ $64 ÷ 8 =$ ☐
㉒ $21 ÷ 7 =$ ☐

*Score 2 points for each correct answer!* **SCORE** **/44** (0-20) (22-38) (40-44)

# Statistics & Probability

There are no statistics & probability activities in this unit.

# Measurement & Space

AC9M4M04

## Angles

**Order these angles from smallest to largest by writing the numbers 1 (smallest) to 6 (largest) in the boxes.**

① ☐      ④ ☐

② ☐      ⑤ ☐

③ ☐      ⑥ ☐

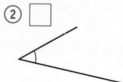

This is a
**right angle:**

⑦ Mark the 27 right angles in this picture with a small square, as shown on this angle.

Score 2 points for each correct answer!

SCORE **/14**  ( 0-4 )  ( 6-10 )  ( 12-14 )

## Problem Solving

AC9M4N08

### Solve it!

Solve these word problems. Show your working out.

① There are 10 biscuits in a pack. Melanie buys 14 packets. How many biscuits are there altogether?

_____

Melanie takes the biscuits to a meeting. There are 70 people at the meeting. How many biscuits can they have each if they are shared equally?

_____

② 100 horses are in a parade. They each have red covers on their hooves and blue covers on their ears. How many red covers altogether?

_____

How many blue covers altogether?

_____

At the end of the parade, they remove half of the red covers and a quarter of the blue covers. How many covers are still on the horses?

_____

_____

**Complete this multiplication and division crossword so that the equations are correct.**

| 6 | × |   | = | 36 |   |   | ÷ | 4 | = | 2 |
|---|---|---|---|----|---|---|---|---|---|---|
| × |   | × |   | ÷  |   |   | × |   |   | × |
| 3 | × |   | = | 9  |   |   | 3 |   | 3 | 10 |
| = |   | = |   | =  |   |   | = |   | = | = |
|   |   |   |   |    | × |   | = | 24 |  |  |
|   |   |   |   |    | × |   |   |   |  |  |
| 5 |   | 9 | = | 45 | 7 | × | 5 | = |  |  |
| × |   | × |   |    | = |   | × |   |  | ÷ |
|   |   | 3 | × | 14 | = |   | 8 | 2 | = | 4 |
| = |   | = |   |    |   |   | = |   |  | = |
| 50 |  |   |   | 2  |   |   |   |  |  | 4 |
|   |   |   |   | =  |   |   |   |  |  |  |
|   |   |   |   | 7  |   |   |   |  |  |  |

# Grammar & Punctuation

AC9E4LA03, AC9E4LY06

## Modal verbs

> Modal (auxiliary) verbs are helper verbs. They give us more information about the verb that follows it.
>
> *Examples:* can, could, will, would, may, might, should, must
>
> Modal verbs can be used to show:
>
> - how likely something is to happen:
>   I **might** sing a song.
> - someone's ability to do something:
>   I **can** sing a song.
> - if something must be done:
>   I **must** sing a song.
> - if permission is given to do something:
>   I **can** sing a song.
> - if something is planned to be done:
>   I **will** sing a song.

**Use modal verbs to complete these sentences.**

① Professional dancers _____ dance for long periods of time.

② You _____ stay within the boundary fences.

③ Our teacher said we _____ read outside today.

④ _____ I come to the show with you?

## Modal verbs for persuasion

> Modal verbs can be used in **persuasive texts** to soften or strengthen arguments.
>
> *Examples:*
>
> Children **can** help with recycling.
> Children **should** help with recycling.
>
> You **could** help with recycling.
> You **must** help with recycling.

**Write another modal verb for the underlined verb to strengthen these arguments.**

⑤ You <u>can</u> be a winner! _____

⑥ I <u>might</u> write to the team leader.
_____

⑦ People <u>can</u> pick up litter. _____

Score 2 points for each correct answer!  SCORE **/14**  (0-4) (6-10) (12-14)

126

# Phonic Knowledge & Spelling

AC9E4LA11, AC9E4LY09, AC9E4LY10

## Prefixes up– and down–

**Say each word in the word bank. They begin with the prefix up– or down–.**

**Remember!** A prefix is a letter or group of letters that is added to the beginning of a word.

| | | | |
|---|---|---|---|
| upstairs | upstream | upright | uproot |
| update | upgrade | upturn | upward |
| downhill | downpour | downpipe | downhearted |
| downfall | downgrade | downstairs | downstream |

**Choose words from the word bank to complete these sentences.**

① We got soaked to the skin during the
_____.

② Suddenly we saw a trout swimming
_____.

③ The plumber had to unblock the
_____.

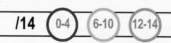

## Antonyms

> Antonyms are words **opposite** in meaning to another word.

**Choose an antonym from the word bank for these words.**

④ upstream _____

⑤ downstairs _____

⑥ uphill _____

⑦ downturn _____

**Match the words in the box to their meanings.**

| | | | |
|---|---|---|---|
| downhearted | upright | download | downgrade |

⑧ to copy and save data from the internet:
_____

⑨ in low spirits: _____

⑩ sitting or standing with a straight back:
_____

⑪ to reduce to a lower grade:
_____

TERM 4 ENGLISH

## The Stranger

**Imaginative text** – Narrative
**Author** – Frances Mackay

Suddenly, I heard a strange shuffling sound behind me. I quickly turned around and caught a glimpse of someone slowly moving past the open door. I walked over and peered outside.

I couldn't see anything and was just about to go back inside when I heard a soft moaning sound. It came from the bushes nearby. I walked over and saw, almost totally hidden in the undergrowth, a man. I stepped back in horror, because the man was dressed in what can only be described as rags and he was bleeding heavily from his head.

As soon as he saw me, he tried to get up, but he quickly fell back down again, clutching at his head.

"Who are you?" I asked. "What's happened?"

"Leave me alone. I'm OK," came the shaky reply.

"But you're bleeding. I'll run and get help." I said.

"No! You can't do that!" the man shrieked.

"OK, I won't. But I'll go inside and get something to stop the bleeding."

I ran back into the house, grabbed a bottle of water, some clean tea towels and a blanket.

When I returned, the man was sitting up. The amount of blood on his face was frightening but the wound itself was only small and he allowed me to clean it up and bandage it as best as I could. He took a huge gulp of water and I laid the blanket around him.

His clothes looked like he'd worn them for years. He was very dirty and smelly. His black hair and beard were filthy and matted with the blood. His bare toes were poking out of the holes in his shoes and he had a large plastic sack beside him. He looked about 60 years old to me, but he could have been younger.

"Thanks, mate," he said at last. "Not many people would help the likes of me. What's your name?"

"Tom."

---

Write or circle the correct answers.

① **Has the author grabbed the reader's attention in the first few sentences?**

a Yes – the beginning is short and to the point.

b Yes – by using phrases such as 'strange shuffling sound' and 'a glimpse of someone', it makes the beginning sound mysterious.

c No – the beginning is very ordinary.

② **Describe the stranger's appearance.**

_____

_____

_____

③ **Why do you think the stranger was so poorly dressed?**

a He didn't like to wash his clothes.

b He was homeless and was living rough.

c He preferred to wear old clothes.

④ **Which word in the text means a quick look?**

_____

⑤ **Which is the odd word/phrase out?**

a peered            c looked closely

b stared            d glared

*Score 2 points for each correct answer!*

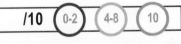

SCORE **/10**  0-2  4-8  10

### My Book Review

Title _____

Author _____

Rating ☆☆☆☆☆

Comment _____

_____

**TERM 4 ENGLISH**

# Number & Algebra

AC9M4N08

## Money in other countries

Australia's money (currency) is in **Australian dollars** and **cents**. Other countries have different currencies and most of them are based on a decimal system. The word **decimal** comes from the Latin word *decimus* which means 'tenth'. So a decimal system is based on **units of 10**.

In Australia, 100 cents = 1 dollar
In the UK, 100 pence = 1 pound

Here are some banknotes from other countries:

**Write the correct answers to these foreign money problems.**

① How many 1 euro coins can be exchanged for a 10 euro note?

_____

② If I buy two items each costing 1000 won, how much change would I receive from 10 000 won?

_____

③ Max has 20 Singapore dollars. How much change will he receive if he buys two books costing 7 Singapore dollars each?

_____

④ How many US dollars are there in two 100 US dollar notes?

_____

⑤ When Su travelled to London, she stayed in a hotel that cost 200 pounds a night. She stayed in the hotel for 4 nights. How many pounds did it cost her altogether?

_____

⑥ You have a 50 baht note. You buy an item costing 35 baht. How much change will you get back?

_____

# Statistics & Probability

AC9M4ST02

## Column graph with multiple values

Tanya carried out a survey of the students in Years 4, 5 and 6 at her school. She asked them to choose their favourite food out of pizza, chicken, hamburger, spaghetti and fish and chips. Here are Tanya's results:

|  | Year 4 | Year 5 | Year 6 |
|---|---|---|---|
| Pizza | 8 | 6 | 10 |
| Chicken | 5 | 3 | 2 |
| Hamburger | 10 | 15 | 12 |
| Spaghetti | 3 | 4 | 2 |
| Fish and chips | 6 | 7 | 4 |

Tanya used the results from her survey to make a column graph. She made a graph that shows the results from all the year groups.

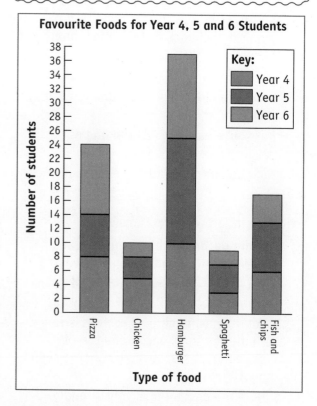

**Favourite Foods for Year 4, 5 and 6 Students**

**Use the table and the graph to answer the questions.**

① What was the most favourite food in Year 4?

_____

② What was the least favourite food in Year 4?

_____

③ How many students in Year 6 preferred pizza? _____

④ How many students in Year 5 preferred spaghetti? _____

⑤ What was the total number of students surveyed in Year 4? _____

⑥ How many students in total prefer hamburgers as their favourite food? _____

⑦ How many students in total prefer chicken as their favourite food? _____

⑧ What was the total number of students surveyed in Year 5? _____

⑨ What was the total number of students surveyed in Year 6? _____

⑩ Which food was the most favourite in all three year groups? _____

⑪ How could Tanya's table be improved?

_____

_____

_____

Score 2 points for each correct answer!

SCORE  **/22**  ( 0-8 )  ( 10-16 )  ( 18-22 )

## Measurement & Space

AC9M4M01

## Capacity

When we measure **capacity**, we use **millilitres (mL)** and **litres (L)**.

1000 millilitres = 1 litre

500 millilitres = ½ litre

250 millilitres = ¼ litre

*Example:*

How would you measure 2750 mL of water? Write the number below each measure you would use.

| 1 L | 500 mL | 200 mL | 100 mL | 50 mL |
|-----|--------|--------|--------|-------|
| 2 | 1 | 1 | 0 | 1 |

How would you measure these quantities of liquids? Write the number below each measure you would use.

① 750 mL of water

| 1 L | 500 mL | 200 mL | 100 mL | 50 mL |
|-----|--------|--------|--------|-------|
| | | | | |

② 850 mL of juice

| 1 L | 500 mL | 200 mL | 100 mL | 50 mL |
|-----|--------|--------|--------|-------|
| | | | | |

③ 950 mL of milk

| 1 L | 500 mL | 200 mL | 100 mL | 50 mL |
|-----|--------|--------|--------|-------|
| | | | | |

④ 8 litres of petrol

| 1 L | 500 mL | 200 mL | 100 mL | 50 mL |
|-----|--------|--------|--------|-------|
| | | | | |

⑤ 10¼ litres of diesel

| 1 L | 500 mL | 200 mL | 100 mL | 50 mL |
|-----|--------|--------|--------|-------|
| | | | | |

**How many 250 mL measures of water do you need to fill these containers?**

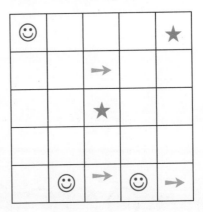

⑥ ½ litre container _____

⑦ 1 litre container _____

⑧ 3 litre watering can _____

⑨ 10 litre drum _____

**A bucket holds 25 litres of water. How many buckets of water will it take to fill these containers?**

⑩ 100 litre drum _____

⑪ 400 litre drum _____

⑫ 1000 litre drum _____

⑬ **A new 350 litre drum of kerosene had 125 litres taken out of it. How much was left in the drum?**

_____

⑭ **30 students were each given 3 litres of juice. How much juice was given out altogether?**

_____

Score 2 points for each correct answer!

SCORE  **/28**  ( 0-12 )  ( 14-22 )  ( 24-28 )

## Problem Solving

AC9M4SP02

### Shape pattern puzzle

Draw a ☺, ★ or → in each of the remaining squares so that no symbol is beside, under or above the same symbol.

| ☺ | | | | ★ |
|---|---|---|---|---|
| | | → | | |
| | | ★ | | |
| | | | | |
| ☺ | → | ☺ | → | |

TERM 4 MATHS

# Grammar & Punctuation

AC9E4LA01

## Contractions

Contractions are two words which have been shortened to make one word. An **apostrophe** (') replaces the missing letters.

*Examples:*   we are = we're
   must not = mustn't

We tend to use contractions in speech and writing when we are in less formal situations, such as with family and friends.

**Replace the underlined words with their contraction. Write the contraction on the line.**

① "<u>You are</u> very late," said Dad.

_____

② I <u>do not</u> know why the dog got out.

_____

③ He <u>is not</u> home today, <u>he is</u> at work.

_____  _____

④ <u>That is</u> the first time <u>she has</u> driven a car.

_____  _____

**Match the contractions in the box to their full form.**

| who've   won't   let's   where's   she'd   they'd |
|---|

⑤ let us _____

⑥ will not _____

⑦ they had / they would _____

⑧ where is _____

⑨ who have _____

⑩ she had / she would _____

# Phonic Knowledge & Spelling

AC9E4LY09, AC9E4LY10

## Prefixes over– and under–

Say each word in the word bank. They all begin with either the prefix **over–** or **under–**.

| overhear | overnight | overturn |
|---|---|---|
| overseas | overgrown | overlook |
| overboard | overweight | |
| underarm | underwear | underground |
| underwater | underline | underpass |
| undertake | underweight | |

**Choose words from the word bank to complete these sentences.**

① The garden of the old, empty house was

_____.

② I couldn't buy new _____
as I didn't have enough money.

## Antonyms

Antonyms are adjectives that are opposite in meaning. *Example:* sweet – sour

**Write the antonyms of these words by changing the prefix to over.**

③ underweight _____
④ underpass _____
⑤ underarm _____
⑥ underfed _____

**Build the words and write the new word.**

⑦ over + turn + ed _____
⑧ under + hand + ed _____
⑨ over + grown _____
⑩ over + dress + ed _____

**Add –ing to these words. Write the new word. Remember your spelling rules!**

⑪ underline

_____

⑫ overcharge

⑬ overlap

_____

⑭ undertake

_____

## What is a Tsunami?

**Informative text** – Report
**Author** – Lisa Thompson

A tsunami is a series of giant waves. Most tsunamis occur when an earthquake or a volcano shakes the ocean floor. This creates strong, underwater waves. Because the waves are so far beneath the surface of the water, these waves cannot be felt on a boat.

The deeper the water, the faster the tsunami travels. But as the tsunami reaches shallow water near the coast, it slows down. The water behind it begins to pile up. At the same time, the shallow water near the shore is sucked back. The tsunami swells to between 10 and 30 metres high and hits the shore with terrible force. This wave could be followed by another an hour later, and then another after that. And the first wave may not be the biggest!

Tsunami is a Japanese word. In English, it means 'harbour wave'. Sometimes tsunamis are called tidal waves. But tsunamis have nothing to do with the tides. Most tsunamis are

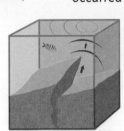
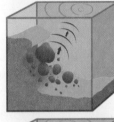
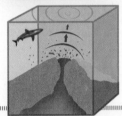

caused by underwater events such as earthquakes, volcanic eruptions or landslides.

The Pacific Ocean is the world's deepest ocean. Ninety per cent of all tsunamis have occurred here because the most dangerous tsunamis usually begin in very deep water. Also, the Pacific has many underwater earthquakes that are caused by movements in the **earth's crust**.

There are two tsunami warning centres in the world. One of them is in Alaska, and the other is in Hawaii. Scientists at these centres watch for strong earthquakes. They also get information from tidal stations, which tell when sea conditions match those of a possible tsunami. Then they warn people to be prepared. But the system doesn't always work. Seventy-five per cent of all tsunami warnings issued since 1948 have been false.

Source: *Wild Waves*, Brainwaves, Blake Education.

---

**Write or circle the correct answers.**

1. **What happens when a volcano or an earthquake shakes the ocean floor?**

   a It creates a storm.

   b It causes boats to capsize.

   c It creates strong, underwater waves.

2. **What is the earth's crust?**

   a the outer layer of the earth

   b any soil that is crusty

   c We are not told.

3. **Give two reasons why 90% of tsunamis occur in the Pacific Ocean.**

   _____

   _____

4. **Where in the world are the two tsunami warning stations?**

   _____

   _____

5. **Which word is an antonym of strong?**

   a powerful      b weak      c mighty

6. **Which word in the text means 'not very deep'?**

   a swells      b shore      c shallow

7. **How effective are the tsunami warnings?**

   _____

   _____

   _____

Score 2 points for each correct answer!   SCORE   **/14**   0-4   6-10   12-14

**My Book Review**

Title _____

Author _____

Rating

Comment _____

_____

TERM 4 ENGLISH

# Number & Algebra

AC9M4N01

## Place value

> *Example:* In the number **1457**, the **4** has a value of **400**.

**What is the value of the digits in red?**

① 2830 _____

② 6715 _____

③ 8940 _____

④ 6792 _____

⑤ 8561 _____

⑥ 23 456 _____

⑦ 14 598 _____

⑧ 54 700 _____

⑨ 72 345 _____

⑩ 123 600 _____

⑪ 543 291 _____

> *Example:*
> If the **7** in **15 574** is changed to a **9**, by how much would the value change?
> The **7** has a value of 70.
> The 9 would have a value of 90.
> 90 – 70 = 20
> The value would change by **20**.

**Write the correct answers.**

⑫ If the **6** in **23 682** is changed to a **9**, by how much would the value change?

_____

⑬ If the **2** in **42 567** is changed to a **5**, by how much would the value change?

_____

⑭ If the **4** in **45 690** is changed to a **6**, by how much would the value change?

_____

⑮ If the **3** in **43 776** is changed to a **9**, by how much would the value change?

_____

**Populations of some Australian towns and cities, June 2015**

| Place | Population June 2015 | Order |
|-------|----------------------|-------|
| Mackay | 85 455 | |
| Tamworth | 42 255 | |
| Ballarat | 99 841 | |
| Bundaberg | 70 588 | |
| Cairns | 147 993 | |
| Devonport | 30 497 | |
| Hervey Bay | 52 288 | |
| Bendigo | 92 888 | |
| Hobart | 209 254 | |
| Alice Springs | 27 972 | |

⑯ Number the places in order from **1** for the **highest** population to **10** for the **lowest** population. Write the numbers in the table.

⑰ Which place had the highest population?

_____

⑱ Which place had the lowest population?

_____

⑲ Which place had a population closer to 100 000 – Ballarat or Bendigo?

_____

⑳ How many more people need to live in Cairns to make the population 148 000?

_____

㉑ If 12 more people lived in Hervey Bay, what would the new population be?

_____

*Score 2 points for each correct answer!* **SCORE** **/42** (0-18) (20-36) (38-42)

## Statistics & Probability

AC9M4ST01

### Temperature

This table shows the average temperatures (°C) for each month of the year in Melbourne.

**Average temperature, Melbourne (°C)**

| J | F | M | A | M | J | J | A | S | O | N | D |
|---|---|---|---|---|---|---|---|---|---|---|---|
| 26 | 26 | 24 | 20 | 17 | 14 | 14 | 15 | 17 | 20 | 22 | 24 |

① Use the information in the table to make a column graph. Add a scale that fits the data and write a suitable title.

**Month**

**Answer the questions about the temperature data.**

② Which months have the highest average temperatures?

_____

③ Which months have the lowest average temperatures?

_____

④ How many months have an average temperature above 20 °C?

_____

⑤ How many months have an average temperature below 20 °C?

_____

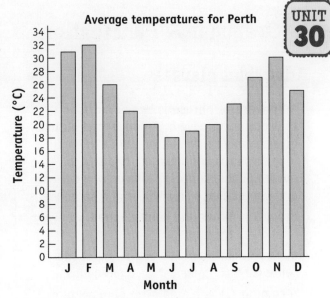

**Average temperatures for Perth**

**Month**

**Answer the questions about the graph above.**

⑥ How many months have an average temperature above 20 °C? _____

⑦ How many months have an average temperature below 20 °C? _____

⑧ Which month has the highest average temperature? _____

⑨ Which month has the lowest average temperature? _____

Score 2 points for each correct answer! **SCORE** **/18**  0-6  8-14 16-18

## Measurement & Space

*There are no measurement & space activities in this unit.*

## Problem Solving

AC9M4N02

### Fraction problems

**Solve these fraction puzzles. Show your working out.**

① $\frac{1}{10}$ of the jelly beans in a bag are red and $\frac{4}{10}$ are blue. What fraction of the jellybeans in the bag are colours other than red or blue?

_____

_____

② A cake recipe requires $1\frac{1}{3}$ cup of sugar for the cake and $\frac{2}{3}$ cup of sugar for the icing. How much sugar is needed altogether?

_____

_____

③ You give $\frac{2}{8}$ of some cookies to Trixie and $\frac{3}{8}$ of the cookies to Ria. What fraction of the cookies do you have left?

_____

_____

TERM 4 MATHS

# Grammar & Punctuation

AC9E4LA08

## Adverbial clauses

An **adverbial phrase** is two or more words that act as an adverb. An **adverbial clause** gives us more information about the main idea and includes a subject and a verb. An adverbial clause begins with a conjunction and can be placed anywhere in a sentence.

*Example:* **When the rain stopped,** <u>we went for a walk</u>.

adverbial clause at the beginning of the sentence　　comma　　main clause

A **comma (,)** is placed after an adverbial clause if it's at the beginning of a sentence.

No comma is needed if the clause is at the end of the sentence.

*Example:* We went for a walk **when the rain stopped**.

**Underline the adverbial clause in each sentence.**

1. We played on the beach until the sun set.

2. Because no one was home, the cat slept on the bed.

3. Once the house is painted, we can lay the new carpet.

4. You should visit the museum before you go back home.

5. Although it was late, Jess continued to watch TV.

**Add commas where they are needed in these sentences.**

6. When school has finished we are going into town.

7. Unless she arrives early I will not see her.

8. Whenever I eat chocolate I always make a mess.

9. After the game we had a picnic.

10. Before I go to school I walk the dog.

*Score 2 points for each correct answer!* **SCORE** | **/20** | 0-8 | 10-14 | 16-20

# Phonic Knowledge & Spelling

AC9E4LY09, AC9E4LY10

## Prefixes re– and de–

Say each word in the word bank. The prefix **re–** means 'again'. The prefix **de–** means to remove, to reverse something or a departure from.

| | | | |
|---|---|---|---|
| remark | remove | reflect | reduce |
| regret | repeat | rebuild | replace |
| delete | describe | depart | depend |
| defend | demolish | deliver | detour |

**Choose words from the word bank to complete these sentences.**

1. Mum did not know what type of cleaner would _____ ink from the sofa.

2. For history, we asked our grandparents to _____ what life was like in the past.

3. The courier couldn't _____ my parcel because of the road works.

**Match the words in the box to their meanings.**

| | | |
|---|---|---|
| remark | demolish | defend |
| repeat | regret | detour |

4. to take a roundabout route: _____

5. to protect from harm: _____

6. to feel sad about something you have done: _____

7. to knock down: _____

8. to do or say something again: _____

9. to say something you have noticed: _____

*Score 2 points for each correct answer!* **SCORE** | **/18** | 0-6 | 8-14 | 16-18

## Kevin's Echidna

**Imaginative text** – Narrative
**Author** – Ross Pearce
**Illustrator** – David Dickson

A leathery, black creature poked out from beneath the rotting log. Its thin, flickering tongue searched the air. The movement caught Kevin's eye.

"No, it couldn't be a snake. Perhaps a lizard?" he thought.

Curved claws scraped aside the leaves, and the furry, funnel-shaped head appeared in full.

Just an echidna, sniffing out some termites. Kevin relaxed now that he knew it wasn't a snake.

The echidna lumbered slowly forward. Its long, black snout searched from side to side for anything edible among the dried leaves and twigs. Suddenly it stopped. Kevin froze, his eyes fixed on the little creature.

The echidna was wary. Kevin could see the cream and black spines, like sharpened knitting needles, lying flat over its back. The tiny, black eyes returned his interest. The boy and the echidna were both still, staring at each other.

Kevin could feel the warm, afternoon sun on his back, but all his other senses were focused on the echidna.

"You're a prickly little creature," Kevin thought. "I wouldn't let you into my place, you're too prickly."

Source: *Kevin's Echidna*, Sparklers, Blake Education.

**Write or circle the correct answers.**

① **List the three adjectives in the first paragraph.**

_____

② **What do echidnas eat?**

a snakes

b We are not told.

c termites

d dried leaves

③ **What does edible mean?**

a small

b fresh

c suitable for eating

④ **Which word in the text tells you how the echidna moved?**

_____

⑤ **What does the sentence: 'The echidna was wary' mean?**

_____

⑥ **Which word in the text means concentrating?**

a focused     b stopped     c searched

⑦ **'The tiny, black eyes returned his interest.' What does this sentence mean?**

a The echidna's eyes were black and tiny.

b The echidna stared back at Kevin.

c The echidna looked away.

Score 2 points for each correct answer!

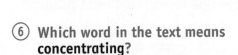

SCORE **/14**  (0-4)  (6-10)  (12-14)

**My Book Review**

Title _____

Author _____

Rating ☆☆☆☆☆

Comment _____

**TERM 4 ENGLISH**

# Number & Algebra

AC9M4N04

## Fraction number lines

> This **number line** shows counting in **halves** as improper fractions and mixed numerals.

① Complete the number line by counting in **mixed numerals** on top of the line and **improper fractions** under the line.

Write these **improper fractions** as whole or mixed numerals.

② $\frac{2}{2}$ = _____

③ $\frac{7}{2}$ = _____

④ $\frac{11}{2}$ = _____

⑤ $\frac{12}{2}$ = _____

⑥ $\frac{15}{2}$ = _____

⑦ $\frac{3}{2}$ = _____

> This **number line** shows counting in **thirds** as improper fractions and mixed numerals.

| 0 | $\frac{1}{3}$ | $\frac{2}{3}$ | 1 | $1\frac{1}{3}$ | $1\frac{2}{3}$ | 2 | $2\frac{1}{3}$ | $2\frac{2}{3}$ | 3 | $3\frac{1}{3}$ | $3\frac{2}{3}$ | 4 |
|---|---|---|---|---|---|---|---|---|---|---|---|---|
| 0 | $\frac{1}{3}$ | $\frac{2}{3}$ | $\frac{3}{3}$ | $\frac{4}{3}$ | $\frac{5}{3}$ | $\frac{6}{3}$ | $\frac{7}{3}$ | $\frac{8}{3}$ | $\frac{9}{3}$ | $\frac{10}{3}$ | $\frac{11}{3}$ | $\frac{12}{3}$ |

⑧ Complete the number line by counting in **mixed numerals** on top of the line and **improper fractions** under the line.

Write these **improper fractions** as whole or mixed numerals.

⑨ $\frac{4}{3}$ = _____

⑩ $\frac{7}{3}$ = _____

⑪ $\frac{9}{3}$ = _____

⑫ $\frac{12}{3}$ = _____

⑬ $\frac{14}{3}$ = _____

⑭ $\frac{16}{3}$ = _____

> This **number line** shows counting in **fifths** as improper fractions and mixed numerals.

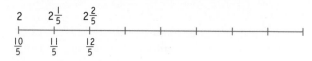

⑮ Complete the number line by counting in **mixed numerals** on top of the line and **improper fractions** under the line.

Write these **improper fractions** as whole or mixed numerals.

⑯ $\frac{5}{5}$ = _____

⑰ $\frac{7}{5}$ = _____

⑱ $\frac{9}{5}$ = _____

⑲ $\frac{12}{5}$ = _____

⑳ $\frac{14}{5}$ = _____

㉑ $\frac{15}{3}$ = _____

Score 2 points for each correct answer! SCORE /42  0-18  20-36  38-42

# Statistics & Probability

AC9M4P01

## What are the chances?

**Which event is more likely to happen? Circle the correct answer.**

① a You will go home after school today.
b You will turn into a frog after school today.

② a There will be a flood tomorrow.
b There will be rain tomorrow.

③ a You will meet an alien tonight.
b You will meet your friend tonight.

④ a You will go on a school trip this year.
b You will fly to the moon this year.

⑤ a An elephant will run down the street.
b A cat will run down the street.

TERM 4 MATHS

TARGETING HOMEWORK 4 © PASCAL PRESS ISBN 9781925726466

**Read the first event. Then circle the event that will not make any difference to the chances of the first event happening.**

⑥ My dad will buy a new car.

   **a** My dad is a good surfer.

   **b** My dad got a pay rise last week.

⑦ A new bridge will be built across the river.

   **a** A survey showed that the current bridge is not strong enough for future traffic.

   **b** I like travelling across bridges.

⑧ I will eat some strawberry ice-cream today.

   **a** My dentist said I am not allowed to eat anything cold today.

   **b** Our local shop sells ice-cream.

⑨ We are flying to Queensland for a holiday in January.

   **a** Queensland is a state in Australia.

   **b** All flights to Queensland in January have been cancelled.

*Score 2 points for each correct answer!* SCORE **/18** ( 0-6 ) ( 8-14 ) ( 16-18 )

## Measurement & Space

AC9M4SP03

## Make it symmetrical

In a **symmetrical shape**, one side is an exact mirror image of the other side. If you fold a shape or pattern along a **line of symmetry**, one half fits exactly over the other.

line of symmetry

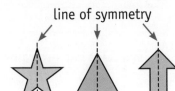

**Draw the other half of each vase so it is symmetrical. Colour the shapes.**

① 

② 

③ 

④ 

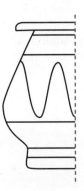

⑤ 

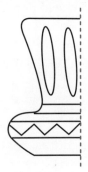

*Score 2 points for each correct answer!* SCORE **/10** ( 0-2 ) ( 4-8 ) ( 10 )

## Problem Solving

AC9M4P02

## Throwing dice

When you throw two dice, how many different combinations give you a total of more than 6? Write the possible combinations.

_____

_____

_____

## Grammar & Punctuation

AC9E4LA04

### Paragraphs

> A **paragraph** is a block of sentences built around a main idea. The first sentence in the paragraph often introduces the main idea. This is followed by sentences giving further details.
>
> Begin a new paragraph when:
> * a new person is introduced
> * one person has stopped speaking and a new person starts speaking
> * there is a change of place or setting
> * time has passed.

**Read through the following extract. Insert a // symbol to show where a new paragraph should begin.** *Hint:* **there are 3.**

①–③ Last weekend we all went to stay at Aunt Bev's house. I love to go there because she lives right on the beach. It was a long journey in the car and Dad was quite grumpy by the time we got there but he soon cheered up when Aunt Bev greeted him with a big smile and a cold drink. In the afternoon, Dad and I walked along the beach to the rock pools at the far end. "Remember last year when you found that big crab?" asked Dad. "Yes," I said, "it scared me half to death when it grabbed my finger! I'm going to be more careful this time."

### Text connectives

> **Text connectives** are words and phrases that join ideas together throughout the text. Some text connectives show that time has passed.
>
> *Examples:* after an hour had passed, suddenly, when we arrived back, eventually, then, after several months

**Choose a suitable connective from those above to show the passing of time in these paragraphs.**

④–⑥ In the morning, we had breakfast and _____4 we headed off for our walk.

_____5, we stopped to have a drink and look at the view. "It's beautiful here," said Tina. "I wish I lived here all the time."

"Yes, that would be great," I agreed.

We continued our walk and _____6 came to the place we had chosen to have our picnic lunch. We spread the rug out on the grass and sat back to relax. "This is just perfect!" said Tina.

*Score 2 points for each correct answer!* SCORE **/12** (0-4) (6-8) (10-12)

## Phonic Knowledge & Spelling

AC9E4LY09, AC9E4LY10

### Suffix –tion

**Say each word in the word bank. When a word ends in –ion it is a noun. The letters in the suffix –tion work together to make a 'shun' sound.**

| | | | |
|---|---|---|---|
| mention | action | lotion | motion |
| station | nation | fiction | option |
| relation | collection | connection | |
| invitation | education | demonstration | |
| completion | competition | | |

**Choose words from the word bank to complete these sentences.**

① The lamp had a loose _____ making the light flicker on and off.

② I didn't want to _____ that my friend's clothes looked tight on her.

**Change these verbs to nouns. Remember the 'e' rule. The first one has been done for you.**

educate ___education___

③ invite _____

④ compete _____

⑤ collect _____

⑥ explain _____

**Circle how many syllables each word has.**

⑦ action  1  2  3  4

⑧ option  1  2  3  4

⑨ invitation  1  2  3  4

⑩ illustration  1  2  3  4

*Score 2 points for each correct answer!* SCORE **/20** (0-8) (10-14) (16-20)

TARGETING HOMEWORK 4 © PASCAL PRESS ISBN 9781925726466

## A Terrible Thing

Imaginative text – Narrative
**Author** – Elizabeth Best
**Illustrator** – Janine Dawson

The next week, Dad went back to work and Peter, Bridget and Lisa started school. Everyone was so nice to Lisa, knowing it was her first day at a new school.

By Friday, Lisa was looking forward to the weekend. But that night something terrible happened.

They'd just finished eating dinner when Mum asked in a surprised voice, "Where's the little mermaid?"

For a moment no-one moved. Then everyone's head swung around. No mermaid sat on her rock on top of the TV. There was an awful silence.

"Peter?" Dad said.

"No, I haven't got it!"

"Bridget?"

"No, Dad!"

"Is someone playing a joke?" Mum said.

"Lisa?" Dad said.

"No, I ... no," said Lisa. Her face went bright red.

"She could've been knocked off the TV," said Mum, peering behind the set.

"Now this isn't funny," said Dad. "Everyone start looking. There must be an explanation."

"Burglars?" said Mum. "It couldn't be. When I got back, all the doors were locked."

Everyone started looking. They turned everything upside down and inside out. Homework was forgotten. Their favourite TV show was forgotten. They looked and looked. The little mermaid was gone.

Source: *Lisa*, Sparklers, Blake Education.

---

Write or circle the correct answers.

① **This story uses several text connectives that tell us that time has passed. List four examples.**

_____

_____

② **What does 'There was an awful silence' mean?**

a  not sure

b  No-one spoke and everyone felt awkward and unsure.

c  The talking stopped.

③ **Lisa's face went bright red when Dad questioned her. What does this tell you about how Lisa was feeling?**

a  She felt embarrassed.

b  She felt hot.

c  She felt sad.

④ **Why was burglary ruled out as a reason for the mermaid having disappeared?**

a  We are not told.

b  All the doors were locked when Mum came home.

c  Burglaries are rare in their neighbourhood.

Score 2 points for each correct answer!  **SCORE**  /8   0-2   4-6   8

### My Book Review

Title _____

Author _____

Rating ☆ ☆ ☆ ☆ ☆

Comment _____

_____

# Number & Algebra

AC9M4N09

## Function machines

Use the rule to complete each function machine.

① 
| Rule: × 5 | |
|---|---|
| IN | OUT |
| 3 | 15 |
| 6 | |
| 7 | 35 |
| 10 | |
| | 45 |
| 8 | |

② 
| Rule: × 4 | |
|---|---|
| IN | OUT |
| 4 | |
| 10 | 40 |
| 6 | |
| | 8 |
| 5 | |
| | 28 |

③ 
| Rule: × 6 | |
|---|---|
| IN | OUT |
| 2 | 12 |
| 8 | |
| | 60 |
| 5 | |
| | 36 |
| 4 | |

④ 
| Rule: × 8 | |
|---|---|
| IN | OUT |
| 2 | 16 |
| 4 | |
| 3 | 24 |
| 10 | |
| | 64 |
| 7 | |

⑤ 
| Rule: × 9 | |
|---|---|
| IN | OUT |
| 3 | 27 |
| 1 | |
| 10 | 90 |
| 8 | |
| | 81 |
| 4 | |

⑥ 
| Rule: × 10 | |
|---|---|
| IN | OUT |
| 5 | 50 |
| 2 | |
| 7 | |
| 10 | |
| | 60 |
| 3 | |

Write the rules and complete the machines.

⑦ 
| Rule: | |
|---|---|
| IN | OUT |
| 3 | |
| 5 | 15 |
| 9 | |
| 10 | 30 |
| | 24 |
| 7 | |

⑧ 
| Rule: | |
|---|---|
| IN | OUT |
| 10 | 20 |
| 5 | |
| 20 | |
| 9 | 18 |
| | 80 |
| 30 | |

⑨ 
| Rule: | |
|---|---|
| IN | OUT |
| 8 | 56 |
| 3 | |
| 10 | 70 |
| 7 | |
| | 35 |
| 9 | |

⑩ 
| Rule: | |
|---|---|
| IN | OUT |
| 3 | 12 |
| | 28 |
| 10 | 40 |
| | 32 |
| 6 | |
| 4 | |

⑪ 
| Rule: | |
|---|---|
| IN | OUT |
| 10 | |
| 5 | 40 |
| 6 | |
| 9 | 72 |
| | 16 |
| | 56 |

⑫ 
| Rule: | |
|---|---|
| IN | OUT |
| 4 | 20 |
| | 50 |
| 6 | 30 |
| 12 | |
| | 25 |
| 7 | |

Score 2 points for each correct answer!  SCORE /24  0-10  12-18  20-24

# Statistics & Probability

There are no statistics & probability activities in this unit.

# Measurement & Space

AC9M4M01

## Direct distance and actual distance on a map

The **direct distance** is the straight-line distance between two places.

The **actual distance** is the distance along a route between two places.

The route between places usually bends around corners and follows curves so is further than the straight-line distance.

You can use a piece of string to measure curved distances on a map.

- Place one end of the string at your starting point.
- Curve it along the route to the end.
- Then use a ruler to measure the length of the string you used.

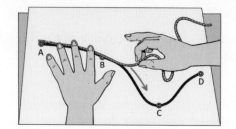

**Use the map to answer the following questions.**

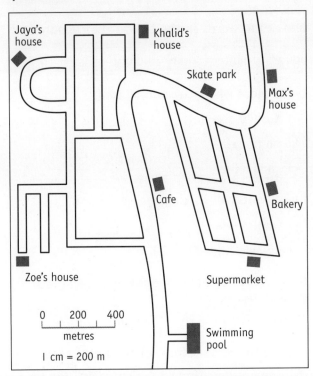

0   200   400
metres
1 cm = 200 m

On the map, use a ruler to measure the direct distances and a piece of string to measure the actual distances. Then use the scale to work out the real distances on the ground.

**Measure to the nearest centimetre.**

*Example:* **From the swimming pool to the cafe**
- direct distance on the map: 4 cm
- direct distance on the ground: 4 × 200 = 800 m
- actual distance on the map: 5 cm
- actual distance on the ground:
  5 × 200 = 1000 m

**From Max's house to the bakery**

1. direct distance on the map      _____
2. direct distance on the ground   _____
3. actual distance on the map      _____
4. actual distance on the ground   _____

**From Zoe's house to the swimming pool**

5. direct distance on the map      _____
6. direct distance on the ground   _____
7. actual distance on the map      _____
8. actual distance on the ground   _____

**From Jaya's house to Zoe's house**

9. direct distance on the map       _____
10. direct distance on the ground   _____
11. actual distance on the map      _____
12. actual distance on the ground   _____

**From Khalid's house to the supermarket**

13. direct distance on the map       _____
14. direct distance on the ground    _____
15. actual distance on the map       _____
16. actual distance on the ground    _____

Score 2 points for each correct answer!   SCORE   **/32**   (0-14)  (16-26)  (28-32)

## Problem Solving

AC9M4N01, AC9M4N02

### Number sort

| 60 | 85 | 13 | 32 |
|---|---|---|---|
| | 81 | 100 | 236 |
| | 567 | 708 | 892 |
| | 1340 | 2500 | 8914 |
| | 7833 | 9015 | |

**List these numbers from the box.**

1. all the even numbers

   _____

2. all the odd numbers

   _____

3. the multiples of 5

   _____

4. all the numbers larger than 1300 but less than 7000

   _____

5. the numbers that are divisible by 2

   _____

6. the number that is 8 less than 900

   _____

7. the number that is 50 greater than 186

   _____

8. the number that is double 1250

   _____

**TERM 4 MATHS**

# Grammar & Punctuation

**Choose the correct verb to complete this sentence.**

① That school of fish (was    were) amazing to watch.

**Underline the nouns or noun groups that the pronouns in bold refer back to.**

② My dad likes to fix cars. **He** is very good at it.

**Add the quotation marks.**

③ How many people came to your party? asked Michelle.

**Write the past tense form of each verb to complete the sentences.**

④ **write** I _____ a funny poem.

⑤ **catch** My dog _____ the ball.

**Write another modal verb for the underlined verb to strengthen this argument.**

⑥ Ben <u>might</u> be the next cricket captain.

_____

**Replace the underlined words with their contractions. Write the contractions on the lines.**

⑦ <u>They are</u> all coming to lunch. <u>It is</u> on Saturday. _____  _____

**Underline the adverbial clause.**

⑧ We played at the park until the sun set.

**Add commas where they are needed.**

⑨ Unless it rains I will meet you at the park.

**Insert a // symbol to show where new paragraphs should begin in this extract. Hint: There are 3.**

⑩–⑫ Last weekend, my friend Amy came to stay with us. We were running late to meet her at the train station. By the time we got there, Amy was standing all alone outside the station. "We're so sorry, Amy," said my mum, "but the traffic was terrible and it took us ages to get across town." "That's OK. I've amused myself by watching the seagulls raiding the rubbish bins!" said Amy.

**Circle the text connective that shows that time has passed.**

⑬ I went to the shops and (therefore afterwards) I had lunch.

Score 2 points for each correct answer!  **SCORE**  /26  (0-10)  (12-20)  (22-26)

# Phonic Knowledge & Spelling

**Match the words in the box to their meanings.**

| quiet    quite    dairy    diary |

① a place where cows are milked: _____

② a daily account: _____

③ no noise: _____

④ completely: _____

**Build words by writing the new word.**

⑤ final + ly = _____

⑥ model + ing = _____

**Choose the correct homophone to complete this sentence.**

⑦ Dad made the (doe    dough) for a pie.

**Choose the correct form of the past tense.**

⑧ The brothers (fought    fighted) all the time.

**Add –ing to these words. Write the new words.**

⑨ throb _____

⑩ phone _____

**Write the antonym of these words.**

⑪ upstream _____

⑫ downstairs _____

**Write the antonyms of these words by changing the prefix to over–.**

⑬ underweight _____

⑭ underpass _____

**Change these verbs to nouns. For example: invite – invitation.**

⑮ collect _____

⑯ act _____

**Circle how many syllables these words have.**

⑰ addition        1    2    3    4    5

⑱ multiplication   1    2    3    4    5

**Make compound words that end in guard.**

⑲ coast_____

⑳ mouth_____

Score 2 points for each correct answer!  **SCORE**  /40  (0-18)  (20-34)  (36-40)

TARGETING HOMEWORK 4 © PASCAL PRESS ISBN 9781925726466

Imaginative text – Narrative
Author – Frances Mackay

## The Future

Jai entered the city just after sunrise. The air was clear and bright but no sunlight could be seen because gigantic skyscrapers towered above him, blotting out the sky. There was a pleasant flowery scent all around him which seemed to waft out of the wire grates in the gutters of the street. The footpaths were like huge conveyor belts, slowly carrying people everywhere so they didn't have to walk. No cars could be seen anywhere but suddenly a fantastic flying craft appeared and gently landed near Jai. Four people got out, all dressed in spotless white suits. Music seemed to be all around him. Lovely, soft, gentle music that soothed him and made him feel happy and calm.

"What an amazing place," he thought, "I wonder where I am?"

**Write or circle the correct answers.**

① **Where was Jai?**

a on another planet

b on Earth in the past

c on Earth in the future

② **What time of day was it?**

a morning

b afternoon

c evening

③ **What line in the text tells you that the air was not polluted?**

④ **What does waft mean?**

a wave

b pass gently through the air

c melt

⑤ **What was unusual about the footpaths?**

_____

⑥ **Which word in the text is another word for huge?**

_____

⑦ **Which is the odd word out?**

a tainted

b spotless

c immaculate

d clean

⑧ **What are skyscrapers?**

a very tall buildings

b spacecraft

c screens that block out the sky

TERM 4 ENGLISH

Score 2 points for each correct answer!

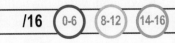

SCORE /16   0-6   8-12   14-16

## Number & Algebra

Write the answers to make the number sentences balance.

① 45 + _____ = 20 + 30

② 100 – 30 = 50 + _____

③ 50 – _____ = 15 + 15

Write these word problems as number sentences. Then work out the answers.

④ Eight people shared 32 party pies. How many pies did they have each?

_____

⑤ 10 ladies had their fingernails painted. How many fingernails got painted in total?

_____

⑥ 9 people each donated $5 to a charity. How much money was donated altogether?

_____

Use the **adding on strategy** to work out the correct change for these purchases.

| | Cost | Amount received | Change |
|---|---|---|---|
| ⑦ | $3.40 | $5.00 | _____ |
| ⑧ | $5.70 | $10.00 | _____ |
| ⑨ | $6.15 | $10.00 | _____ |

Write the correct answers to these foreign money problems.

⑩ How many 1 euro coins can be exchanged for a 20 euro note?

_____

⑪ If I buy two items that each cost 4000 won, how much change would I receive from 10 000 won?

_____

⑫ Fi has 20 Singapore dollars. How much change will she receive if she buys two books costing 8 Singapore dollars each?

_____

What is the value of the digits in red?

⑬ 1457 _____   ⑯ 5940 _____

⑭ 2830 _____   ⑰ 23 956 _____

⑮ 6715 _____   ⑱ 15 598 _____

Write the correct answers.

⑲ If the **4** in **15 574** is changed to a **9**, by how much would the value change?

_____

⑳ If the **6** in **23 682** is changed to an **8**, by how much would the value change?

_____

㉑ If the **2** in **42 567** is changed to a **9**, by how much would the value change?

_____

㉒ Complete the number line by counting in **mixed numerals** on top of the line and **improper fractions** under the line.

Write these improper fractions as whole or mixed numeral.

㉓ $\frac{5}{3}$ = _____

㉔ $\frac{9}{3}$ = _____

㉕ $\frac{13}{3}$ = _____

*Score 2 points for each correct answer!* SCORE **/50** (0-22) (24-44) (46-50)

## Statistics & Probability

Order these events from least likely to most likely by numbering them from 1 (least likely) to 6 (most likely).

① ☐ I will drink something today.

② ☐ I will speak to a friend this week.

③ ☐ I will get a cold this year.

④ ☐ I will eat mushrooms on toast for breakfast every day.

⑤ ☐ I will travel to New York one day.

⑥ ☐ I will be an alien when I wake up tomorrow.

**Read the two events. What will probably happen next? Circle the correct answer.**

⑦ • Ria and Eve will have lunch in town tomorrow.
  • Ria woke up with a bad headache.
  **a** The lunch will most likely be cancelled.
  **b** The lunch is likely to go ahead.

⑧ • Mum will take me to the beach tomorrow.
  • Today Mum had to go away for work for a week.
  **a** The beach trip is likely to go ahead.
  **b** The beach trip is unlikely to go ahead.

This is a graph of the average temperatures for Sydney.

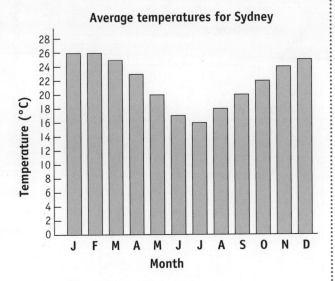

Average temperatures for Sydney

**Answer the questions about the graph.**

⑨ How many months have an average above 20 °C? ____

⑩ How many months have an average below 20 °C? ____

⑪ Which months have the highest average temperature?

_____

⑫ Which month has the lowest average temperature?

_____

⑬ What is the difference between the highest average temperature and the lowest average temperature in degrees Celsius? _____

Score 2 points for each correct answer! SCORE /26 (0-10) (12-20) (22-26)

## Measurement & Space

**Use this bus timetable to answer the questions.**

| Red Springs | 7:10 am | 8:30 am | 9:50 am | 11:10 am | 12:30 pm | 1:50 pm | 3:10 pm |
|---|---|---|---|---|---|---|---|
| Bus station | 7:45 am | 9:05 am | 10:25 am | 11:45 pm | 1:05 pm | 2:25 pm | 3:45 pm |

① You catch the bus at Red Springs at 1:50 pm. What time do you arrive at the bus station? _____

② You need to be at the bus station by 9:30 am. Which bus should you catch at Red Springs? _____

③ How long does the journey take from Red Springs to the bus station? _____

**Which two small shapes make up the larger shape? Circle the correct answers.**

④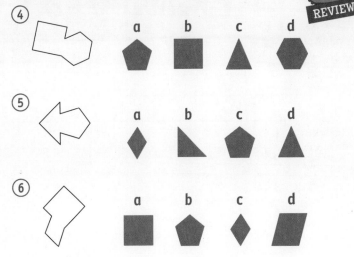
  a  b  c  d

⑤
  a  b  c  d

⑥
  a  b  c  d

**Are these angles equal to, greater than or smaller than a right angle? Write equal, greater than or smaller than.**

⑦ _____

⑨ _____

⑧ _____

⑩ _____

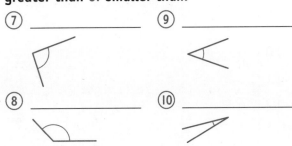

**How would you measure these quantities of liquids? Write the number below each measure you would use.**

| Quantity | 1 L | 500 mL | 200 mL | 100 mL | 50 mL |
|---|---|---|---|---|---|
| 750 mL of water | | 1 | 1 | | 1 |
| ⑪ 950 mL of juice | | | | | |
| ⑫ 650 mL of milk | | | | | |

⑬ **Draw the other half of this shape to make it symmetrical.**

Score 2 points for each correct answer! SCORE /26 (0-10) (12-20) (22-26)

# MY READING LIST

Name: _____

| | Title | Author | Rating | Date |
|---|---|---|---|---|
| 1 | | | ☆☆☆☆☆ | |
| 2 | | | ☆☆☆☆☆ | |
| 3 | | | ☆☆☆☆☆ | |
| 4 | | | ☆☆☆☆☆ | |
| 5 | | | ☆☆☆☆☆ | |
| 6 | | | ☆☆☆☆☆ | |
| 7 | | | ☆☆☆☆☆ | |
| 8 | | | ☆☆☆☆☆ | |
| 9 | | | ☆☆☆☆☆ | |
| 10 | | | ☆☆☆☆☆ | |
| 11 | | | ☆☆☆☆☆ | |
| 12 | | | ☆☆☆☆☆ | |
| 13 | | | ☆☆☆☆☆ | |
| 14 | | | ☆☆☆☆☆ | |
| 15 | | | ☆☆☆☆☆ | |
| 16 | | | ☆☆☆☆☆ | |
| 17 | | | ☆☆☆☆☆ | |
| 18 | | | ☆☆☆☆☆ | |
| 19 | | | ☆☆☆☆☆ | |
| 20 | | | ☆☆☆☆☆ | |
| 21 | | | ☆☆☆☆☆ | |
| 22 | | | ☆☆☆☆☆ | |
| 23 | | | ☆☆☆☆☆ | |
| 24 | | | ☆☆☆☆☆ | |
| 25 | | | ☆☆☆☆☆ | |
| 26 | | | ☆☆☆☆☆ | |
| 27 | | | ☆☆☆☆☆ | |
| 28 | | | ☆☆☆☆☆ | |
| 29 | | | ☆☆☆☆☆ | |
| 30 | | | ☆☆☆☆☆ | |
| 31 | | | ☆☆☆☆☆ | |
| 32 | | | ☆☆☆☆☆ | |

TARGETING HOMEWORK 4 © PASCAL PRESS ISBN 9781925726466

# Answers - Homework Year 4

## Unit 1 ENGLISH: Grammar & Punctuation
1. <u>Our supermarket</u> **sells** organic fruit and vegetables.
2. <u>The battered old car</u> **crawled** up the hill.
3. Yesterday, <u>Penny</u> **cycled** all the way into town.
4. Jamie painted <u>the kitchen ceiling and walls</u>.
5. A huge ship sailed into <u>the harbour</u> last night.
6. How    7 Who    8 Did    9 Has

## Unit 1 ENGLISH: Phonic Knowledge & Spelling
1. crust
2. thick
3. grab
4. stamp, crack
5. shell, spend
6. bring, mist
7. trot, stop
8. shrug, truck
9. tested, testing
10. stopped, stopping
11. stepbrother
12. stepladder

## Unit 1 ENGLISH: Reading & Comprehension
1. a. provide with food
2. b. a swamp
3. b. come out
4. algae, bacteria, microorganisms
5. b. 4
6. a. a very small plant or animal
7. b. trumpets
8. b. a complete change in form from one stage of the life cycle to another

## Unit 1 MATHS: Number & Algebra
1. 62, 63, 64, 65
2. 500, 501, 502, 503
3. 1236, 1237, 1238, 1239
4. 4996, 4995, 4994, 4993
5. 9863, 9862, 9861, 9860
6. b. 59
7. c. 1800
8. a. 24 906
9. b. 78 599
10. 25, 47, 63, 72, 98
11. 708, 718, 780, 781, 788
12. 5040, 5090, 5490, 5904, 5940
13. 24 600, 24 605, 24 650, 24 690, 24 700
14. eighty-nine
15. one hundred and fifty-two
16. seven hundred and eight
17. one thousand, five hundred
18. five thousand, six hundred and eight
19. twelve thousand, five hundred and four

## Unit 1 MATHS: Statistics & Probability
1. Friday
2. Wednesday
3. 29
4. 40
5. Thursday
6. Tuesday and Wednesday
7. 7
8. 7
9. 227
10. $454

## Unit 1 MATHS: Measurement & Space
1. b. 115 cm
2. b. 4 m
3. b. 18 cm
5. 4 cm
7. 2 cm
9. 8 cm
10-17

## Unit 1 MATHS: Problem Solving
1. Red 42 cm, Pink 36, Green 32 cm, Yellow 24 cm, Purple 20 cm

## Unit 2 ENGLISH: Grammar & Punctuation
1. (5) Remove the pancake from the pan and eat!
2. (2) Beat the ingredients together in a bowl.
3. (3) Brush some butter onto a hot pan.
4. (1) Gather your ingredients.
5. (4) Pour some batter into the pan and cook until lightly golden.
6. S    7 C    8 E    9 Q

## Unit 2 ENGLISH: Phonic Knowledge & Spelling
1. Excuse
2. safe
3. chase, trade
4. wise, slide
5. nose, vote
6. prune, flute
7. whined, whining
8. exploded, exploding
9. spicy
10. hazy
11. stony
12. slimy

## Unit 2 ENGLISH: Reading & Comprehension
1. b. feel anxious for the characters
2. a. a storm with destructive winds and heavy rainfall
3. c. a tree
4. Mainly for safety in case something smashed through the window.
5. c. whispered
6. b. The wind and rain had come inside the house.
7. a. The bathroom was small and the walls were less likely to collapse.

## Unit 2 MATHS: Number & Algebra
1–6

|  | Ten thousands | Thousands | Hundreds | Tens | Ones |
|---|---|---|---|---|---|
| 25 |  |  |  | 2 | 5 |
| 89 |  |  |  | 8 | 9 |
| 984 |  |  | 9 | 8 | 4 |
| 5906 |  | 5 | 9 | 0 | 6 |
| 12 891 | 1 | 2 | 8 | 9 | 1 |
| 24 785 | 2 | 4 | 7 | 8 | 5 |

7. 9
8. 20
9. 500
10. 80
11. 0
12. 900
13. 1000
14. 0
15. 900
16. 2000
17. 70 000
18. 0

19. 312 + 186
= (300 + 10 + 2) + (100 + 80 + 6)
= 400 + 90 + 8
= 498

20. 541 + 357
= (500 + 40 + 1) + (300 + 50 + 7)
= 800 + 90 + 8
= 898

21. 730 + 269
= (700 + 30 + 0) + (200 + 60 + 9)
= 900 + 90 + 9
= 999

22. 785 – 463
700 – 400 = 300
80 – 60 = 20
5 – 3 = 2
300 + 20 + 2 = 322

23. 498 – 164
400 – 100 = 300
90 – 60 = 30
8 – 4 = 4
300 + 30 + 4 = 334

24. 668 – 102
600 – 100 = 500
60 – 0 = 60
8 – 2 = 6
500 + 60 + 6 = 566

## Unit 2 MATHS: Measurement & Space
1. 3:00
2. 7:15
3. 8:25
4. 9:45
5. 4:50
6. 3:05
7. 1:30
8. 7:40
9. ½ past 8
10. ¼ past 7
11. 9 o'clock
12. ¼ to 7
13. 25 past 2
14. 10 to 9
15. 20 past 2
16. 20 to 5
17.
18.
19.
20.
21.
22.
23.
24.

## Unit 2 MATHS: Problem Solving

| 1 + | 5 | 7 |
|---|---|---|
| 5 | 10 | 12 |
| 6 | 11 | 13 |

| 2 + | 5 | 7 |
|---|---|---|
| 10 | 15 | 17 |
| 4 | 9 | 11 |

| 3 × | 5 | 4 |
|---|---|---|
| 3 | 15 | 12 |
| 4 | 20 | 16 |

## Unit 3 ENGLISH: Grammar & Punctuation
1. People: scientist, teacher, family, grandad
2. Animals: tadpole, joey, shark, spider
3. Places: park, zoo, school, hotel

**4** Things: fridge, calculator, ferry, bicycle

**5** A       **6** C       **7** C

## Unit 3 ENGLISH: Phonic Knowledge & Spelling

**1** weigh      **2** explain      **3** eight

**4–6** The word list can include any of these words:

**4** dray, bray, stay, flay, tray, slay, play

**5** drain, brain, stain, train, grain, slain, plain

**6** shake, drake, brake, stake, snake, flake, slake

**7** plain      **9** reign      **11** main

**8** way      **10** tail

## Unit 3 ENGLISH: Reading & Comprehension

**1** b. She wants to gain the attention of the reader.

**2** c. cousin Mimi

**3** c. willing

**4** d. 4

**5** a. rude and curt

**6** … fans may be disappointed with this book and its lack of atmosphere.

## Unit 3 MATHS: Number & Algebra

**1** 21, 23, 25, 27, 29, 31, 33, 35

**2** 562, 564, 566, 568, 570, 572, 574, 576, 578, 580, 582, 584

**3** 4531, 4533, 4535, 4537, 4539

**4** 13 382, 13 384, 13 386, 13 388, 13 390

| | | | | | |
|---|---|---|---|---|---|
| **5** even | **9** even | **13** odd | **17** 805 | **21** 4500 |
| **6** even | **10** odd | **14** even | **18** 24 | **22** 24 |
| **7** odd | **11** odd | **15** 12 679 | **19** 766 | |
| **8** even | **12** even | **16** 24 562 | **20** 5901 | |

## Unit 3 MATHS: Statistics & Probability

**1**

**2** a. Birthday Months of the Children in Sam's School

**3** April

**4** December

**5** No

**6** January and November

**7** b. In what month is your birthday?

## Unit 3 MATHS: Measurement & Space

**1** tennis ball: 1

**2** cricket ball: 5

**3** cricket bat: 8

**4** tennis racquet: 6

**5** badminton racquet: 3

**6** softball bat: 4

**7** dart board: 9

**8** basketball: 7

**9** table tennis bat: 2

**10** dart board

**11** tennis ball

**12** basketball, dart board, cricket bat

**13** tennis ball, cricket ball, tennis racquet,

badminton racquet, table tennis bat, softball bat

**14** 338 g

**15** 1 163 g or 1 kg 163 g

**16** 270 g

**17** tennis racquet

## Unit 3 MATHS: Problem Solving

Possible answers:

| | | |
|---|---|---|
| 5 + 4 + 8 = 17 | 58 + 4 = 62 | 85 × 4 = 340 |
| 48 + 5 = 53 | 84 + 5 = 89 | 45 × 8 = 360 |
| 45 + 8 = 53 | 85 + 4 = 89 | 84 × 5 = 420 |
| 54 + 8 = 62 | 58 × 4 = 232 | 54 × 8 = 432 |
| | 48 × 5 = 240 | |

## Unit 4 ENGLISH: Grammar & Punctuation

**1** P      **2** C      **3** C      **4** P

**5** Michael plays basketball for the Franklin Dodgers.

**6** My dog, Max, likes to play with my friend's dog, Spot.

**7** We like to eat lunch at Ted's Café in Border Street.

| | | | |
|---|---|---|---|
| **8** Mercedes | **10** Star Wars | **12** Africa | **14** Amazon |
| **9** Everest | **11** Paris | **13** Paul | **15** Cockatoo |

## Unit 4 ENGLISH: Phonic Knowledge & Spelling

**1** deer/creature

**2** cheer

**3** coffee

**4** sweep

**5** creep

**6** spear

**7** gear

**8** peaches

**9** guesses

**10** leashes

**11** lynxes

## Unit 4 ENGLISH: Reading & Comprehension

**1** b. 36

**2** hemisphere

**3** a. the language of Ancient Rome

**4** c. Australia was unknown then and the words mean 'Unknown South Land'.

**5** Cape of Good Hope

**6** b. a type of metal

**7** a. He wanted to prove that he had been there.

**8** c. mapping

## Unit 4 MATHS: Number & Algebra

| | | | | |
|---|---|---|---|---|
| **1** 12 | **5** 15 | **9** 12 | **13** 28 | **17** 27 |
| **2** 4 | **6** 5 | **10** 2 | **14** 7 | **18** 27 |
| **3** 3 | **7** 3 | **11** 2 | **15** 7 | **19** 9 |
| **4** 4 | **8** 5 | **12** 6 | **16** 7 | **20** 3 |

**21**

| × | 2 | 3 | 4 | 5 |
|---|---|---|---|---|
| 1 | 2 | 3 | 4 | 5 |
| 2 | 4 | 6 | 8 | 10 |
| 3 | 6 | 9 | 12 | 15 |
| 4 | 8 | 12 | 16 | 20 |
| 5 | 10 | 15 | 20 | 25 |
| 6 | 12 | 18 | 24 | 30 |
| 7 | 14 | 21 | 28 | 35 |
| 8 | 16 | 24 | 32 | 40 |
| 9 | 18 | 27 | 36 | 45 |
| 10 | 20 | 30 | 40 | 50 |

**22** The numbers end in 2, 4, 6, 8 and 0. The pattern repeats.

**23** The numbers end in 4, 8, 2, 6 and 0. The pattern repeats.

**24** The numbers end in 0 and 5. The pattern repeats.

**25** 20, 22, 24, 26

**26** 42, 45, 48, 51

**27** 56, 60, 64, 68

**28** 75, 80, 85, 90

**29** 132, 134, 136, 138

**30** 168, 172, 176, 180

## Unit 4 MATHS: Measurement & Space

| | | |
|---|---|---|
| **1** triangle | **8** irregular | **15** octagon |
| **2** regular | **9** pentagon | **16** irregular |
| **3** triangle | **10** irregular | **17** nonagon |
| **4** irregular | **11** hexagon | **18** regular |
| **5** quadrilateral | **12** irregular | **19** decagon |
| **6** regular | **13** heptagon | **20** regular |
| **7** quadrilateral | **14** regular | |

## Unit 4 MATHS: Problem Solving

| 12 | 9 | 15 | 6 | 27 |
|---|---|---|---|---|
| 30 | 6 | 24 | 12 | 21 |
| 3 | 18 | 30 | 15 | 3 |
| 27 | 12 | 6 | 24 | 30 |
| 6 | 9 | 21 | 12 | 27 |
| 15 | 24 | 30 | 6 | 18 |

| 20 | 15 | 25 | 10 | 45 |
|---|---|---|---|---|
| 50 | 10 | 40 | 20 | 35 |
| 5 | 30 | 50 | 25 | 5 |
| 45 | 20 | 10 | 40 | 50 |
| 10 | 15 | 35 | 20 | 45 |
| 25 | 40 | 50 | 10 | 30 |

## Unit 5 ENGLISH: Grammar & Punctuation

**1** A large, heavy **parcel** was delivered to our **neighbour**.

**2** The **rain** poured into the old, haunted **house**.

**3** The **model** wore a long, flowing **dress** at the **photoshoot**.

**4** An **elephant** with huge **feet** stomped into the **circus ring**.

**5** The **clown** wore huge brown shoes, a funny hat and a red nose.

**6** Mike and his best friend are staying with us on Saturday and Sunday.

**7** The supermarket had apples, bananas and melons on special offer.

**8** My brother is a tall boy with red hair and a freckled face.

## Unit 5 ENGLISH: Phonic Knowledge & Spelling

| | | | |
|---|---|---|---|
| **1** whole | **4** download | **7** workload | **10** whole |
| **2** borrow | **5** shipload | **8** truckload | **11** toe |
| **3** nose/elbow | **6** overload | **9** rode | |

## Unit 5 ENGLISH: Reading & Comprehension

**1** b. the sound a frog makes and to die

**2** The word **wash** has two meanings: to wash yourself with soap and to float into shore.

**3** croak

**4** two

**5** b. It uses words that can be difficult to pronounce correctly if you say them quickly.

**6** a. sour

**7** c. to make money

**8** She was trying to make her batter better by using butter that was less bitter.

TARGETING HOMEWORK 4 © PASCAL PRESS ISBN 9781925726466

## Unit 5 MATHS: Number & Algebra

1. 130, 135, 150
2. 258, 261, 267
3. 1335, 1330, 1325
4. 1832, 1836, 1840
5. 2996, 2992, 2988
6. 896, 898, 890, rule = +2
7. 5991, 5988, 5985, rule = −3
8. 12 090, 12 085, 12 080, rule = −5
9. 96, 106, 116, rule = +10
10. 556, 552, 548, rule = −4
11.–14. double 8, 8 lots of 2 half of 24, 24 ÷ 2 9 times 4, half of 72 7 × 3, (2 × 10) + 1

## Unit 5 MATHS: Statistics & Probability

Answers may vary, but these are the most likely responses:

1. unlikely/impossible
2. certain
3. certain
4. likely
5. unlikely/impossible
6. likely
7. likely
8. impossible
9. 5 (certain)
10. 2 (very unlikely)
11. 1 (impossible)
12. 3 (likely)
13. 4 (very likely)

## Unit 5 MATHS: Measurement & Space

1. 100 mL
2. 500 mL
3. 300 mL
4. 450 mL

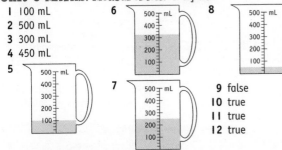

9. false
10. true
11. true
12. true

## Unit 5 MATHS: Problem Solving

It is not possible to find four numbers that cannot be reduced to zero, although some numbers will need to be reduced more times than the example given.

## Unit 6 ENGLISH: Grammar & Punctuation

1. The footballers **practised** their skills every Thursday.
2. I **studied** the painting on the wall.
3. Two huge elephants **charged** at the tourists.
4. Georgie and Jack **played** cricket at the park.

5–14 Jamal's mother **finished**[5] mixing the ingredients for his birthday cake, **turned**[6] the oven on and put the cake in. She then **opened**[7] a large bar of chocolate, **broke**[8] it into pieces and **put**[9] it in a bowl. She then **scooped**[10] out some ice cream into ten small bowls and **placed**[11] them on the table. "Right, I'm finished," she **said**[12]. "I **hope**[13] Jamal and his friends **enjoy**[14] his birthday treats."

## Unit 6 ENGLISH: Phonic Knowledge & Spelling

1. wind
2. right
3. tie
4. drying, dries, dried
5. spying, spies, spied
6. prying, pries, pried
7. trying, tries, tried

## Unit 6 ENGLISH: Reading & Comprehension

1. c. jumped
2. b. She wanted to look her best for her friend.
3. creased, crinkles
4. c. embarrassed

## Unit 6 MATHS: Number & Algebra

1. $\frac{4}{6}$ or $\frac{2}{3}$
2. $\frac{1}{3}$
3. $\frac{2}{8}$ or $\frac{1}{4}$
4. $\frac{1}{8}$
5. $\frac{5}{8}$
6. $\frac{3}{5}$

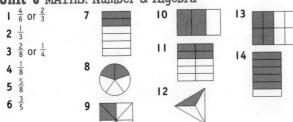

## Unit 6 MATHS: Measurement & Space

1. 8 °C, 12 °C, 35 °C, 40 °C
2. 12 °C, 17 °C, 18 °C, 20 °C
3. 0 °C, 25 °C, 32 °C, 100 °C
4. 28 °C
5. 15 °C
6. 110 °C
7. 200 °C
8. 92 °C
9. 105 °C
10. twenty-seven degrees Celsius
11. one hundred and nine degrees Celsius
12. one hundred and eighty-one degrees Celsius
13. 10 °C
14. 40 °C
15. 22 °C
16. 46 °C

## Unit 6 MATHS: Problem Solving

Ben has 6 choices:
- tomato & ham
- tomato & pineapple
- tomato & anchovies
- cheese & anchovies
- cheese & ham
- cheese & pineapple

## Unit 7 ENGLISH: Grammar & Punctuation

1. Watch
2. Wash
3. Run

4–11 Rock cakes

Collect the ingredients: flour,[4] sugar,[5] butter,[6] dried fruit,[7] egg and milk.

Mix the flour,[8] sugar and melted butter in a bowl.

Beat the egg and milk together.

Add the milk mixture to the flour mixture,[9] stir until smooth and then add the dried fruit.

Using a spoon,[10] scoop up some of the mixture,[11] shape it into a ball and place it on a baking tray.

Continue until all the mixture has been used. Bake in a moderate oven until brown.

## Unit 7 ENGLISH: Phonic Knowledge & Spelling

1. wood
2. jewel
3. good
4. food, mood, broom
5. few, dew, stew
6. book, took, look
7. boot, root, shoot
8. toothpaste
9. toothache
10. toothbrush
11. toothpick
12. wooden
13. roofing
14. goodness
15. chewed
16. sooner

## Unit 7 ENGLISH: Reading & Comprehension

1. b. the head of state such as a king or queen
2. c. the rules for governing Australia
3. a. a town or district that has local government
4. b. to reject
5. c. order to leave
6. An election takes place to elect a new council.

## Unit 7 MATHS: Number & Algebra

1. b. $3.60
2. a. $12.50
3. b. $22.75
4. b. $61.85
5. b. $80.25
6. a. $104.50
7. b. $238.75

8–16

| Price | Nearest 5 cents | Change from $20.00 |
|---|---|---|
| $5.31 | $5.30 | $14.70 |
| $8.59 | $8.60 | $11.40 |
| $10.75 | $10.75 | $9.25 |
| $16.49 | $16.50 | $3.50 |
| $11.27 | $11.25 | $8.75 |
| $17.18 | $17.20 | $2.80 |
| $14.36 | $14.35 | $5.65 |
| $10.33 | $10.35 | $9.65 |
| $8.84 | $8.85 | $11.15 |

17. $4.05
18. $7.40
19. $7.70
20. $7.45

## Unit 7 MATHS: Statistics & Probability

1 e. My favourite shoe shop doesn't sell red shoes.
2 d. I only have yellow and green pencils.
3 f. My teacher cancelled the maths test this week.
4 a. No new cars come in blue.
5 b. Ben takes out a blue marble.
6 b. I pack one pink and one black pair of shoes.

## Unit 7 MATHS: Measurement & Space

| | | |
|---|---|---|
| 1 D | 3 B and C | 5 A |
| 2 B | 4 A and D | 6 D |

7–9 Possible answers:

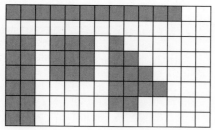

| | |
|---|---|
| 10 A = 5 squares | 12 C = 8 squares |
| 11 B = 6 squares | 13 D = 18 squares |

## Unit 7 MATHS: Problem Solving

start   You end up with a symmetrical shape of two triangles.

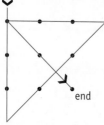

end

## Unit 8 ENGLISH: Grammar & Punctuation

1 Jasmine is going to university this year.
2 The boys were playing football in the park.
3 Michelle has cut her hair shorter.
4 My brother will travel to Europe next month.
5 Our class will sing at a concert tomorrow. (future)
6 Jamie was building a cubby house. (past)
7 I am reading an exciting book. (present)
8 I shall ride my bike to Nan's on Monday. (future)

## Unit 8 ENGLISH: Phonic Knowledge & Spelling

| | | |
|---|---|---|
| 1 flour | 5 download | 9 rendezvous |
| 2 mountain | 6 downfall | 10 ballet |
| 3 down | 7 downgrade | 11 café |
| 4 growl/howl | 8 downpipe | 12 croissant |

## Unit 8 ENGLISH: Reading & Comprehension

1 b. started
2 c. unaffected
3 Canberra, Ballarat
4 True
5 a. a prisoner
6 b. search
7 c. email
8 It came from a convict word meaning 'a thief's stolen goods'.

## Unit 8 MATHS: Number & Algebra

1 5 × 10 = 50 strawberries
2 2 × 30 = 60 hamburgers
3 3 × 8 = 24 figurines
4 100 × 4 = 400 elephant feet
5 5 × 9 = 45 potatoes
6 7 × 5 = 35 sausage rolls
7 48 ÷ 2 = 24 pairs of shoes
8 25 ÷ 5 = 5 stacks of chairs
9 18 ÷ 3 = 6 hairclips in each container
10 40 ÷ 5 = 8 taxis

## Unit 8 MATHS: Measurement & Space

1 caravan park
2 14
3 Surf Parade
4 Sea View Road
5 Sea View Road
6 a. near the lighthouse
7 4
8 Welton Bridge
9 Surf Parade, Sea View Road
10 c. church
11 north
12 south
13 south

## Unit 8 MATHS: Problem Solving

| × | 40 | 5 |
|---|---|---|
| 20 | 800 | 100 |
| 3 | 120 | 15 |

800 + 100 = 900
120 + 15 = 135
Total = 1035

### TERM 1 REVIEW

## Term 1 ENGLISH: Grammar & Punctuation

1 Yesterday, our class visited the museum.
2 Beth painted the bedroom ceiling and walls.

| | | | | | |
|---|---|---|---|---|---|
| 3 How | 5 S | 7 Q | 9 A |
| 4 What | 6 C | 8 E | 10 C |

11 Harry Potter was written by J. K. Rowling.
12 The man wore shiny black shoes, a top hat and a bow tie.
13 Chop the tomatoes, lettuce, spring onions and celery into small pieces.
14 The boys were playing cricket in the park. (past)
15 New Zealand – country
16 Ford – car
17 Las Vegas – city

## Term 1 ENGLISH: Phonic Knowledge & Spelling

| | |
|---|---|
| 1 stack, lamp | 10 speeches |
| 2 shell, spend | 11 drying, dries, dried |
| 3 checked, checking | 12 ties: a piece of fabric worn under a collar; to fasten |
| 4 dragged, dragging | 13 few, dew, stew, chew |
| 5 voted, voting | 14 toothpick |
| 6 plane | 15 bookshelf |
| 7 sleigh | 16 pancake |
| 8 spicy | |
| 9 atlases | |

## Term 1 ENGLISH: Reading & Comprehension

1 a gold miner
2 California (USA)
3 b. to sell canvas cloth
4 famous
5 b. a cart, often drawn by horses
6 He didn't give up when things went wrong and he tried another way which succeeded.

## Term 1 MATHS: Number & Algebra

1 b. 79
2 c. 1600
3 a. 44 806
4 9
5 60
6 5000
7 8000
8 512 = 500 + 10 + 2
175 = 100 + 70 + 5
600 + 80 + 7 = 687
9 600 – 200 = 400
90 – 30 = 60
4 – 2 = 2
400 + 60 + 2 = 462
10 5411, 5413, 5415, 5417, 5419
11 12
12 4
13 3
14 4
15 30
16 6
17 6
18 6
19 140, 145, 160
20 658, 661, 667
21 2335, 2330, 2325
22 $\frac{3}{8}$
23 $\frac{2}{6}$ or $\frac{1}{3}$
24 $5.55
25 $9.55
26 30 ÷ 5 = 6 groups
27 32 ÷ 4 = 8 groups

## Term 1 MATHS: Statistics & Probability

1 certain
2 impossible
3 very unlikely
4 very likely
5 certain
6 c. Tanya takes out a green marble.
7

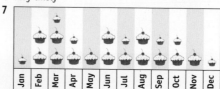

| | | |
|---|---|---|
| 8 March | 10 35 | 12 b. In which month were you born? |
| 9 January and December | 11 no | |

## Term 1 MATHS: Measurement & Space

| | | |
|---|---|---|
| 1 8:00 | 10 767 g | 16  |
| 2 5:15 | 11 c | |
| 3 6:25 | | |
| 4 7:45 | | |
| 5 3:50 | 12 400 mL | 17  |
| 6 12:05 | 13 25 °C | |
| 8 3 cm | 14 40 °C | |
| 9 tennis ball, table tennis bat, basketball, cricket bat | 15 18 squares | |

## Unit 9 ENGLISH: Grammar & Punctuation

1 Matty threw the ball so hard **it** went flying over the fence.
2 Jack wanted to go fishing so **he** asked his mum if **he** could go.
3 She        4 me        5 us        6 you

## Unit 9 ENGLISH: Phonic Knowledge & Spelling

| | | | |
|---|---|---|---|
| 1 drawer | 6 bored | bored | 13 core, more, sore, shore, store |
| 2 caught | 7 draw | 11 coarser | |
| 3 shore | 8 applauded | 12 saw, law, paw, jaw, claw | |
| 4 paws | 9 prawns | | |
| 5 roar | 10 ignoring, | | |

## Unit 9 ENGLISH: Reading & Comprehension

1 b. the readers of *Water Watchers Daily*
2 c. persuade
3 b. to use something up
4 b. people who use a lot of water
5 Any three from:
 – using dual-flush toilets
 – having shorter showers
 – not doing the washing until you have a full load
 – using dirty bath water or water from the washing machine to water the garden or wash the car
6 d. save
7 She wanted to convince readers of the newspaper to urge members of their community to save water.

## Unit 9 MATHS: Number & Algebra

1 548 + 237
 = (500 + 40 + 8) + (200 + 30 + 7)
 = 700 + 70 + 15
 = 700 + 70 + 10 + 5
 = 700 + 80 + 5
 = 785
2 652 + 229
 = (600 + 50 + 2) + (200 + 20 + 9)
 = 800 + 70 + 11
 = 800 + 70 + 10 + 1
 = 800 + 80 + 1
 = 881
3 428 + 285
 = (400 + 20 + 8) + (200 + 80 + 5)
 = 600 + 100 + 13
 = 600 + 100 + 10 + 3
 = (600 + 100) + 10 + 3
 = 700 + 10 + 3
 = 713
4 587 + 146
 = (500 + 80 + 7) + (100 + 40 + 6)
 = 600 + 120 + 13
 = 600 + 100 + 20 + 10 + 3
 = (600 + 100) + (20 + 10) + 3
 = 700 + 30 + 3
 = 733

## Unit 9 MATHS: Statistics & Probability

| | |
|---|---|
| 1 b. don't include | 8 b. don't include |
| 2 a. include | 9 b. Ask all the students in her class. |
| 3 b. don't include | |
| 4 a. include | 10 a. a questionnaire sheet, a clipboard and a pencil |
| 5 b. don't include | |
| 6 a. include | 11 c. tally charts and graphs |
| 7 b. don't include | |

## Unit 9 MATHS: Measurement & Space

| | | | |
|---|---|---|---|
| 1 4 cm | 3 3 km | 5 17 cm | 7 25 cm |
| 2 200 cm | 4 50 mm | 6 500 m | 8 6 km |
| 9 100 cm – 30 cm = 70 cm | | 12 142 cm – 135 cm = 7 cm | |
| 10 1000 m – 600 m = 400 m | | 13 250 m ÷ 50 m = 5 laps | |
| 11 25 mm × 4 = 100 mm | | 14 42 cm ÷ 6 = 7 cm | |

## Unit 9 MATHS: Problem Solving

$\frac{1}{2}$ of 200 = 10 × 10
the sum of 12 and 13 = quarter of 100
100 ÷ 5 = 5 × 4
160 – 40 = 50 + 50 + 20
double 24 = 100 – 52

## Unit 10 ENGLISH: Grammar & Punctuation

1 his, his    2 their    3 your    4 my    5 its
6 Yesterday, I went to see <u>my doctor</u>.
7 Jack has a younger sister, <u>Georgia</u>.
8 <u>My brother and I</u> took a bus to see **our** friend in hospital.
9 "Can I get some milk for **you**, <u>Luke</u>?" asked Tom.
10 <u>Mustafa and Greg</u> hung **their** coats in Ali's wardrobe.

## Unit 10 ENGLISH: Phonic Knowledge & Spelling

| | | | |
|---|---|---|---|
| 1 wash | 3 glasses | 5 pretzel | 7 waltz |
| 2 class | 4 waltzes | 6 fest | |

## Unit 10 ENGLISH: Reading & Comprehension

1 natural
2 renewable
3 hard-wearing
4 a. exciting
5 Will Wood and Wendy Wool
6 warm, natural tones; can be cut into lots of different shapes; hard-wearing; renewable
7 b. Georgina

## Unit 10 MATHS: Number & Algebra

| | | | | |
|---|---|---|---|---|
| 1 24 | 5 21 | 9 54 | 13 56 | 17 30 |
| 2 4 | 6 7 | 10 9 | 14 7 | 18 30 |
| 3 6 | 7 7 | 11 9 | 15 7 | 19 6 |
| 4 4 | 8 3 | 12 6 | 16 8 | 20 5 |
| 21 | | | | |

| × | 6 | 7 | 8 | 9 |
|---|---|---|---|---|
| 1 | 6 | 7 | 8 | 9 |
| 2 | 12 | 14 | 16 | 18 |
| 3 | 18 | 21 | 24 | 27 |
| 4 | 24 | 28 | 32 | 36 |
| 5 | 30 | 35 | 40 | 45 |
| 6 | 36 | 42 | 48 | 54 |
| 7 | 42 | 49 | 56 | 63 |
| 8 | 48 | 56 | 64 | 72 |
| 9 | 54 | 63 | 72 | 81 |
| 10 | 60 | 70 | 80 | 90 |

22 The last digits in the 6 times table repeat in the pattern 6, 2, 8, 4, 0.
23 The last digits in the 8 times table repeat in the pattern 8, 6, 4, 2, 0.
24 The first digit increases by 1 each time. The second digit decreases by 1 each time. Both digits add to 9.
25 36, 42, 48, 54
26 72, 80, 88, 96
27 56, 45, 36, 27
28 189, 196, 203, 210
29 186, 180, 174, 168
30 368, 360, 352, 344

## Unit 10 MATHS: Measurement & Space

| | | | | |
|---|---|---|---|---|
| 1 120 | 6 420 | 11 600 | 16 3 | 21 4 |
| 2 180 | 7 60 | 12 540 | 17 7 | 22 6 |
| 3 300 | 8 120 | 13 2 | 18 9 | 23 5 |
| 4 600 | 9 240 | 14 4 | 19 1 | 24 10 |
| 5 480 | 10 300 | 15 6 | 20 3 | |

## Unit 10 MATHS: Problem Solving

1 5 hours                2 5 × 60 = 300 minutes
3 24 × 60 = 24 × 6 = 144, add zero = 1440
4 Early by 20 minutes
5 12:55 pm
6 12 noon

## Unit 11 ENGLISH: Grammar & Punctuation

Possessive pronouns are bold type in Q1–5.
1 I think <u>these garden magazines</u> are **yours**.
2 <u>That tall house</u> over there is **ours**.
3 The boys claimed that <u>the skateboard</u> was **theirs**.
4 <u>Those coats</u> are **theirs** and so are <u>the shoes</u>.

5 mine
6 mine, yours
7 hers

8 Are those plates yours or ours?
9 Is this coat yours?

## Unit 11 ENGLISH: Phonic Knowledge & Spelling
1 heard   3 warm   5 workbook   7 workload
2 work   4 learn   6 workshop   8 workforce

9–11 Answers will vary but most words should begin with 'w'.
*Example:* Wilbur Worm warmed himself under the wobbly wharf whilst working in his workbook.

## Unit 11 ENGLISH: Reading & Comprehension
1 8 months
2 b. settlement
3 Captain Arthur Phillip
4 convict
5 crew
6 marine
7 officer
8 a. *Scarborough*
9 c. *Supply*
10 Master John Marshall

## Unit 11 MATHS: Number & Algebra
1 $\frac{4}{4}$   4 $\frac{1}{2}$   7 $\frac{4}{8}$   10 $\frac{2}{6}$   13 $\frac{2}{8}$   16 $\frac{2}{10}$
2 $\frac{6}{8}$   5 $\frac{6}{9}$   8 $\frac{3}{6}$   11 $\frac{4}{6}$   14 $\frac{4}{8}$   17 $\frac{6}{10}$
3 $\frac{2}{6}$   6 $\frac{2}{10}$   9 $\frac{5}{10}$   12 $\frac{6}{6}$   15 $\frac{4}{10}$   18 $\frac{8}{8}$

## Unit 11 MATHS: Statistics & Probability
1 pop   3 35   5 5   7 16
2 rap   4 9   6 2   8 19

## Unit 11 MATHS: Measurement & Space
1 50 g, 10 g, 10 g, 10 g
2 50 g, 10 g, 5 g
3 100 g, 10 g, 10 g, 10 g, 1 g, 1 g
4 100 g, 50 g, 10 g, 5 g
5 400 g
6 600 g
7 350 g
8 230 g

## Unit 11 MATHS: Problem Solving
1 9 × 24
  Split to multiply.
  9 × 20 = 180, 9 × 4 = 36
  180 + 36 = 216 cakes
2 85 ÷ 5 = 17 rows

## Unit 12 ENGLISH: Grammar & Punctuation
Nouns are bold type in Q1–6.
1 The boys played an <u>awesome</u> computer game. (computer game)
2 The <u>old, dilapidated</u> house had stood empty for years. (house)
3 The sheets had a <u>fresh, clean</u> smell after washing. (smell)
4 Our <u>dirty</u> shoes were left outside. (shoes)
5 Nan's <u>old</u> sofa was <u>uncomfortable</u> so she sold it. (sofa)
6 The <u>ferocious</u> dog growled at the intruder. (dog)
7 ugly   9 true   11 fresh   13 brave
8 loose   10 young   12 poor

## Unit 12 ENGLISH: Phonic Knowledge & Spelling
1 circle   4 circuit   7 unfurl
2 service   5 impersonal   8 uncertain
3 purchase   6 non-allergic

## Unit 12 ENGLISH: Reading & Comprehension
1 b. rules and laws that prevented black people having the same rights as white people
2 African National Congress
3 population
4 campaigned
5 riots
6 freedom
7 c. 46
8 b. He wanted equal rights for black people.
9 a. refused
10 1994

## Unit 12 MATHS: Number & Algebra
1 250
2 480
3 280
4 360
5 360
6 400
7 6 × (40 + 9)
  = (6 × 40) + (6 × 9)
  = 240 + 54
  = 294

8 4 × (60 + 8)
  = (4 × 60) + (4 × 8)
  = 240 + 32
  = 272
9 5 × (70 + 6)
  = (5 × 70) + (5 × 6)
  = 350 + 30
  = 380
10 7 × (50 + 9)
  = (7 × 50) + (7 × 9)
  = 350 + 63
  = 413
11 8 × (80 + 7)
  = (8 × 80) + (8 × 7)
  = 640 + 56
  = 696
12 9 × (40 + 3)
  = (9 × 40) + (9 × 3)
  = 360 + 27
  = 387
13 84 ÷ 4
  = (80 ÷ 4) + (4 ÷ 4)
  = 20 + 1
  = 21
14 96 ÷ 3
  = (90 ÷ 3) + (6 ÷ 3)
  = 30 + 2
  = 32
15 63 ÷ 3
  = (60 ÷ 3) + (3 ÷ 3)
  = 20 + 1
  = 21

## Unit 12 MATHS: Measurement & Space
1 5   2 4   3 5   4 6

5   6   7   8

## Unit 12 MATHS: Problem Solving

## Unit 13 ENGLISH: Grammar & Punctuation
1 taller, tallest
2 fatter, fattest
3 happier, happiest
4 longer
5 wettest
6 noisier
7 good, better
8 best
9 worst
10 bad, worse

## Unit 13 ENGLISH: Phonic Knowledge & Spelling
1 finger/blister
2 spider
3 fingernail
4 gingerbread
5 spiderweb
6 singer
7 farmer
8 easier, easiest
9 angrier, angriest
10 funnier, funniest

## Unit 13 ENGLISH: Reading & Comprehension
1 Tomo Machines & Co
2 b. to attract the attention of the reader
3 c. families
4 a. outstanding
5 smarter, quieter, more energy-efficient
6 Any three from: smarter, quieter, more energy-efficient, smaller, more powerful, less expensive

## Unit 13 MATHS: Number & Algebra
1 $4\frac{3}{5}$   3 $3\frac{2}{3}$   5 $4\frac{1}{2}$   7 $1\frac{2}{4}$   9 $2\frac{3}{4}$   11 $1\frac{3}{4}$
2 $2\frac{2}{4}$   4 $1\frac{4}{5}$   6 $5\frac{1}{3}$   8 3   10 $2\frac{1}{4}$   12 2

## Unit 13 MATHS: Statistics & Probability
1 b. Thomas' favourite sport is football.
2 a. Emma learnt to ride last year.
3 a. Jake's best friend is Paul.
4 a. It was a lovely sunny day.
5 b. Dad cooked spaghetti for tea.
6 a. Our neighbour is a champion swimmer.
7 a. My favourite TV program is Sneaky Peaky.
8 b. Georgie's nan likes watching tennis.

## Unit 13 MATHS: Measurement & Space
1 500 mL
2 1500 mL
3 2000 mL
4 1300 mL
5 2 × 7 = 14 litres in a week
6 250 ÷ 10 = 25 cups
7 100 ÷ 2 = 50 buckets

TARGETING HOMEWORK 4 © PASCAL PRESS ISBN 9781925726466

## Unit 13 MATHS: Problem Solving

| | | | | | | | | | |
|---|---|---|---|---|---|---|---|---|---|
| $\frac{1}{5}$ | $\frac{3}{6}$ | $\frac{5}{8}$ | 1 | $1\frac{3}{4}$ | $2\frac{1}{4}$ | $2\frac{2}{4}$ | $2\frac{3}{4}$ | 3 | $2\frac{1}{2}$ |
| $\frac{1}{6}$ | $\frac{2}{5}$ | $\frac{3}{5}$ | $\frac{4}{5}$ | 1 | 2 | $2\frac{3}{5}$ | 3 | 4 | $4\frac{1}{5}$ |
| $\frac{1}{4}$ | 1 | $\frac{4}{6}$ | $1\frac{2}{4}$ | $1\frac{3}{4}$ | $2\frac{3}{4}$ | $3\frac{5}{6}$ | $3\frac{1}{4}$ | $3\frac{6}{10}$ | $4\frac{5}{6}$ |
| $\frac{1}{8}$ | $\frac{2}{4}$ | $\frac{3}{8}$ | 2 | $1\frac{2}{4}$ | $2\frac{1}{4}$ | $3\frac{7}{8}$ | $2\frac{3}{4}$ | $3\frac{2}{4}$ | $4\frac{7}{8}$ |
| $\frac{1}{10}$ | $\frac{3}{4}$ | $\frac{2}{5}$ | $1\frac{1}{4}$ | $2\frac{2}{5}$ | 3 | 4 | $3\frac{3}{4}$ | $3\frac{5}{6}$ | 4 |
| $\frac{1}{4}$ | $\frac{2}{10}$ | 1 | 2 | $1\frac{2}{6}$ | $1\frac{8}{10}$ | $3\frac{6}{8}$ | $3\frac{9}{10}$ | 4 | 5 |
| $\frac{1}{8}$ | $\frac{3}{8}$ | 2 | $2\frac{1}{5}$ | 2 | $1\frac{9}{10}$ | $3\frac{1}{2}$ | $3\frac{7}{8}$ | $4\frac{1}{4}$ | $4\frac{1}{5}$ |
| $\frac{1}{4}$ | $\frac{2}{4}$ | $\frac{3}{4}$ | 1 | $1\frac{3}{4}$ | $2\frac{4}{5}$ | 3 | $3\frac{5}{6}$ | $4\frac{2}{4}$ | 4 |
| $\frac{1}{3}$ | $\frac{2}{3}$ | 1 | $2\frac{1}{4}$ | 3 | $3\frac{1}{4}$ | $3\frac{3}{5}$ | 4 | $4\frac{1}{4}$ | $4\frac{3}{4}$ |

## Unit 14 ENGLISH: Grammar & Punctuation

1 most delicious    3 more physical   5 least useful
2 more beautiful   4 less sweet   6 less precious

## Unit 14 ENGLISH: Phonic Knowledge & Spelling

1 healthy         7 breadbasket
2 leather         8 breadline
3 weather       9 breadfruit
4 spread         10 headstrong (2)
5 ahead, redhead, thread   11 breakfast (2)
6 steady, unsteady, already   12 deafening (3)

## Unit 14 ENGLISH: Reading & Comprehension

1 b. dead bodies wrapped in cloth
2 to tell the reader how to pronounce the word
3 c. an ancient Egyptian writing using pictures
4 c. the Rosetta stone
5 a. 23 years (from 1799 to 1822)
6 b. known
7 a. modern

## Unit 14 MATHS: Number & Algebra

1

| | Number of cakes | | | | | |
|---|---|---|---|---|---|---|
| | 1 | 2 | 3 | 4 | 5 | 6 |
| Large hearts | 2 | 4 | 6 | 8 | 10 | 12 |
| Small hearts | 6 | 12 | 18 | 24 | 30 | 36 |
| Bows | 2 | 4 | 6 | 8 | 10 | 12 |
| Cream beads | 10 | 20 | 30 | 40 | 50 | 60 |

2, 3, 4

| | Number of cakes | | | | | |
|---|---|---|---|---|---|---|
| | 1 | 2 | 3 | 4 | 5 | 6 |
| Large hearts | 2 | 4 | 6 | 8 | 10 | 12 |
| Small hearts | 6 | 12 | 18 | 24 | 30 | 36 |
| Bows | 2 | 4 | 6 | 8 | 10 | 12 |
| Cream beads | 10 | 20 | 30 | 40 | 50 | 60 |

5

| Cost ($ each) | Number of items | | | | | |
|---|---|---|---|---|---|---|
| | 1 | 2 | 3 | 4 | 5 | 6 |
| Large hearts | 5 | 10 | 15 | 20 | 25 | 30 |
| Small hearts | 2 | 4 | 6 | 8 | 10 | 12 |
| Bows | 7 | 14 | 21 | 28 | 35 | 42 |
| Cream beads | 0.05 | 0.10 | 0.15 | 0.20 | 0.25 | 0.30 |

6 $28.10     7 $70.25     8 $84.30

## Unit 14 MATHS: Measurement & Space

1 30 °C    3 70 °C    5 250 °C
2 5 °C     4 18 °C    6 50 °C

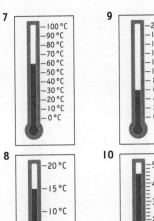

13–17

| Start temperature | Change: Up = + Down = − | End temperature |
|---|---|---|
| 35 °C | − 8 °C | 27 °C |
| 5 °C | + 16 °C | 21 °C |
| 40 °C | + 21 °C | 61 °C |
| 100 °C | − 56 °C | 44 °C |
| 32 °C | − 12 °C | 20 °C |

## Unit 14 MATHS: Problem Solving

There are ten possible solutions.

| | | | | |
|---|---|---|---|---|
| 0 + 6 + 9 | 1 + 5 + 9 | 2 + 4 + 9 | 2 + 6 + 7 | 3 + 5 + 7 |
| 0 + 7 + 8 | 1 + 6 + 8 | 2 + 5 + 8 | 3 + 4 + 8 | 4 + 5 + 6 |

All others, such as 6 + 5 + 4, are repeats as 6 + 5 + 4 is the same as 4 + 5 + 6.

## Unit 15 ENGLISH: Grammar & Punctuation

1 "Look out!" yelled the shop assistant.
2 Max said, "Dogs are my favourite type of pet."
3 "You are so funny," laughed Jake.
4 "Suddenly," said Max, "the door swung open."
5 "When she arrives," said Eli, "we'll surprise her."
6 "Once," laughed Emma, "I put a spider in Tom's shoe!"

## Unit 15 ENGLISH: Phonic Knowledge & Spelling

1 bridge     5 changed, changing    8 birdcage
2 gel                                    9 gemstone
3 dodge     6 drawbridge    10 dodgeball
4 judged, judging   7 hedgehog

## Unit 15 ENGLISH: Reading & Comprehension

1 b. paintings
2 to keep bad spirits off the building
3 b. ordinary
4 b. prawns
5 So that Meh could not see him disappear.
6 c. magically travel very quickly

## Unit 15 MATHS: Number & Algebra

1 40            7 7
2 8             8 80 + 25 = **105**
3 25           9 45 − 8 = 25 + 12
4 70           10 60 − 12 = **48 beads**
5 60           11 15 + 35 = 40 + 10
6 5

## Unit 15 MATHS: Statistics & Probability

1 27     3 20     5 10     7 1
2 b. 2   4 23     6 6      8 4

ANSWERS

## Unit 15 MATHS: Measurement & Space

1. 10 square centimetres or 10 cm²
2. 14 square centimetres or 14 cm²
3. 32 square centimetres or 32 cm²
4. 3
5. 1 and 2
6. 2
7. 8 cm wide × 4 cm long
8. 4 cm²

## Unit 15 MATHS: Problem Solving

1. 47 m²
2. $40 × 47. The easy way is to work out 4 × 47 first, then add a zero.
   4 × 47 = 4 × (40 + 7)
   = (4 × 40) + (4 × 7)
   = 160 + 28
   = 188 (add a zero)
   Total = $1880
3. 20 × 47
   The easy way is to work out 2 × 47 first, then add a zero.

2 × 47 = 2 × (40 + 7)
= (2 × 40) + (2 × 7)
= 80 + 14
= 94 (add a zero)
Total = $940
Or, $20 is half $40, so you could halve $1880 to get the answer.
4. 50 × 2 = 100
   Total = $100
5. Total cost
   = $1880 + $940 + $100
   = $2920

---

## Unit 16 ENGLISH: Grammar & Punctuation

1. Mum said that lunch was ready.
2. He said that he was learning French.
3. She said that she was not sure.
4. Sara said that she was going into town.

## Unit 16 ENGLISH: Phonic Knowledge & Spelling

1. thief
2. field
3. receive
4. ceiling
5. knives
6. giraffes
7. wives
8. beliefs

## Unit 16 ENGLISH: Reading & Comprehension

1. stormy
2. b. someone whose job it is to manage a lighthouse
3. downpour
4. hazy
5. exact
6. a. an instrument for seeing things in the distance more clearly

---

## Unit 16 MATHS: Number & Algebra

1–7

| Words | Fraction | Decimal |
|-------|----------|---------|
| three-tenths | $\frac{3}{10}$ | 0.3 |
| four-tenths | $\frac{4}{10}$ | 0.4 |
| five-tenths | $\frac{5}{10}$ | 0.5 |
| six-tenths | $\frac{6}{10}$ | 0.6 |
| seven-tenths | $\frac{7}{10}$ | 0.7 |
| eight-tenths | $\frac{8}{10}$ | 0.8 |
| nine-tenths | $\frac{9}{10}$ | 0.9 |

8. 0.5, 0.8, 1.7, 1.9, 2.4
9. 1.6, 1.8, 2.0, 2.2, 2.3
10. 0.1, 0.3, 0.8, 2.5, 2.8
11. 2.7, 3.2, 4.5, 5.0, 5.6
12. 0.1, 0.4, 0.6
13. 2.2, 2.4, 2.7, 2.8
14. 3.7, 3.8, 4.1, 4.3

15–21

| Words | Fraction | Decimal |
|-------|----------|---------|
| four-hundredths | $\frac{4}{100}$ | 0.04 |
| five-hundredths | $\frac{5}{100}$ | 0.05 |
| six-hundredths | $\frac{6}{100}$ | 0.06 |
| seven-hundredths | $\frac{7}{100}$ | 0.07 |
| eight-hundredths | $\frac{8}{100}$ | 0.08 |
| nine-hundredths | $\frac{9}{100}$ | 0.09 |
| twenty-four hundredths | $\frac{24}{100}$ | 0.24 |

## Unit 16 MATHS: Measurement & Space

1. 3 km
2. 4 km
3. 3 km
4. 3 km
5. 2 km
6. 4 km
7. 7 km
8. 6 km
9. 8 km
10. 6 km

## Unit 16 MATHS: Problem Solving

◆ = 3, ★ = 4, ☺ = 5

---

## Term 2 ENGLISH: Grammar & Punctuation

1. Max wanted to go swimming so **he** asked his mum if **he** could go.
2. Please take **me** to the beach with you.
3. Yesterday, I went to see <u>my friend</u>. **She** is really nice.
4. The <u>red bike</u> is **mine**, but the <u>blue bike</u> is **hers**.
5. Are those books **yours** or **ours**?
6. The **old, dilapidated** fence finally fell down. (fence)
7. taller, tallest
8. thinner, thinnest
9. happier, happiest
10. most delicious
11. "Watch out!" yelled the police officer.
12. Tom said that he was going fishing today.

## Term 2 ENGLISH: Phonic Knowledge & Spelling

1. pause
2. prawns
3. ignoring, nudged
4. clusses
5. waltzes
6. tasks
7. foxes
8. brave – fearful
9. young – old
10. ugly – beautiful
11. poor – rich
12. impersonal
13. uncertain
14. breakfast (2)
15. unpleasant (3)
16. healthy, wealthy, stealthy
17. judged, judging
18. changed, changing
19. field
20. receive
21. siege
22. lives
23. giraffes
24. thieves
25. chiefs

## Term 2 ENGLISH: Reading & Comprehension

1. b. The flea is much better at jumping high than humans.
2. c. a plant or animal that gets its food from another living thing by living on or inside it
3. rubbery pads on their back legs
4. released
5. b. proportion
6. d. loosened
7. force
8. 30 centimetres
9. 6
10. no

## Term 2 MATHS: Number & Algebra

1. 648 + 337
   = (600 + 40 + 8) + (300 + 30 + 7)
   = 900 + 70 + 15
   = 900 + (70 + 10) + 5
   = 900 + 80 + 5
   = 985
2. 24
3. 4
4. 6
5. 4
6. 21
7. 7
8. 7
9. 3
10. 36, 42, 48, 54
11. 72, 80, 88, 96
12. $\frac{2}{6}$
13. $\frac{2}{10}$
14. 6 × 48
    = 6 × (40 + 8)
    = (6 × 40) + (6 × 8)
    = 240 + 48
    = 288
15. $1\frac{1}{4}$
16. $1\frac{3}{4}$
17. $2\frac{1}{4}$
18. 3
19. 52
20. 28
21. 50
22. 66
23. 55 – 15 = 25 + 15
24. 0.2, 0.5, 1.9, 2.4, 2.7

## Term 2 MATHS: Statistics & Probability

1. 33
2. b. 2
3. 25
4. 8
5. football
6. tennis
7. 3
8. 8
9. picture graph

## Term 2 MATHS: Measurement & Space

1. 6 cm
2. 400 cm
3. 5 km
4. 70 mm
5. 180 seconds
6. 300 seconds
7. 120 minutes
8. 240 minutes
9. 2 minutes
10. 3 hours
11. 600 g
12. 230 g
13. 1400 mL
14. 700 mL
15.
16.
17. Area = 9 square centimetres or 9 cm²
18. Area = 14 square centimetres or 14 cm²
19. 4 km
20. 12 km
21. 9 km

---

## Unit 17 ENGLISH: Grammar & Punctuation

1 fact 2 opinion 3 fact
4 Any one of the following: My favourite / The best
5 Any one of the following: I think / I believe / I feel / It's my belief / I strongly believe / I am convinced
6 Any one of the following: My favourite/ The best
7 b. happy 8 a. confident 9 a. worried

## Unit 17 ENGLISH: Phonic Knowledge & Spelling

1 juggle
2 chicken
3 wriggle
4 thicken
5 tremble
6 rumble
7 shuffle
8 dazzle, puzzle, nozzle, drizzle
9 shuffle, sniffle, ruffle, raffle
10 rumble, crumble, nibble, bobble
11 juggled, juggling, juggler
12 thickened, thickening, thickener
13 tumbled, tumbling, tumbler

## Unit 17 ENGLISH: Reading & Comprehension

1 a. a written version
2 b. overcrowded gaols, cheaper to transport them, may prevent criminals from committing crimes again
3 c. major
4 a. people who are considered to be soft-hearted and kind
5 fact
6 opinion

## Unit 17 MATHS: Number & Algebra

1 true 5 false 9 a. odd 13 b. even
2 true 6 b. even 10 b. even 14 a. odd
3 false 7 b. even 11 b. even 15 a. odd
4 true 8 a. odd 12 b. even 16 b. even

## Unit 17 MATHS: Statistics & Probability

1 He asked all the students in his class to choose their favourite from the food choices and recorded their answers in a tally chart.
2 10 3 8 4 32
5–7 • A picture graph does not have a scale on the vertical axis. You count the pictures instead.
• The horizontal axis should be labelled 'Type of food'.
• The pictures of each food should be lined up and the same size to show they are of equal value.

8

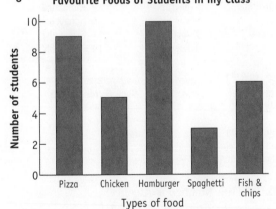

**Favourite Foods of Students in my Class**

## Unit 17 MATHS: Measurement & Space

1 Sara crosses over Walker Street heading north into **Centenary Park**. She walks through the park and comes out through **North Gate**. She crosses over **Merrifield** Street, walks up **Cross** Road and turns **right** into School Road.
2 Sara turns left, heading west. She turns right into **Richard** Street and walks north up to Merrifield Street where she turns **right**. She turns **left** into Cross Road and then **right** into School Road.
3 Sara turns right, heading **east**. She turns left into **Baker** Street and walks north. She then turns **left** into School Road.
4–8 School Road, Merrifield Street, Walker Street, Gattney Street, Malden Street
9 Baker Street and Bunker Street

## Unit 17 MATHS: Problem Solving

1 9 2 6 3 5 4 8 5 7 6 3

## Unit 18 ENGLISH: Grammar & Punctuation

1 so 2 but 3 and / but 4 or
5 <u>Jackie</u> prefers netball **but** <u>Milly</u> prefers soccer. (different)
6 <u>Mum</u> bought some wool **so** <u>she</u> can knit me a jumper. (same)
7 <u>Dad</u> mowed the lawn **and** <u>I</u> picked up the grass. (different)
8 <u>Mia</u> used to have a bike **but** <u>her mother</u> sold it. (different)

## Unit 18 ENGLISH: Phonic Knowledge & Spelling

1 able 3 station 5 stable 7 trifle
2 stable 4 ruby 6 rifle 8 kind
9 able, cable, table, stable stamen
10 station, stable, staple,

## Unit 18 ENGLISH: Reading & Comprehension

1 A force is a push or pull that changes the speed, direction or shape of something.
2 b. slows it down
3 Any two from the following: keep pedalling, pump up the tyres, don't apply the brakes, wear streamlined clothing
4 a. increase
5 c. something designed to give little resistance to the flow of air or water
6 movement energy

## Unit 18 MATHS: Number & Algebra

1 96, 102, 108
2 140, 147, 154
3 1182, 1176, 1170
4 1274, 1282, 1290
5 2992, 2984, 2976
6 1350, 1360, 1370
7 2027, 2036, 2045
8 Rule: + 9. 917, 926, 935
9 Rule: – 10. 4970, 4960, 4950
10 Rule: + 6. 12 118, 12 124, 12 130
11 Rule: – 7. 779, 772, 765
12 Rule: + 10. 5060, 5070, 5080
13–16 double 9, 9 lots of 2 one-sixth of 36, 36 ÷ 6 the product of 9 and 8, (7 × 10) + 2 140 divided by 10, half of 28
17–24 More than one answer is possible. Sample answers:
17 6 × 6 = 36; 9 × 4 = 36
18 10 × 5 = 50; 2 × 25 = 50
19 10 × 10 = 100; 4 × 25 = 100
20 7 × 8 = 56; 2 × 28 = 56
21 10 × 4 = 40; 8 × 5 = 40
22 10 × 8 = 80; 4 × 20 = 80
23 70 ÷ 10 = 7; 21 ÷ 3 = 7
24 60 ÷ 10 = 6; 12 ÷ 2 = 6

## Unit 18 MATHS: Measurement & Space

1 am
2 pm
3 pm
4 pm
5 pm
6 am
7 1 hour
8 1½ hours
9 4 hours
10 1 hour
11 ¾ hour (45 minutes)
12 2 hours
13 1 hour
14 1¼ hours (75 minutes)
15 ¾ hour (45 minutes)
16 ¾ hour (45 minutes)
17 4:00 pm
18 5:45 pm
19 1½ hours
20 3:15 pm

## Unit 18 MATHS: Problem Solving

| Time | Task |
|------|------|
| 8:30 am | Feed the cat. |
| 9:00 am | Take the dog for a walk. |
| 10:30 am | Take Jake to football practice. |
| 12:30 pm | Pick up Jake and give him some lunch. |
| 2:30 pm | Take the cat to the vet. |
| 3:15 pm | Pick up Melissa from the train station. |
| 6:00 pm | Cook tea for everyone. |
| 9:00 pm | Put Jake to bed. |
| 10:30 pm | Make Maxine a cup of tea. |

## Unit 19 ENGLISH: Grammar & Punctuation

Adverbs are bold type in Q1–5.
1 Jason <u>drank</u> his coffee **silently**.
2 I **accidentally** <u>stepped</u> on the dog's tail.
3 We <u>bought</u> a birthday cake **yesterday**.
4 Dad **always** <u>sings</u> in the shower.
5 bravely
6 regularly
7 cruelly
8 noisily
9 hungrily
10 busily
11 regularly
12 brightly

## Unit 19 ENGLISH: Phonic Knowledge & Spelling

1 monkey
2 reply
3 family
4 monkeys
5 cities
6 libraries
7 journeys
8 turkeys
9 families
10 busy, busier, busiest, busily
11 sturdy, sturdier, sturdiest, sturdily

## Unit 19 ENGLISH: Reading & Comprehension

1 San Domingo in the Philippines
2 It has a near perfect cone shape.
3 b. the ejection of molten rock from a volcano
4 a. side    5 assured    6 lava    7 plumes

## Unit 19 MATHS: Number & Algebra

1 $40 \times 2 = 80$, $7 \times 2 = 14$
   $80 + 14 = 94$
2 $50 \times 2 = 100$, $9 \times 2 = 18$
   $100 + 18 = 118$
3 $60 \times 2 = 120$, $4 \times 2 = 8$
   $120 + 8 = 128$
4 $100 \times 2 = 200$, $50 \times 2 = 100$, $3 \times 2 = 6$
   $200 + 100 + 6 = 306$
5 $400 \times 2 = 800$, $50 \times 2 = 100$, $8 \times 2 = 16$
   $800 + 100 + 16 = 916$
6 $200 \div 2 = 100$, $60 \div 2 = 30$, $4 \div 2 = 2$
   $100 + 30 + 2 = 132$
7 $400 \div 2 = 200$, $20 \div 2 = 10$, $8 \div 2 = 4$
   $200 + 10 + 4 = 214$
8 $600 \div 2 = 300$, $40 \div 2 = 20$, $2 \div 2 = 1$
   $300 + 20 + 1 = 321$

## Unit 19 MATHS: Statistics & Probability

1 39    2 white    3 blue    4 7
5 tally chart, bar graph, pie chart
6 Answers will vary but must be supported by a reason.
7 Answers will vary but may include:
   • How many red cars went past Tom's school?
   • Which colours had more than 5 cars?
   • Which colours had fewer than 5 cars?
   • How many more silver cars passed than red cars?
   • 1 car out of 39 cars was blue. What proportion of the cars were black?

## Unit 19 MATHS: Measurement & Space

1 1.5 kg
2 1.6 kg
3 1.8 kg
4 2.4 kg
5 3.5 kg
6 5.7 kg
7 1600 g
8 2300 g
9 4500 g
10 5800 g
11 6400 g
12 8900 g
13 1.1 kg = 1100 g
14 4.8 kg = 4800 g
15 3.3 kg = 3300 g
16 2.3 kg = 2300 g

## Unit 19 MATHS: Problem Solving

1 The elephant has a mass of $2.5 \times 2000 = 5000$ kg.
   Add 5000 and 2000 = 7000
   Subtract 7000 from 7700 = 700
   The giraffe has a mass of 700 kg.
2 $2000 - 45 = 1955$
   The hippo now has a mass of 1955 kg.

## Unit 20 ENGLISH: Grammar & Punctuation

1 Our friends will arrive in half an hour. (when)
2 The snake slithered through the tall grass. (where)
3 My brother can run almost as fast as I can. (how)
4 I made a cake for my sister's birthday. (why)
5–8 Some sentences have several possibilities:
5 We saw a rabbit: on the other side of the street / in the afternoon / in the forest.
6 The police car stopped: on the other side of the street / in the forest.
7 We finally arrived home: in the afternoon.
8 Mum cleaned the table: with a soft cloth / in the afternoon.

## Unit 20 ENGLISH: Phonic Knowledge & Spelling

1 knight, sword    2 wrong    3 knit, knot/wreck
4 Answers will vary but the sentence must have most words that begin with a silent 'k' or silent 'w'.
5 know    6 wrung

## Unit 20 ENGLISH: Reading & Comprehension

1 c. one of the main areas of land in the world
2 Pacific and Atlantic Oceans
3 a. 2½ times    4 b. disagreed

## Unit 20 MATHS: Number & Algebra

1 $\frac{13}{5}$
2 $2\frac{3}{5}$
3 $\frac{7}{2}$
4 $3\frac{1}{2}$
5 $\frac{11}{6}$
6 $1\frac{5}{6}$
7 $\frac{13}{4}$
8 $3\frac{1}{4}$
9 $\frac{11}{4}$
10 $\frac{10}{3}$
11 $\frac{9}{2}$
12 $\frac{28}{5}$
13 $\frac{17}{6}$
14 $\frac{19}{4}$
15 $1\frac{1}{4}$
16 $1\frac{2}{5}$
17 $1\frac{2}{4}$
18 $2\frac{2}{3}$
19 $2\frac{1}{2}$
20 $1\frac{4}{5}$

## Unit 20 MATHS: Measurement & Space

1 less than
2 less than
3 less than
4 greater than
5 greater than
6 less than
7 equal
8 less than
9 a
10 a
11 c
12 c
13 b
14 b

## Unit 20 MATHS: Problem Solving

1

2

| Dots | Lines |
| --- | --- |
| 2 | 1 |
| 3 | 3 |
| 4 | 6 |
| 5 | 10 |
| 6 | 15 |

3 The difference between the number of lines increases in consecutive numbers: 2, 3, 4, 5

## Unit 21 ENGLISH: Grammar & Punctuation

1 main    2 main    3 subordinate
4 a. When she had finished breakfast, Alex went for a walk.
5 b. Lions are carnivorous mammals that live in Africa.

## Unit 21 ENGLISH: Phonic Knowledge & Spelling

1 thumb/limb, climb
2 lamb, nestle
3 limb
4 listen
5 nestling
6 combing
7 rustling
8 listening
9 thumbnail
10 honeycomb
11 firebomb
12 doorjamb

## Unit 21 ENGLISH: Reading & Comprehension

1 b. a test to see if a person is suitable to act in a play or film
2 big-budget film
3 David Copperfield
4 The Tailor of Panama
5 Harry Potter and the Philosopher's Stone
6 opinion
7 fact
8 c. competing

## Unit 21 MATHS: Number & Algebra

1 $\frac{5}{10}$, 0.5
2 $\frac{6}{10}$, 0.6
3 $\frac{4}{10}$, 0.4
4 $\frac{7}{10}$, 0.7
5 $\frac{1}{10}$, 0.1
6 $\frac{9}{10}$, 0.9
7 $\frac{3}{10}$, 0.3
8 $\frac{16}{100}$, 0.16
9 $\frac{42}{100}$, 0.42
10 $\frac{59}{100}$, 0.59
11 $\frac{91}{100}$, 0.91
12 $\frac{77}{100}$, 0.77

## Unit 21 MATHS: Statistics & Probability

1 a. true
2 b. false
3 a. true
4 off
5 tails
6 cold
7 adult
8 summer
9 closed
10 There should be more red jelly beans in the jar than blue or green jelly beans.

## Unit 21 MATHS: Measurement & Space

1 no
2 yes
3 no
4 no
5 yes
6 yes
7 yes
8 yes
9 yes
10 no

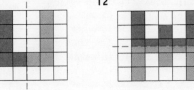

II      I2

## Unit 21 MATHS: Problem Solving

1 $\frac{6}{10}$ of a chocolate bar      4 0.7 of a cake
2 $\frac{9}{10}$ of $5.00      5 0.80 of a pie
3 0.85 of a pizza

## Unit 22 ENGLISH: Grammar & Punctuation

1 As soon as    2 Later that day    3 Firstly
4–12 Last week[4], we went to visit my grandma who lives in a small apartment by the beach. Although[5] she is happy to live alone, she loves to have visitors and enjoys baking cakes for us when we visit.
We left home at 9 o'clock[6] and we should have arrived at Grandma's by 10, but things just didn't happen that way. Firstly[7], there were roadworks and we had to wait twenty minutes before we could move on. Then[8], we had to pull in to buy petrol and that was when Mum discovered she'd come without the gift we had bought for Grandma. So[9], we had to go to the flower shop to buy some flowers.
We all clambered back into the car. Unfortunately[10], the car wouldn't start and Dad had to phone for a tow truck.
An hour later[11], the truck arrived to take us to the repair garage. We all had to sit at the garage for hours before the car was fixed. Consequently[12], it was 3 o'clock by the time we arrived at grandma's, but I really enjoyed those cakes when we finally ate them!

## Unit 22 ENGLISH: Phonic Knowledge & Spelling

1 voyage      4 spoil, coil, boil, toil      6 avoid
2 appoint      7 hoist
3 oyster      5 enjoy, decoy, annoy, ahoy      8 appoint
     9 moist

## Unit 22 ENGLISH: Reading & Comprehension

1 c. a long-established custom or way of life
2 d. unintentionally
3 b. It is normally something that only boys do.
4 b. The next day after school; c. Finally; d. And then

## Unit 22 MATHS: Number & Algebra

1 $1.45      hamster wheel ($9.60)
2 $4.35      6 3 balls ($7.50)      7 10
3 $2.20      or 2 balls + lead ($8.55)      8 $5
4 $29      or 2 leads + ball      9 two dog bowls
5 bird cage and      10 $13.89

## Unit 22 MATHS: Statistics & Probability

1 22 °C      5 b. The highest temperature recorded that day.
2 25 °C
3 Monday      6 9 °C
4 Thursday      7 5 °C
8

| | Sun | Mon | Tue | Wed | Thu | Fri | Sat |
|---|---|---|---|---|---|---|---|
| Max. temp. (°C) | 25 | 28 | 26 | 22 | 19 | 23 | 27 |

## Unit 22 MATHS: Problem Solving

1 Brisbane 31 °C, Melbourne 23 °C
2 25 °C      4 17 °C      6 21 °C
3 120 °C      5 15 °C

## Unit 23 ENGLISH: Grammar & Punctuation

1 baby's      4 artists'
2 Dad's      5 I washed my dad's car.
3 horses'      6 Emily's shoes were new.

## Unit 23 ENGLISH: Phonic Knowledge & Spelling

1 compare    5 stare    9 flair    13 hairbrush
2 wear    6 fair    10 stare    14 hairdresser
3 pear    7 wear    11 bear    15 hairstyle
4 hair    8 hair    12 fair    16 hairpiece

## Unit 23 ENGLISH: Reading & Comprehension

1 a. to alert people to the government's decision of keeping farmland trees as carbon sinks
2 b. a large area of forest that will be kept to absorb carbon dioxide from the atmosphere
3 fact      5 d. discourage      7 regenerate
4 opinion      6 atmosphere

## Unit 23 MATHS: Number & Algebra

| 1 | 2 | 3 | 4 | 5 | 6 | 7 | 8 | 9 | 10 |
|---|---|---|---|---|---|---|---|---|---|
| 11 | 12 | 13 | 14 | 15 | 16 | 17 | 18 | 19 | 20 |
| 21 | 22 | 23 | 24 | 25 | 26 | 27 | 28 | 29 | 30 |
| 31 | 32 | 33 | 34 | 35 | 36 | 37 | 38 | 39 | 40 |
| 41 | 42 | 43 | 44 | 45 | 46 | 47 | 48 | 49 | 50 |
| 51 | 52 | 53 | 54 | 55 | 56 | 57 | 58 | 59 | 60 |
| 61 | 62 | 63 | 64 | 65 | 66 | 67 | 68 | 69 | 70 |
| 71 | 72 | 73 | 74 | 75 | 76 | 77 | 78 | 79 | 80 |
| 81 | 82 | 83 | 84 | 85 | 86 | 87 | 88 | 89 | 90 |
| 91 | 92 | 93 | 94 | 95 | 96 | 97 | 98 | 99 | 100 |

2 The patterns go vertically down the 100-square in a column. The difference between each number in the column is 10.
4 The pattern makes diagonal lines across the 100-square.
6 40, 80
8 The pattern goes vertically down the 100-square in a column. The numbers all end in 3. The first numbers count consecutively; 1, 2, 3, 4, etc.
10 The pattern goes vertically down the 100-square in a column. The numbers all end in 7. The first numbers count consecutively; 1, 2, 3, 4, etc.
11 Circle: 56, 92      15 a. true      20 a. true
12 Circle: 360, 782      16 b. false      21 =
13 Circle: 1346, 3978      17 b. false      22 >
     18 a. true      23 =
14 Circle: 24 500, 89 202      19 b. false      24 <

## Unit 23 MATHS: Statistics & Probability

1 activity / adventure      5 63
2 caravan and staying with family      6 caravan
     7 5
3 hotel and activity      8 4
4 caravan

## Unit 23 MATHS: Problem Solving

Answers, from 0 continuing clockwise:
×6: 0, 12, 48, 30, 36, 54, 18, 42
×7: 0, 14, 56, 35, 42, 63, 21, 49
×9: 0, 18, 72, 45, 54, 81, 27, 63

## Unit 24 ENGLISH: Grammar & Punctuation

1 my new bike      7 some yellow roses      12 vegetable peeler
2 every tall building      8 their baby daughter      13 microwave oven
3 the dog's kennel      14 cutting board
4 that girl's hat      9 oven glove      15 measuring cup
5 your red car      10 ice-cream scoop      16 frying pan
6 an old friend      11 carving knife      17 mixing bowl
     18 wooden spoon

## Unit 24 ENGLISH: Phonic Knowledge & Spelling

1 always      7 alright      13 unafraid
2 afraid      8 already      14 alertness
3 ahead/alone      9 altogether      15 amazement
4 aloud/alone      10 almighty      16 amusing
5 always      11 almost      17 amazing
6 although      12 also      18 alerted

## Unit 24 ENGLISH: Reading & Comprehension

1 Sulawesi or Indonesia      4 Yolngu      8 true
     5 preserve      9 false
2 perahu or prau      6 true      10 b. unfriendly
3 trepang      7 false
11 They traded with each other. The Yolngu copied the Macassans' canoe design.

## Unit 24 MATHS: Number & Algebra
1. 6 × 9 = 56
2. 40 ÷ 5 = 8
3. 8 × 10 = 80
4. 32 ÷ 4 = 8
5. 50 × 4 = 200
6. 88 ÷ 2 = 44
7. 4 × 9 = 36
8. 8 × 4 = 32

## Unit 24 MATHS: Measurement & Space

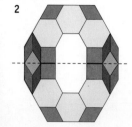

1    2

3–4 Answers will vary but must be coloured symmetrically.

## Unit 24 MATHS: Problem Solving
Answers will vary, but no tile should touch another tile of the same colour.

---

### TERM 3 REVIEW

## Term 3 ENGLISH: Grammar & Punctuation
1. opinion
2. fact
3. angry
4. so
5. but
6. Maggie **sang** a song **softly**.
7. The concert will commence <u>in one hour</u>. (when)
8. The horse galloped <u>through the lush forest</u>. (where)
9. subordinate
10. main
11. Although
12. Tom's brother is older than he is.
13. **my** new shoes
14. **every** house
15. **the** dog's lead
16. **that** boy's bike
17. The rabbits' hutch needs cleaning.

## Term 3 ENGLISH: Phonic Knowledge & Spelling
1. juggled, juggling, juggler
2. donkeys
3. cities
4. busier, busiest, busily
5. know
6. spoil, coil, boil, toil
7. wheelchair
8. hairbrush
9. sandcastle
10. almost
11. altogether
12. stable
13. bridle
14. kind
15. wear

## Term 3 ENGLISH: Reading & Comprehension
1. No, it was a school day.
2. potatoes
3. a girl (she asked)
4. d. packet
5. No, they ran out last year.
6. potatoes, peas, beans, cauliflower, carrots, lettuce
7. ones that don't need sticks
8. No
9. No
10. She was going to change and then help her gran.

## Term 3 MATHS: Number & Algebra
1. true
2. true
3. false
4. 140, 147, 154
5. 1176, 1168, 1160
6. Rule: + 9, 908, 917, 926
7. Rule: – 5, 4985, 4980, 4975
8. Rule: + 6, 12 118, 12 124, 12 130
9. 30 × 2 = 60, 6 × 2 = 12
   60 + 12 = 72
10. 400 ÷ 2 = 200, 80 ÷ 2 = 40, 2 ÷ 2 = 1
    200 + 40 + 1 = 241
11. $3\frac{5}{6}$
12. $\frac{23}{6}$
13. $\frac{7}{4}$
14. $\frac{8}{3}$
15. $1.45
16. $1.00
17. $4.75
18. 10 × 12 = 120 football cards
19. $\frac{6}{10}$, 0.6
20. $\frac{3}{10}$, 0.3
21. $\frac{12}{100}$, 0.12
22. $\frac{60}{100}$, 0.60

## Term 3 MATHS: Statistics & Probability
1. a. true
2. b. false
3. off
4. heads
5. closed
6. hot
7. dog
8. goldfish
9. 43
10. 22
11. 6

## Term 3 MATHS: Measurement & Space
1. am
2. pm
3. pm
4. 3 hours
5. $1\frac{1}{2}$ (1 hour and 30 minutes)
6. $\frac{3}{4}$ hour (45 minutes)
7. 6:45 pm
8. 1.3 kg
9. 2.5 kg
10. 3.3 kg
11. 2800 g
12. 5500 g
13. 1400 g
14. 4.6 kg
15. 4600 g
16. equal
17. greater than
18. greater than
19. less than
20. 8 cm²
21. 16 cm²
22. 20 cm²
23.

## Unit 25 ENGLISH: Grammar & Punctuation
1. stars – galaxy
2. keys – bunch
3. wolves – pack
4. sailors – crew
5. bees – swarm
6. was
7. have
8. is
9. is

## Unit 25 ENGLISH: Phonic Knowledge & Spelling
1. guitar
2. mosquito
3. disguise
4. mouthguard
5. coastguard
6. safeguard
7. lifeguard
8. a barren place: desert
9. a daily account: diary
10. a place where cows are milked: dairy
11. no noise: quiet
12. sweet food eaten at the end of a meal: dessert
13. completely: quite

## Unit 25 ENGLISH: Reading & Comprehension
1. b. to add humour to the story
2. Great Uncle Pillion, Grandad Throttle, Ariel's father, Norton and Harley
3. c. doing stunts on a motorbike.
4. a. not in the right shape
5. The first letters of each word spell 'I'm Batty'.

## Unit 25 MATHS: Number & Algebra
1. 15
2. 2
3. 30
4. 25
5. 35 – 8 = 15 + 12
6. 30 + 20 = 40 + 10
7. 30 – 15 = 40 – 25
8. 45 + 55 = 200 – 100
9. 30 + 10 = 34 + 6
10. 100 – 40 = 30 + 30

## Unit 25 MATHS: Statistics & Probability
1. c. Monday – 25, Tuesday – 15, Wednesday – 19, Thursday – 14, Friday – 26, Saturday – 9, Sunday – 5
2. a. yes
3. b. no

## Unit 25 MATHS: Measurement & Space
1. 24
2. 30
3. 60
4. 90
5. 7 minutes
6. 75
7. 9:40
8. 2.5 mins
9. 1440 minutes
10. 3:00
11. 10:30
12. half past one
13. 2
14. 31st March

## Unit 25 MATHS: Problem Solving
8 triangles are needed.
2 triangles = 1 circle, 2 triangles = 1 square
2 squares + 2 circles = 8 triangles

## Unit 26 ENGLISH: Grammar & Punctuation
1. My <u>mum</u> likes to knit jumpers. **She** is very good at it.
2. Last year, we visited <u>London</u>. **It** was a very busy city.
3. My cat has eight <u>kittens</u>. **They** are adorable.
4. My favourite food is <u>roast lamb</u>. **It** is delicious.
5. "Why are **you** crying, <u>Sarah</u>?" asked the teacher.
6. "May **I** join you?" asked <u>Tim</u>.
7. "Please join **me** for lunch," said <u>Luke</u> to Sam.
8. "I will meet **you** at the shop," shouted Max to his <u>sister</u>.

TARGETING HOMEWORK 4 © PASCAL PRESS ISBN 9781925726466

## Unit 26 ENGLISH: Phonic Knowledge & Spelling

1 tunnel
2 final, medal
3 globally
4 angelic
5 modelling
6 labelled
7 –le words: trouble, juggle, ankle, title
8 –al words: plural, general, final, animal
9 –el words: model, angel, fuel, cancel

## Unit 26 ENGLISH: Reading & Comprehension

1 b. a place where generations of people have lived
2 a. something very special that deserves respect
3 a game like touch football: purru-purru
4 permanent camps: kudgen
5 dance ceremonies around a fire: corroborees
6 b. insufficient
7 spears and nets

## Unit 26 MATHS: Number & Algebra

1 8 × 9 = 72 chairs
2 35 ÷ 7 = 5 pies
3 10 × 4 = 40 paws
4 9 × 7 = $63
5 45 ÷ 9 = 5 balloons
6 6 × 9 = 54 cupcakes
7 8 × 4 = 32 children
8 9 × 2 = 18 legs
9 2 × 9 = 18 + 5 = 23 marbles
10 100 ÷ 10 = 10 slices

## Unit 26 MATHS: Measurement & Space

1 3:25 pm
2 9:30 am
3 35 minutes
4 1 hour 20 minutes
5 3:30 pm
6 25 minutes
7 9:25 am

8–12

| Springtown | Bus station |
|---|---|
| 8:20 am | 8:55 am |
| 9:40 am | 10:15 am |
| 11:00 am | 11:35 am |
| 12:20 pm | 12:55 pm |
| 1:40 pm | 2:15 pm |
| 3:00 pm | 3:35 pm |
| 4:20 pm | 4:55 pm |

13 2:25 pm
14 40 minutes
15 1 hour 20 minutes
16 10:25 am

## Unit 26 MATHS: Problem Solving

## Unit 27 ENGLISH: Grammar & Punctuation

1 Julia cried out, "Wait for me!"
2 "Why didn't you come to my party?" asked Peta.
3 'Slow Reader' is a poem in the book *Please Mrs Butler* by Allan Ahlberg.
4 "Please help me with the dishes," said Mum.
5 "Where are you going?" asked Maxine. (correct)
6 "Paul said," I am going to be late. (incorrect)
   The correct sentence is: Paul said, "I am going to be late."
7 The first chapter in 'The Paper Wish' is called Make a Wish. (incorrect)
   The correct sentence is: The first chapter in *The Paper Wish* is called 'Make a Wish'.
8 Lee replied, "I am going fishing on Sunday." (correct)

## Unit 27 ENGLISH: Phonic Knowledge & Spelling

1 tough/ rough
2 dough
3 cough
4 bough
5 doe
6 thought
7 brought

## Unit 27 ENGLISH: Reading & Comprehension

1 c. to grab the attention of the reader because it is **their** future that needs protection
2 O      3 O      4 F
5 The use of repetition may help to persuade the reader to the author's point of view. It tries to instil the message into the reader's mind by repeating it.
6 unique
7 drastic
8 unpredictable
9 toxic

## Unit 27 MATHS: Number & Algebra

1 $1.40
2 $4.60
3 $2.90
4 $3.70
5 $6.60
6 $9.70
7 $3.05
8 $6.10
9 $14.05
10 $10.25

## Unit 27 MATHS: Statistics & Probability

1–6 Answers may vary.
   The least likely statement is: I will be a hippopotamus when I wake up tomorrow.
   The most likely statement is: I will eat something today.
   You are more likely to speak to a friend this week and get a cold this year than eat pancakes every day for breakfast.
7 a. The picnic will most likely be cancelled.
8 b. The bike ride is most unlikely to go ahead.
9 a. It is most unlikely that we will watch the play.

## Unit 27 MATHS: Measurement & Space

1 b. and f.
2 a. and d.
3 c. and e.
4 a. and d.
5 b. and e.
6 c. and f.

## Unit 27 MATHS: Problem Solving

1

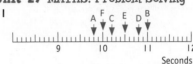

2 A      3 B      4 1.2 seconds      5 0.8 seconds

## Unit 28 ENGLISH: Grammar & Punctuation

1 laugh – laughed
2 begin – began
3 think – thought
4 catch – caught
5 say – said
6 hang – hung
7 fall – fell
8 look – looked
9 lay
10 ate
11 found
12 knelt

## Unit 28 ENGLISH: Phonic Knowledge & Spelling

1 nephew
2 whimper
3 thorough
4 photo
5 photograph
6 paragraph
7 geography
8 autograph
9 graphics
10 pictograph
11 telegraph
12 throbbing
13 phoning
14 whispering
15 whinging
16 whisking
17 whining
18 graphing
19 phrasing

## Unit 28 ENGLISH: Reading & Comprehension

1 A
2 B
3 b. father and daughter
4 polite and formal
5 friendly and informal
6 assess
7 compensated
8 purchased
9 to ask her grandparents to visit in order to calm her father down

## Unit 28 MATHS: Number & Algebra

1 9 × 2 = 18
   2 × 9 = 18
   18 ÷ 2 = 9
   18 ÷ 9 = 2
2 6 × 10 = 60
   10 × 6 = 60
   60 ÷ 6 = 10
   60 ÷ 10 = 6
3 4 × 5 = 20
   5 × 4 = 20
   20 ÷ 4 = 5
   20 ÷ 5 = 4
4 7 × 4 = 28
   4 × 7 = 28
   28 ÷ 7 = 4
   28 ÷ 4 = 7
5 8 × 9 = 72
   9 × 8 = 72
   72 ÷ 8 = 9
   72 ÷ 9 = 8

6 6 × 3 = 18
   3 × 6 = 18
   18 ÷ 3 = 6
   18 ÷ 6 = 3
7 9 × 10 = 90
   10 × 9 = 90
   90 ÷ 9 = 10
   90 ÷ 10 = 9
8 9 × 6 = 54
   6 × 9 = 54
   54 ÷ 9 = 6
   54 ÷ 6 = 9
9 4 × 8 = 32
   8 × 4 = 32
   32 ÷ 4 = 8
   32 ÷ 8 = 4
10 7 × 8 = 56
   8 × 7 = 56
   56 ÷ 7 = 8
   56 ÷ 8 = 7

11 4
12 15
13 18
14 50
15 1
16 2
17 21
18 5
19 25
20 6
21 8
22 3

## Unit 28 MATHS: Measurement & Space

1 5
2 2
3 4
4 6
5 3
6 1

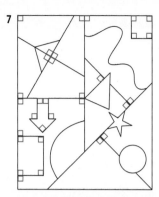

## Unit 28 MATHS: Problem Solving

1. 10 × 14 = 140 biscuits altogether
   140 ÷ 70 = 2 biscuits each
2. 100 × 4 = 400 red covers
   100 × 2 = 200 blue covers
   400 ÷ 2 = 200 red covers still on the horses
   200 − (200 ÷ 4) = 150 blue covers still on the horses

| 6 | × | 6 | = | 36 | | 8 | ÷ | 4 | = | 2 |
|---|---|---|---|----|---|---|---|---|---|---|
| × |   | × |   |    |   | × |   | × |   | × |
| 3 | × | 3 | = | 9  |   | 3 |   | 3 |   | 10 |
| = |   | = |   | =  |   | = |   | = |   | = |
| 18 |  | 18 |  | 4  | × | 6 | = | 24 | 12 | 20 |
|   |   |   |   | ×  |   |   |   |   |   |   |
| 5 | × | 9 | = | 45 |   | 7 | × | 5 | = | 35 | 16 |
| × |   | × |   | =  |   | × |   |   |   | ÷ |
| 10 |  | 3 | × | 14 | = | 42 | 8 | ÷ | 2 | = | 4 |
| = |   | = |   | ÷  |   |   |   | = |   | = |
| 50 |  | 27 |  | 2  |   | 40 |  |   |   | 4 |
|   |   |   |   | =  |   |   |   |   |   |   |
|   |   |   |   | 7  |   |   |   |   |   |   |

## Unit 29 ENGLISH: Grammar & Punctuation

1. can/must
2. should/must
3. can/could/will/might/may
4. May/Can
5. You <u>will</u> be a winner!
6. I <u>will/must</u> write to the team leader.
7. People <u>must/should</u> pick up litter.

## Unit 29 ENGLISH: Phonic Knowledge & Spelling

1. downpour
2. upstream/ downstream
3. downpipe
4. downstream
5. upstairs
6. downhill
7. upturn
8. download
9. downhearted
10. upright
11. downgrade

## Unit 29 ENGLISH: Reading & Comprehension

1. b. Yes – by using phrases such as 'strange shuffling sound' and 'a glimpse of someone', it makes the beginning sound mysterious.
2. The stranger had matted black hair and beard. He wore old clothes that looked like rags. He was dirty and smelly. His toes were poking out of the holes in his shoes. He was bleeding from a cut on his head. He carried a plastic sack.
3. b. He was homeless and living rough.
4. glimpse
5. d. glared

## Unit 29 MATHS: Number & Algebra

1. 10 dollars
2. 8000 won
3. 6 Singapore
4. 200
5. 800 pounds
6. 15 baht

## Unit 29 MATHS: Statistics & Probability

1. hamburgers
2. spaghetti
3. 10
4. 4
5. 32
6. 37
7. 10
8. 35
9. 30
10. hamburger
11. The table could have a total column for the numbers of students in each year group and the total numbers for each food type.

## Unit 29 MATHS: Measurement & Space

1.

| | 1 L | 500 mL | 200 mL | 100 mL | 50 mL |
|---|---|---|---|---|---|
| | | 1 | 1 | | 1 |

2.

| | 1 L | 500 mL | 200 mL | 100 mL | 50 mL |
|---|---|---|---|---|---|
| | | 1 | 1 | 1 | 1 |

3.

| | 1 L | 500 mL | 200 mL | 100 mL | 50 mL |
|---|---|---|---|---|---|
| | | 1 | 2 | | 1 |

4.

| | 1 L | 500 mL | 200 mL | 100 mL | 50 mL |
|---|---|---|---|---|---|
| | 8 | | | | |

5.

| | 1 L | 500 mL | 200 mL | 100 mL | 50 mL |
|---|---|---|---|---|---|
| | 10 | | 1 | | 1 |

6. 2
7. 4
8. 12
9. 40
10. 4
11. 16
12. 40
13. 225 litres
14. 90 litres

## Unit 29 MATHS: Problem Solving

There are several possible answers. Here is one solution:

| ☺ | ★ | ☺ | → | ★ |
|---|---|---|---|---|
| ★ | ☺ | → | ★ | ☺ |
| ☺ | → | ★ | ☺ | → |
| → | ★ | ☺ | → | ★ |
| ★ | ☺ | → | ☺ | → |

## Unit 30 ENGLISH: Grammar & Punctuation

1. You're
2. don't
3. isn't, he's
4. That's, she's
5. let's
6. won't
7. they'd
8. where's
9. who've
10. she'd

## Unit 30 ENGLISH: Phonic Knowledge & Spelling

1. overgrown
2. underwear
3. overweight
4. overpass
5. overarm
6. overfed
7. overturned
8. underhanded
9. overgrown
10. overdressed
11. underlining
12. overcharging
13. overlapping
14. undertaking

## Unit 30 ENGLISH: Reading & Comprehension

1. c. It creates strong, underwater waves.
2. a. the outer layer of the earth
3. The Pacific Ocean is the world's deepest ocean and tsunamis occur in deep water. The Pacific has many underwater earthquakes.
4. Alaska, Hawaii
5. b. weak
6. c. shallow
7. Not very effective because 75% of all tsunami warnings since 1948 have been false.

## Unit 30 MATHS: Number & Algebra

1. 800
2. 10
3. 8000
4. 2
5. 500
6. 400
7. 4000
8. 50 000
9. 2000
10. 100 000
11. 40 000
12. 300
13. 3000
14. 20 000
15. 6000

TARGETING HOMEWORK 4 © PASCAL PRESS ISBN 9781925726466

16

| Place | Population – June 2015 | Order |
|---|---|---|
| Mackay | 85 455 | 5 |
| Tamworth | 42 255 | 8 |
| Ballarat | 99 841 | 3 |
| Bundaberg | 70 588 | 6 |
| Cairns | 147 993 | 2 |
| Devonport | 30 497 | 9 |
| Hervey Bay | 52 288 | 7 |
| Bendigo | 92 888 | 4 |
| Hobart | 209 254 | 1 |
| Alice Springs | 27 972 | 10 |

17 Hobart  19 Ballarat  21 52 300
18 Alice Springs  20 7

## Unit 30 MATHS: Statistics & Probability

1

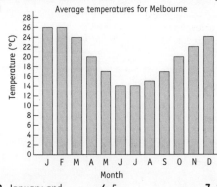

Average temperatures for Melbourne

2 January and February  4 5  7 2
3 June and July  5 5  8 February
6 8  9 June

## Unit 30 MATHS: Problem Solving

1 $\frac{1}{10} + \frac{4}{10} = \frac{5}{10}$ are coloured red or blue, so $\frac{5}{10}$ must be other colours.
2 $1\frac{1}{3} + \frac{2}{3} = 2$ cups of sugar
3 $\frac{2}{8} + \frac{3}{8} = \frac{5}{8}$
$\frac{8}{8} - \frac{5}{8} = \frac{3}{8}$, so there must be $\frac{3}{8}$ left over.

## Unit 31 ENGLISH: Grammar & Punctuation

1 We played on the beach <u>until the sun set</u>.
2 <u>Because no one was home</u>, the cat slept on the bed.
3 <u>Once the house is painted</u>, we can lay the new carpet.
4 You should visit the museum <u>before you go back home</u>.
5 <u>Although it was late</u>, Jess continued to watch TV.
6 When school has finished, we are going into town.
7 Unless she arrives early, I will not see her.
8 Whenever I eat chocolate, I always make a mess.
9 After the game, we had a picnic.
10 Before I go to school, I walk the dog.

## Unit 31 ENGLISH: Phonic Knowledge & Spelling

1 remove  4 detour  7 demolish
2 describe  5 defend  8 repeat
3 deliver  6 regret  9 remark

## Unit 31 ENGLISH: Reading & Comprehension

1 leathery, black, thin  Kevin might harm him.
2 c. termites  6 a. focused
3 c. suitable for eating  7 b. The echidna stared back at him.
4 lumbered
5 The echidna was not sure if

## Unit 31 MATHS: Number & Algebra

1
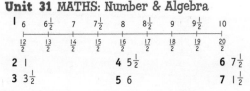

2 1  4 $5\frac{1}{2}$  6 $7\frac{1}{2}$
3 $3\frac{1}{2}$  5 6  7 $1\frac{1}{2}$

8
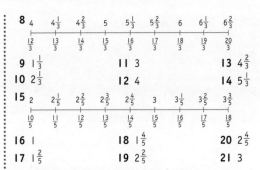

9 $1\frac{1}{3}$  11 3  13 $4\frac{2}{3}$
10 $2\frac{1}{3}$  12 4  14 $5\frac{1}{3}$

15
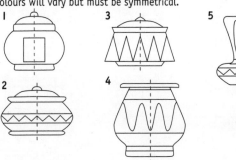

16 1  18 $1\frac{4}{5}$  20 $2\frac{4}{5}$
17 $1\frac{2}{5}$  19 $2\frac{2}{5}$  21 3

## Unit 31 MATHS: Statistics & Probability

1 a. You will go home after school today.
2 b. There will be rain tomorrow.
3 b. You will meet your friend tonight.
4 a. You will go on a school trip this year.
5 b. A cat will run down the street.
6 a. My dad is a good surfer.
7 b. I like travelling across bridges.
8 b. Our local shop sells ice-cream.
9 a. Queensland is a state in Australia.

## Unit 31 MATHS: Measurement & Space

Colours will vary but must be symmetrical.

## Unit 31 MATHS: Problem Solving

1 + 6  4 + 4, 4 + 5, 4 + 6
2 + 5, 2 + 6  5 + 5, 5 + 6
3 + 4, 3 + 5, 3 + 6  6 + 6

## Unit 32 ENGLISH: Grammar & Punctuation

1–3 Last weekend we all went to stay at Aunt Bev's house. I love to go there because she lives right on the beach. It was a long journey in the car and Dad was quite grumpy by the time we got there but he soon cheered up when Aunt Bev greeted him with a big smile and a cold drink. [1]//In the afternoon, Dad and I walked along the beach to the rock pools at the far end. [2]// "Remember last year when you found that big crab?" asked Dad. [3]// "Yes," I said, "it scared me half to death when it grabbed my finger! I'm going to be more careful this time."
4–6 In the morning, we had breakfast and <u>then</u>[4] we headed off for our walk.
<u>After an hour had passed</u>[5], we stopped to have a drink and look at the view. "It's beautiful here," said Tina. "I wish I lived here all the time."
"Yes, that would be great," I agreed.
We continued our walk and <u>eventually</u>[6] came to the place we had chosen to have our picnic lunch. We spread the rug out on the grass and sat back to relax. "This is just perfect!" said Tina.

## Unit 32 ENGLISH: Phonic Knowledge & Spelling

1 connection  5 collection  9 invitation (4)
2 mention  6 explanation  10 illustration (4)
3 invitation  7 action (2)
4 competition  8 option (2)

## Unit 32 ENGLISH: Reading & Comprehension

1 Any four from: The next week, By Friday, that night, They'd just finished eating dinner when, For a moment, Then
2 b. No-one spoke and everyone felt awkward and unsure.
3 a. She felt embarrassed.
4 b. All the doors were locked when Mum came home.

## Unit 32 MATHS: Number & Algebra

**1**

| IN | OUT |
|----|-----|
| 3 | 15 |
| 6 | 30 |
| 7 | 35 |
| 10 | 50 |
| 9 | 45 |
| 8 | 40 |

**2**

| IN | OUT |
|----|-----|
| 4 | 16 |
| 10 | 40 |
| 6 | 24 |
| 2 | 8 |
| 5 | 20 |
| 7 | 28 |

**3**

| IN | OUT |
|----|-----|
| 2 | 12 |
| 8 | 48 |
| 10 | 60 |
| 5 | 30 |
| 6 | 36 |
| 4 | 24 |

**4**

| IN | OUT |
|----|-----|
| 2 | 16 |
| 4 | 32 |
| 3 | 24 |
| 10 | 80 |
| 8 | 64 |
| 7 | 56 |

**5**

| IN | OUT |
|----|-----|
| 3 | 27 |
| 1 | 9 |
| 10 | 90 |
| 8 | 72 |
| 9 | 81 |
| 4 | 36 |

**6**

| IN | OUT |
|----|-----|
| 5 | 50 |
| 2 | 20 |
| 7 | 70 |
| 10 | 100 |
| 6 | 60 |
| 3 | 30 |

**7** Rule: ×3

| IN | OUT |
|----|-----|
| 3 | 9 |
| 5 | 15 |
| 9 | 27 |
| 10 | 30 |
| 8 | 24 |
| 7 | 21 |

**8** Rule: ×2

| IN | OUT |
|----|-----|
| 10 | 20 |
| 5 | 10 |
| 20 | 40 |
| 9 | 18 |
| 40 | 80 |
| 30 | 60 |

**9** Rule: ×7

| IN | OUT |
|----|-----|
| 8 | 56 |
| 3 | 21 |
| 10 | 70 |
| 7 | 49 |
| 5 | 35 |
| 9 | 63 |

**10** Rule: ×4

| IN | OUT |
|----|-----|
| 3 | 12 |
| 7 | 28 |
| 10 | 40 |
| 8 | 32 |
| 6 | 24 |
| 4 | 16 |

**11** Rule: ×8

| IN | OUT |
|----|-----|
| 10 | 80 |
| 5 | 40 |
| 6 | 48 |
| 9 | 72 |
| 2 | 16 |
| 7 | 56 |

**12** Rule: ×5

| IN | OUT |
|----|-----|
| 4 | 20 |
| 10 | 50 |
| 6 | 30 |
| 12 | 60 |
| 5 | 25 |
| 7 | 35 |

## Unit 32 MATHS: Measurement & Space

1 3 cm
2 600 m
3 3 cm
4 600 m
5 5 cm
6 1000 m
7 10 cm
8 2000 m
9 5 cm
10 1000 m
11 7 cm
12 1400 m
13 7 cm
14 1400 m
15 11 cm
16 2200 m

## Unit 32 MATHS: Problem Solving

1 60, 32, 100, 236, 708, 892, 1340, 2500, 8914
2 85, 13, 81, 567, 7833, 9015
3 60, 85, 100, 1340, 2500, 9015
4 1340, 2500
5 32, 60, 100, 236, 708, 892, 1340, 2500, 8914
6 892
7 236
8 2500

### TERM 4 REVIEW

## Term 4 ENGLISH: Grammar & Punctuation

1 was
2 **My dad** likes to fix cars. **He** is very good at it.
3 "How many people came to your party?" asked Michelle.
4 wrote
5 caught
6 Ben <u>must/will/should</u> be the next cricket captain.
7 They're, It's
8 We played at the park <u>until the sun set</u>.
9 Unless it rains, I will meet you at the park.

**10–12** Last weekend, my friend Amy came to stay with us. We were running late to meet her at the train station. //[10] By the time we got there, Amy was standing all alone outside the station. //[11] "We're so sorry, Amy," said my mum, "but the traffic was terrible and it took us ages to get across town." //[12] "That's ok. I've amused myself by watching the seagulls raiding the rubbish bins!" said Amy.

13 afterwards

## Term 4 ENGLISH: Phonic Knowledge & Spelling

1 dairy
2 diary
3 quiet
4 quite
5 finally
6 modelling
7 dough
8 fought
9 throbbing
10 phoning
11 downstream
12 upstairs
13 overweight
14 overpass
15 collection
16 action
17 addition (3)
18 multiplication (5)
19 coastguard
20 mouthguard

## Term 4 ENGLISH: Reading & Comprehension

1 c. on Earth in the future
2 a. morning
3 The air was clear and bright.
4 b. pass gently through the air
5 They were like conveyor belts.
6 gigantic
7 a. tainted
8 a. very tall buildings

## Term 4 MATHS: Number & Algebra

1 5
2 20
3 20
4 32 ÷ 8 = 4 party pies each
5 10 × 10 = 100 fingernails
6 9 × 5 = $45
7 $1.60
8 $4.30
9 $3.85
10 20
11 2000 won
12 4 Singapore dollars
13 400
14 30
15 700
16 5000
17 900
18 5000
19 5
20 200
21 7000

**22**

$$1 \quad 1\tfrac{1}{3} \quad 1\tfrac{2}{3} \quad 2 \quad 2\tfrac{1}{3} \quad 2\tfrac{2}{3} \quad 3 \quad 3\tfrac{1}{3} \quad 3\tfrac{2}{3}$$
$$\tfrac{3}{3} \quad \tfrac{4}{3} \quad \tfrac{5}{3} \quad \tfrac{6}{3} \quad \tfrac{7}{3} \quad \tfrac{8}{3} \quad \tfrac{9}{3} \quad \tfrac{10}{3} \quad \tfrac{11}{3}$$

23 $1\tfrac{2}{3}$
24 3
25 $4\tfrac{1}{3}$

## Term 4 MATHS: Statistics & Probability

1 6 – I will drink something today
2 5 – I will speak to a friend this week
3 4 – I will get a cold this year
4 2 – I will eat mushrooms on toast for breakfast every day
5 3 – I will travel to New York one day
6 1 – I will wake up as an alien tomorrow
7 a. The lunch will most likely be cancelled.
8 b. The beach trip is unlikely to go ahead.
9 7
10 3
11 January and February
12 July
13 10 °C

## Term 4 MATHS: Measurement & Space

1 2:25 pm
2 8:30 am
3 35 minutes
4 b, d
5 b, c
6 a, c
7 equal
8 greater than
9 smaller than
10 smaller than

**11–12**

| Quantity | 1 L | 500 mL | 200 mL | 100 mL | 50 mL |
|----------|-----|--------|--------|--------|-------|
| 950 mL of juice | | 1 | 2 | | 1 |
| 650 mL of milk | | 1 | | 1 | 1 |

13
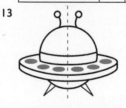

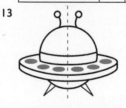

TARGETING HOMEWORK 4 © PASCAL PRESS ISBN 9781925726466